The Eucharist in
Modern Philosophy

The Eucharist in Modern Philosophy

Xavier Tilliette, SJ

Translation and Introduction by
Jonathan Martin Ciraulo

Foreword by Cyril O'Regan

The Catholic University of America Press
Washington, D.C.

Originally published as *Philosophies eucharistiques de Descartes à Blondel*

© Les Éditions du Cerf, 2006
English Translation copyright © 2023
The Catholic University of America Press
All rights reserved

Cataloging-in-Publication Data available from the Library of Congress
ISBN: 978-0-8132-3596-7
eISBN: 978-0-8132-3597-4

Contents

To the blessed memory of Fathers Liégé and Duhayle, OP

To His Holiness Benedict XVI
As a tribute of gratitude
And with filial devotion.

Foreword

Although he is not as well known in Catholic theological circles as he ought to be, the distinguished Jesuit philosopher, Xavier Tilliette (1921–2018), was for decades a powerful proponent for the dialogue between faith and reason and theology and philosophy. He was also one of its foremost executors, as illustrated in tome after tome on the positive as well as the negative engagement of modern philosophers with the truths of the Christian faith. This *Communio* thinker, friend of Hans Urs von Balthasar, Henri de Lubac, Louis Bouyer, Cardinal Joseph Ratzinger, and admirer of Jean-Luc Marion, was a proponent of Christian philosophy, but conditionally so. While he advocated for the genuine intimacy and mutual complementarity of faith and reason, he also wanted to underscore in each case their genuine autonomy. Unlike Gilson, Maritain, and others, and without prejudice to the enduring value of the achievement of Aquinas, he was concerned that the Catholic Church not marry itself to one philosophy or one act of synthesis of theology and philosophy, however magnificent, and that it remain attentive to as broad a spectrum of philosophies as possible. In particular, he was concerned to resist the kind of tendentious parochialism in Catholic thought that would allow it to dispense with the encounter with modern philosophy. Not for him the univocal dismissal of modern philosophy as typified by Neoscholasticism. He was anxious to explore some of the more significant movements in modern philosophy, for example, German Idealism (especially Schelling), phenomenology (Husserl, Merleau-Ponty, Jean-Luc Marion), and certain forms of existentialism (Jaspers, Marcel), as genuine dialogue partners with the Catholic faith.

In this respect both his advocacy and his work are in line with *Fides et Ratio* (1998), in which Pope John Paul II both privileges the relation between theology and philosophy, while insisting that the "Church has no philosophy," and is open to adopting and adapting philosophical insights whatever their origin, whether ancient (Plato, Aristotle) or modern (phenomenology, personalism, existentialism, etc.). As with past encyclicals, such as *Aeterni Patris* (1879), in *Fides et Ratio* Aquinas is honored. The honor rendered in the encyclical over a hundred years later, however, was different than that in the earlier one, which essentially set the table for Catholic theology for over half a century. Aquinas's philosophical thought and integration of reason and faith is promoted as first among equals for the Church. Gone, however, is any suggestion that Aquinas represents the sole or exclusive option that he came to be in the hardening of the Church's position toward modern philosophy during the Modernist crisis. For John Paul II, Catholic faith, then, necessarily requires a philosophical pluralism. This is precisely the position of Tilliette. The Jesuit philosopher has no illusions regarding the change in the general intellectual climate of modernity, and he recognizes that Catholic thinkers can no longer assume from philosophy the kind of hospitality to Christian faith that was common in the medieval period. Skepticism is rampant. Moreover, philosophy has a tendency to function imperialistically. Nonetheless, on pain of becoming an intellectual ghetto and constituting a "separated theology"—to use de Lubac's phrase— the Church must not only tolerate but also welcome dialogue with modern philosophy. Tilliette is convinced that the Christian failure to encounter modern philosophy betrays the wellsprings of the Christian tradition, which from the beginning engaged with the given culture in a way productive to the faith. Augustine both sums up what had long been the practice of the Church and prescribes for the future when he speaks of Christianity's ability to take up the *spolia Aegyptiorum* in his classic *De doctrina christiana*.

Tilliette's wide-ranging work is characterized, on the one hand, by the removal of shibboleths regarding the dialogue of faith and reason and, on the other, by offering incentives for their mutual encounter. One such shibboleth is that modern philosophy is uniformly hostile to Christian faith. Two examples of how Tilliette's work clears away the shibboleths, then, are, first, without being in the slightest way naïve about German Idealism's tendency to misrepresent and distort Christian truths, he is convinced that Christian thinkers and the Catholic Church more generally have something to gain from an encounter with modes of philosophy that themselves are forms of encounter with Christianity. Second, as has been the case for French Catholics from Gilson to Marion, there is the peculiar case of Descartes. While it is, undoubtedly, true that the effective history of Descartes's philosophy—especially its narrowing into Cartesianism—has not proved particularly happy for Catholicism, Tilliette is anxious to underscore that in his intentions at least Descartes is supportive not only of some basic truths of Christianity, but of highly particular truths such as the truth of transubstantiation. Tilliette also offers both theology and philosophy, in particular modern philosophy, incentives for encounter. In its encounter with Christian truths, philosophy becomes deeper and wiser; correlatively, the encounter with modern philosophy or philosophies provides Christian truths the opportunity to rise to new levels of illumination, while the Church gains new levels of self-understanding and a fresh voice for the apologetic and even evangelizing task. Again, in his own double-track work of, on the one hand, uncovering the depth and breadth of the encounter in German Idealism between philosophy and Christian truth as a parable of what can go right and wrong in this encounter, and, on the other, more thematic explorations of Christ as both a fact of history and a construct of faith, Tilliette carries out a conversation between philosophy and theology that illustrates the mutual benefit to both.

This small book stages the encounter between modern philosophy or, better, modern philosophies and the mystery of the Eucharist as rendered in Catholic practice and thought. Although the book is quite expansive in its range, Tilliette does not attempt to be comprehensive. First, he makes the interpretive decision to engage only those modern thinkers whose attitude to the Eucharist is relatively positive rather than negative, including those favorably disposed to the Catholic doctrine of transubstantiation as formulated at the Council of Trent. Tilliette's stance here is well captured in and by a distinction made by a figure whom Tilliette does not bring to the fore, but who is beloved by interlocutors such as Bouyer and Ratzinger. The figure is Newman, the distinction that between inquiry and investigation. In the *Development of Doctrine* Newman underscores the importance of this distinction in the dialogue between Christian faith and philosophy. It cannot be inconsequential, Newman thinks, whether in philosophy's engagement with Christian truths it refuses to adapt its method of rational scrutiny to the givens of faith (inquiry), or it does so adapt and bears the responsibility of elucidating and understanding faith rather than being solely preoccupied with delving into its warrants (investigation). For Newman, investigation characterizes in general the way the early Church dealt with the goods of reason. Of course, outside the purview of this text that marks Newman's conversion (1845), one can adduce the example of high Scholasticism as a crucial instance of this productive dialogue in which philosophy is a serious conversation partner but is not permitted to rule in a hegemonic fashion. Second, in this book, with the exception of Leibniz and Weil, the cast of characters that Tilliette treats at length is almost exclusively Catholic, and, with some notable exceptions, largely French. Given his marvelous competence in German Idealism, in which there is significant discussion of the Eucharist and even more discussion of the symbol of which the Eucharist was regarded as an instance, the latter point is particularly worth noting. It may very well have been the case, however, that Tilliette felt he had sufficiently covered such material in his tomes on Schelling. In any event, Tilliette does provide a token of his enormous competence in this area in his very brief discussion of Franz von Baader, a thinker who is at once a disseminator of German Idealism and one of its major Christian critics, a thinker steeped in German Romanticism who, though serious about preserving orthodoxy, often played fast and loose with it. Third, and related to both of these points, is what I might refer to as Tilliette's avowal of orthodoxy in principle, but toleration of heterodoxy in fact when it comes to the formulation of Christian beliefs, sacramental or otherwise. Tilliette is not being contradictory. The goal is, indeed, orthodoxy. Yet, in order for orthodoxy to be meaningful and apologetically effective, Christian faith has to be open to new and different philosophical vocabularies and grammars. In the short run, even with the best intentions these new vocabularies and grammars may destabilize orthodoxy and lead to heterodoxy. Nonetheless, Tilliette is convinced that heterodoxy will be temporary and will prove productive—if only in the long run—in the fashioning or refashioning of an orthodox understanding of Christian truth or Christian mysteries.

When it comes to understanding where Tilliette stands on the relation between orthodoxy and heterodoxy, while once again it would be apposite here to invoke Newman and the *Development of Doctrine* it is probably more useful to invoke the two prime representatives of the nineteenth-century Tübingen School, that is, Adam Möhler and Johann Sebastian Drey. Möhler provides an analogue insofar as he is anxious to capture the entire Christian phenomenon of which the Eucharist is a constitutive element. Doctrinal formulation is important, but it is normed by the Christian phenomenon or mystery to which it intends to be adequate but which necessarily exceeds it. Much in the manner that we see operative here in this text, theologically things go wrong for the reflection on faith when there is an over-concentration on a particular aspect of the phenomenon tied together with the sense that explanation in the strict sense is the goal. If the genius of heresy is the genius of mistaking the part for the whole, the form of heresy is the mistaken confidence that important aspects of faith submit without remainder to rational rule. Drey provides a different kind of analogue for Tilliette. Drey thinks of heterodoxy as fortuitous and productive. In challenging regnant and often stagnant forms of orthodoxy that have ceased to sound in the Christian community and resound outside and thus degenerated into a "hyperorthodoxy," heterodoxy provides a challenge and goad for Christian thought to think more deeply and to conceptualize more sharply the truths of the faith. This is essential, of course, if the Church is to affirm something to be true, but also important in an apologetic situation in which the Church has to give a bold and persuasive account of itself to the world.

While Tilliette's overall approach is descriptive rather than evaluative, in *The Eucharist in Modern Philosophy*, which represents a translation of *Philosophies eucharistiques de Descartes à Blondel* (2006), he leaves us in no doubt that the conversation between Catholicism and modern philosophy can sputter out when the application of refined conceptual tools to the Eucharist proves too little and too much (Descartes) or when the conceptual tools are so wedded to a complicated metaphysics that it essentially makes the obscure more obscure (Leibniz). Importantly, however, Tilliette thinks that one should respect the attempts by Descartes and Leibniz and their followers to find a different philosophical grammar than that of Aristotle to account for the exchange of substance from bread and wine into the body and blood of Christ at the Eucharist. Although, on Tilliette's view, Descartes's actual deployment of his philosophy is not successful, he does not accept Pascal's construction of Descartes's philosophy as entirely—even if implicitly—hostile to Christian faith. Furthermore, while Leibniz's bona fides as a Christian can be taken for granted in the way his clarity cannot, pointing to how Blondel availed himself of some of Leibniz's key concepts, especially the concept of *vinculum*, demonstrates that Leibniz's concepts had—and maybe still have—not only a certain pregnancy, but also a definite—even if limited—Catholic utility. Unembarrassed by the Tridentine view of transubstantiation, Tilliette's fundamental problem with the physics or mechanics of transformation of substance and preservation of species, upheld in different ways by Descartes and Leibniz, is rather that it risks what Whitehead called the fallacy of abstract concreteness. Specifically, the objection is that in both cases their philosophies concern themselves exclusively with a single aspect of the multivalent phenomenon of the Eucharist rather than the entire phenomenon or entire "mystery" in its biblical, phenomenological, and christological presuppositions. In addition, both fail to point to and develop the relationship of the Eucharist to spirituality, to Christian formation and life, to the Church both as cause and effect, to the cosmos, and finally to eschatology, which is inscribed in the rite of the Eucharist. This larger frame is embraced in very different ways by the likes of Rosmini, de Chardin, and Blondel, who, arguably, are the three central figures in *The*

Eucharist in Modern Philosophy. All three respect the whole Eucharistic phenomenon or mystery and the subtlety of its connections to other topoi of
theology, not excluding the doctrine of the Trinity.

I enthusiastically recommend this little book by Tilliette, written at the
end of a long and illustrious academic career. The voice is far more personal
than that of his tomes, and it is markedly without anxiety about its com-
pleteness. Indeed, its charm lies in part in its very incompleteness. Still,
there can be no doubt that the work has a deeply personal meaning for Tilliette, who flags the phenomenon or mystery that for him then and throughout his life was the center of his Catholic faith. Another advantage of this
work is that while the text is chronological in sequence, the short chapters
on thinkers admit of being read in isolation. Indeed, reading them in this
way after one has read the book through gives real evidence of the meaning
of the selected authors for Tilliette, as well as the very different attractions
they have for him. Together the readings give a testimonial to the Eucharist
as a central mystery of Christian faith and the beating heart of the Catholic
Church. The book is in vitally important respects a memorial. It is a memorial of the Eucharist in the modern age where we might not tend to expect
it and in some cases least expect to find it. Of course, the memories that
sustain the Eucharist in the modern age are a testimony to the power of
anamnetic quality of the Eucharist itself. It is also a memorial in a kind of
Pascalian sense of a personal testimony and witness.

In some respects Tilliette's turn to the Eucharist at the end of a lifelong
engagement with modern philosophy and contemporary culture reminds
of yet another great nineteenth-century Tübingen theologian, Franz Anton
Staudenmaier (1800–1856), though importantly without the latter's return
to Scholasticism and concomitant vitriolic critique of the German Idealism
that he had once embraced. In the end, however, Tilliette's approach to the
conjunction of faith and reason and theology and philosophy is very much
his own and not reducible to the analogies with the major figures of the
Tübingen School, Newman, or for that matter his interlocutors. Like other
Catholic French thinkers steeped in German philosophy such as Jean Wahl,
Gaston Fessard, Claude Bruaire, and Jean-Luc Marion, his work in general
has an inescapable French esprit. This is particularly so in the present work,
because its subject matter is the Eucharist, which has been a mainstay of
French spirituality since Pierre Bérulle and the rise of the French School of
spirituality, in which the Eucharist was both the theological and adorative
center. As already indicated, a majority of the thinkers covered in *The*

Eucharist in Modern Philosophy are French. Yet not all the figures covered are philosophers in the strict sense. The text also moves outside philosophy and speaks to the way the Eucharist is taken up in adorative fashion in Paul Claudel, and is also at the very least recalled in the poetry of Baudelaire, Rimbaud, Verlaine, and Mallarmé, each of whom finds himself stalled in his attempts to move beyond his Catholicism. *The Eucharist in Modern Philosophy* emanates from a deep wisdom, while also exhibiting a certain playfulness, as if the Eucharist is far too deep, far too mysterious, to be matched by any single attempt of reason to be adequate to it.

The translation by Jonathan Ciraulo is first rate. I applaud this extraordinarily accomplished young theologian and great scholar of Hans Urs von Balthasar for capturing the nuances of Tilliette's thought in supple and clear prose. I applaud him even more for capturing the creative élan of Tilliette's tour of modern philosophy's (and poetry's) encounter with the mystery of the Eucharist. The wonderfully lively translation is complemented by an eloquent Introduction that introduces Tilliette to Anglophone readers as well as skillfully mapping Tilliette's buoyant text. In terms of reflecting on a kaleidoscopic array of modern thinkers who encounter and speak of and to the Eucharist, in this book, written when he was over eighty, Tilliette gets as far as the early Marion. One would love to know whether he was familiar with the work of Louie-Marie Chauvet and Marion's protégé, Jean-Yves Lacoste, and if so, what he thought of them. It also would have been fascinating to know whether he had read Catherine Pickstock's *After Writing*. We know well that English would not have handicapped this profound philosopher who was also a renowned linguist. In any event, this translation of Tilliette whets the appetite for more, indeed, "more" on a number of deep and complementary fronts. First, it invites a more comprehensive account of the engagement of modern philosophy and the Eucharist before the late twentieth century that might make us see what options there are before us beyond phenomenology and beyond postmodernism. In this respect, one could not afford to ignore the contribution—however problematic—of German Idealism. A reading of Tilliette's rich scholarship on Schelling would be essential to the task. Second, we might want to see the connection in Tilliette's work between his presenting the encounter between modern philosophy and the Eucharist and what he does in a more scholarly and comprehensive way in presenting the encounter between modern philosophy and Christ. The reason for this extension is simple: Tilliette makes clear throughout this little book that the horizon of the Eucharist is just as important as its focal features that engaged Descartes and Leibniz. Thus what this book seems to call for and his books on the relation between philosophy and Christ seem to demonstrate is the imbrication of the Eucharist with the other mysteries and articles of faith. In doing so, in a non-theological register, Tilliette recalls not only Hans Urs von Balthasar, but also Louis Bouyer. Tilliette is a hopeful thinker who is confident that the best of reason opens up faith and mystery rather than closes them down. There is much to be critiqued in modern philosophy, even more to be filtered. As long as Christian thinkers, and more specifically Catholic thinkers, adopt the boldness of profession and confession that they are called to, there is nothing to fear. Reason is capable of overcoming its worst instincts and, in any event, reason is ordered to faith that does not annul reason, but rather allows it to grow into its maturity as a testimony to wonder, excess, and an origin that requires a form of remembering that salutes and celebrates that which transcends it.

Cyril O'Regan

Translator's Introduction

The work of Xavier Tilliette, SJ (1921–2018), has been a consistent and trenchant assertion that Tertullian's question, "what has Athens to do with Jerusalem?," is a purely theoretical inquiry, at least in the modern era. Regardless of the endless speculation of how theology and philosophy *should* interact, for which there are innumerable proposals, Tilliette's work shows how, in the various streams of modern philosophy, they have in fact been far more closely related than is usually acknowledged. Although he is highly invested in philosophy's influence on and support for theology, the majority of his work has been dedicated to historical analyses of how theological data, from the historical Jesus to the idea of an institutional Church, is far more than an ancillary aspect of the story of modern philosophy. This is fairly obvious in figures such as Hegel or Blondel, but Tilliette also provides detailed commentary on how Descartes, Spinoza, Kant, Fichte, Jaspers, as well as a host of more minor figures variously measured, or in some cases were measured by, Christian Revelation. Even the relative absence of Christ in an individual's philosophy, as in Heidegger's,[1] or the stipulated opposition between Christianity and philosophy, as in Kierkegaard,[2] simply confirms the tensile relationship between philosophy and theology, even if it is by way of negation.

Tilliette is not primarily a speculative or constructive thinker, though the taxonomies that he uses to categorize these various thinkers betray his creativity and capacity for critical judgment. But there is perhaps no other writer who has so closely surveyed and presented the ways in which the data of Christian revelation appear throughout the philosophies of the modern era, as well as the enormous benefits that theology gains from philosophical reflection, no matter how heterodox. He happily notes when, as is quite often the case, philosophers either partially or majorly distort the givens of the Christian faith, but he is never ungenerous toward even the most blasphemous of philosophers. While his tone is usually that of the dispassionate historian, he never hesitates to note when fruitful speculation degenerates into gnostic reevaluations. And though Tilliette has many notable influences, it is clear that he is an almost unwavering Blondelian,

---

1 See *Le Christ des philosophes: Du Maître de sagesse au divin Témoin* (Namur: Culture et Vérité, 1993), 394–401.

2 *Le Christ*, 165–76.

as is evident not only in this volume, but in his texts on Christology. Thus the generosity that he extends to even those who radically alter and even reconfigure Christianity stems from a confidence that thought itself moves, ineluctably though never without opposition, toward the God-man, Jesus Christ, and the concrete cult that he established, the Eucharist.

Xavier Tilliette was born in 1921 in Corbie, in the north of France, and entered the Jesuit novitiate in 1938, being ordained a priest in 1951.[3] After finishing his doctorate at the Sorbonne, with a thesis on Schelling, he taught philosophy primarily at l'Institut Catholique de Paris and the Pontifical Gregorian University in Rome. He was a visiting professor at numerous European universities, particularly in Germany and Italy, and was the recipient of many honors, including from the Académie française and the Institut de France. This book in particular earned both a Humboldt Prize and the Victor-Delbos Prize, both in 2006. Tilliette, though of a younger generation, has a place among the great Jesuit theologians and philosophers of the twentieth century, many of whom were his mentors and friends: Teilhard de Chardin, Henri de Lubac, Gaston Fessard, Jean Daniélou, Hans Urs von Balthasar, and Karl Rahner. It is impossible here to comment upon the enormous scope of his writings, as they range from Descartes and Malebranche to German Idealism and Russian Sophiology, to existentialism and phenomenology.[4] There is very little in modern philosophy that escaped Tilliette's attention. Yet, his thought was not scattered, even if it managed to go in a bewildering number of directions. What unites much of his work is the acknowledgment of the "impurity" of philosophy, its frequent return to the realm of dogmatics, without simply transforming into theology. This is seen quite evidently in his numerous books on Schelling, about whom he is easily one of the most authoritative commentators.[5]

---

3 Simone Stancampiano has written a brief biography and provided a representative bibliography in "Xavier Tilliette: Fede e sapere in dialogo," available online at http://www.giornaledifilosofia.net/public/scheda.php?id=78. Tilliette also wrote a long reflection about his life, particularly his time in formation as a Jesuit, in the excellent book on his work, *Xavier Tilliette inedito*, ed. Antonio Russo (Milan: Franco Angeli, 2020), 83–161. There one can see his major influences, as well as his dedication to the Society of Jesus.

4 The most comprehensive list of Tilliette's works is *Bibliografia di Xavier Tilliette*, ed. M. Monaco (Trieste: Edizioni Università di Trieste, 2002).

5 To name only a few of his most important works on Schelling: *Schelling: Une philosophie en devenir*, vol. 1, *Le système vivant, 1794–1821* and vol. 2, *La derniere philosophie, 1821–1854* (Paris: Vrin, 1970), *L'absolu et la philosophie: Essais sur Schelling* (Paris: Presses Universitaires de France), 1987), *La mythologie comprise: L'interprétation schellingienne du paganisme* (Paris: Vrin, 2002), and *Schelling: Biographie* (Paris: Calmann-Lévy, 1999).

The Eucharist in Modern Philosophy is derivative of Tilliette's expansive writings on the question of philosophical Christology.[6] From there, from his minute analysis of how the historical figure of Jesus, or perhaps just the idea of a Christ, has reverberated throughout modern philosophy, Tilliette has extended this primary line of investigation to include modern philosophy's relationship to scripture,[7] the Church,[8] and the subject of this volume, the Eucharist.[9] This work is, though not his first,[10] his most detailed analysis of the surprising survival of eucharistic philosophies in the modern era. Here he focuses on both those whose eucharistic speculations are more or less well known, especially Descartes, Leibniz, and Blondel, but also a whole host of other philosophers whose engagement with sacramental discourse is rather limited or perhaps only intimated, but are still nonetheless of particular interest, such as Hamann and Fichte. By no means is his analysis comprehensive, but his selection is representative of the wide-ranging philosophical interest in the sacraments, an interest that only seems to be growing. For instance, other than the important exception of his treatment of Jean-Luc Marion, Tilliette deals with phenomenology only sparingly, and does not discuss Heidegger's own evident antipathy to the sacraments. Yet it is phenomenology in the tradition of Heidegger that is perhaps showing the greatest capacity for taking the Eucharist as a genuine philosophical topic, as is seen in the work of Jean-Yves Lacoste,[11] Emmanuel Falque,[12]

---

6 See especially *Le Christ des philosophes: Du Maître de sagesse au divin Témoin*, but also *Le Christ de la Philosophie* (Paris: Cerf, 1990), *La Christologie idéaliste* (Paris: Desclée, 1986), *La Semaine sainte des philosophes* (Paris: Desclée, 1992), and *Jésus romantique* (Paris: Desclée, 2002).

7 *Les philosophes lisent la Bible* (Paris: Cerf, 2001).

8 *L'Église des philosophes, de Nicolas de Cuse à Gabriel Marcel* (Paris: Cerf, 2006).

9 This book has also been previously translated into Italian and Portuguese: *Eucaristia e Filosofia*, trans. Giuliano Sansonetti (Brescia: Morcelliana, 2008) and *Eucaristia e Filosofia*, trans. Ubenai Lacerda (Rio de Janeiro: Editora Santuario, 2011). The original French title is *Philosophies eucharistiques de Descartes à Blondel* (*Eucharistic Philosophies from Descartes to Blondel*), though the simpler *The Eucharist in Modern Philosophy* has been chosen to eliminate some confusion, as Tilliette's analysis extends through much later in the twentieth century after Blondel.

10 Two previous essays that cover much of the same ground as this book should be noted: "Problèmes de philosophie eucharistique," *Gregorianum* 64, no. 2 (1983): 273–305 and "Problèmes de philosophie eucharistique II," *Gregorianum* 65, no. 4 (1984): 605–34. Tilliette was an expert on Paul Claudel and wrote the preface to the critical edition of Claudel's meditation on the Mass, *La Messe là-bas* (Presses universitaires de Franche-Comté, 2009).

11 See *L'intuition sacramentelle et autres essais* (Ad Solem, 2015).

12 See *The Wedding Feast of the Lamb: Eros, the Body, and the Eucharist*, trans. George Hughes (New York: Fordham University Press, 2016).

Jean-Luc Nancy,[13] Michel Henry,[14] and Jean-Louis Chrétien.[15] Far beyond
being the sole province of French phenomenology, there are even more
"Eucharistic philosophies," however brief or even antagonistic, that can be
discovered in the work of countless other recent and contemporary philosophers, for example, Xavier Zubiri,[16] Robert Sokolowski,[17] Giorgio
Agamben,[18] and Slavoj Žižek.[19] And although Tilliette's selection of philosophers as opposed to theologians reflects the obscurity of the borderlands
between the disciplines (why, for instance are Teilhard de Chardin and Gustave Martelet included here, and not, say, Karl Rahner?[20]), one could add
the philosophically inflected Eucharistic texts by theologians such as
Edward Schillebeeckx,[21] Louis-Marie Chauvet,[22] and Catherine Pickstock,[23]
among many others.

As is evident to anyone familiar with sacramental theology, the pairing
of the Eucharist and philosophical reflection is not a novelty of the modern
era. Perhaps the most significant catalyst for the development of Eucharistic

13 E.g., Nancy begins his *Corpus* (New York: Fordham University Press, 2008) by citing the *hoc est corpus meum*, 2. See also *The Disavowed Community*, trans. Philip Armstrong (New York: Fordham University Press, 2016), 24–50, which also implicates Maurice Blanchot as a thinker of the Eucharist.

14 Henry, though he writes about the flesh of Christ, explicitly mentions the Eucharist only rather infrequently. See, for instance, *Words of Christ*, trans. Christina M. Gschwandtner (Grand Rapids, MI: Eerdmans, 2012), 124.

15 For instance, Chrétien explores the possibility of speech being Eucharistic in *The Ark of Speech*, trans. Andrew Brown (New York: Routledge, 2003).

16 Xavier Zubiri, "Reflexiones Teológicas Sobre La Eucaristía," *Estudios Eclesiásticos* 56, no. 216–17 (1981): 41–60.

17 *Eucharistic Presence: A Study in the Theology of Disclosure* (Washington, DC.: The Catholic University of America Press, 1994).

18 Agamben's writing on the sacraments is found throughout his *Homo Sacer* books, collected as *The Omnibus Homo Sacer* (Stanford, CA: Stanford University Press, 2017).

19 See *The Monstrosity of Christ: Paradox or Dialectic?* with John Milbank, ed. Creston Davis (Cambridge, MA: MIT Press, 2009), 289–91.

20 Though Rahner wrote voluminously on the sacraments, see particularly his hugely influential "The Theology of the Symbol," in *Theological Investigations IV*, trans. Kevin Smyth (London: Darton, Longman & Todd, 1974), 221–52.

21 For instance, *L'économie sacramentelle du salut: Réflexion théologique sur la doctrine sacra-mentaire de saint Thomas, à la lumière de la tradition et de la problématique sacramentelle contemporaine*, trans. Yvon van der Have (Fribourg: Academic Press Fribourg, 2004) and *The Eucharist* (London: Sheed and Ward, 1968).

22 *Symbol and Sacrament: A Sacramental Reinterpretation of Christian Existence*, trans. Patrick Madigan and Madeleine Beaumont (Collegeville, MN: The Liturgical Press, 1995).

23 *After Writing: On the Liturgical Consummation of Philosophy* (Oxford: Blackwell, 1997).

doctrine (and the same is true for many other doctrinal *topoi*), at every major stage of its elaboration and contention, has been new conceptual tools and commitments supplied by philosophy. Though we need not reduce theological development to the philosophical pressures placed upon it, which would indeed be a massively reductive reading, it does remain the case that the elaboration of Eucharistic doctrine has ever been accompanied by philosophical friends and enemies. The eleventh-century Berengarian controversy, that archetypical sacramental debate, cannot be adequately understood without noting the rise of "dialectics" and the influence of Augustine's semiology, just as the story of Thomas Aquinas's deployment of transubstantiation and sacramental secondary causality is not complete without accounting for the Aristotelian origins of much of his technical vocabulary. The same principle holds for Reformation debates and twentieth-century proposals of "transsignification" or "transfinalization," whereby adjustments to sacramental doctrine are demanded by changing metaphysical landscapes.

Philosophical pressure, whether by way of inspiration or opposition, will thus always be the fate of theological reflection, including sacramental discourse. As Hans Urs von Balthasar said epigrammatically: *ohne Philosophie keine Theologie.*[24] Yet, what Tilliette traces throughout his other christological texts, and in this eucharistic one, is that in the modern era the pressure is applied in both directions: *ohne Theologie keine Philosophie.* Though undoubtedly questions of sacramentality would have been an implicit question in the work of much of premodern philosophers, such as Aquinas's more explicitly philosophical texts, in modernity the Eucharist is itself named as a formal object of philosophical inquiry. This can be read as perhaps the end result of a slow process of removing any *disciplina arcani* regarding the hidden mysteries of the Christian faith, at least as those are understood as external norms regarding the scope of access to Christianity's most cherished rites. Now, the Eucharist is as much the patrimony of the philosopher, the sociologist, and the anthropologist as it is of the theologian. There is no doubt that this has led to no little sacrilege, and some of that intellectual sacrilege is indeed recounted within this volume. Yet, as the Eucharist has become an object of analysis beyond the faculty of theology, there have also been enormous gains. Eucharistic thought and faith is now

---

24 "Without philosophy, no theology" (*Theologik I: Wahrheit der Welt* [Einsiedeln: Johannes Verlag, 1985], vii).

more subtle, perhaps more aware of the spiritual and intellectual implications inherent in the sacrament thanks to polymaths like Pascal and poets
like Paul Claudel, to say nothing of the intense Eucharistic piety of the
unbaptized Simone Weil. And even when the attempts of Descartes and
Leibniz to square their own systems with the demands of dogma lead ultimately to admitted failures, or when Hegel and Feuerbach entirely disman-
tle the Catholic sense of the sacrament, there are still gains in Eucharistic
clarity, even if only by way of contrast and warning. Even for these we can
give thanks, as Tilliette does in this volume. As he writes here in the concluding chapter, "The best eucharistic theory is not the one that isolates
some aspects from others, and which decomposes the sacrament into a multiplicity of objective givens, but is rather the one that embraces the amplitude of the mystery and synthesizes as many aspects as possible." However
cut off from the whole, however distorted, the philosophers of the Eucharist
surveyed here provide aspects and entryways into the Eucharistic mystery,
to which the theologian should respond by saying more rather than less.

Tilliette was a widely respected and highly influential philosopher in
Europe, though, with few exceptions,[25] his work is relatively unknown among
English-speaking philosophers and theologians. It is my hope that this first
translation of one of Tilliette's monographs will encourage further engagement
with this prodigious proponent of "catholic philosophy," to use Blondel's term.
He is a thinker as committed to philosophy's "method of immanence" as he is
to theology's transcendent object, and should thus be of interest to practitioners
of both disciplines who acknowledge that there is no genuine theology without
philosophy or philosophy without theology. But even more so, my hope is that
this volume might demonstrate the vehemence of sacramental discourse, the
perdurance of the question of concrete cult, even in an age that has seemingly
forgotten that bread and wine can become flesh and blood.

Jonathan Martin Ciraulo

---

25 Tilliette has been translated into English primarily in various articles in *Communio*: "Henri
de Lubac: The Legacy of a Theologian," *Communio: International Catholic Review* 19, no. 3 (Fall
1992): 332–41; "Notes and Reflections on the Virtue of Hope," *Communio: International Catholic
Review* 23, no. 3 (Fall 1996): 441–47; "The Chastity of Jesus," *Communio: International Catholic
Review* 24, no. 1 (Spring 1997): 51–56; and "Trinity and Creation," *Communio: International Catholic Review* 28, no. 2 (Summer 2001): 296–310. An excellent short summary of his larger books
on the relationship between Christology and philosophy is "Is a Philosophical Christology Possible?" in *Problems and Perspectives of Fundamental Theology*, ed. René Latourelle and Gerald
O'Collins, trans. Matthew J. O'Connell (New York: Paulist Press, 1982), 135–50.

Author's Preface

The history of eucharistic doctrines shows both the elaboration of the dogma up to the definitions of the Council of Trent and the persistent recurrence of problems associated with the mystery, as well as problems that are adjacent to it. Indeed, the eucharistic mystery, *mysterium fidei*, because it implies the memorial of the Passion, the holy sacrifice, communion or the act of eating, consecration and the priesthood, lends itself to intense and difficult theological research. This doctrinal history is, indeed, marked by discussions, disputes, quarrels, and refutations, which were aggravated by the Protestant schism and the heresies that followed.

We wish here to examine this long controversy chronologically from the angle of philosophy. The letter of the dogma is firmly elaborated in the Middle Ages and it benefited from the powerful thought of St. Thomas Aquinas and scholasticism. The vitality of the theologians of the Council of Trent, particularly the Jesuit Diego Laynez, provided a solid fulcrum for the discussions, which was exacerbated by the new heresies. Orthodoxy, however, provided solid defenders as well, including philosophers who did not intend to yield to the reassessments of a hostile reason.

Eucharistic theology is, indeed, closely linked to philosophical explanation. The notions that it brings into play are borrowed from the language of scholasticism, and the mishaps of the dispute of universals and of nominalism are strongly linked to eucharistic theories. On the Catholic side, the doctrine is solidly anchored, but it is philosophy that, under the impulse of Descartes and then of Leibniz, is modernized and opened up to unprecedented paths. This necessarily has repercussions on the eucharistic controversies brought on by the division of the Churches.

Our approach here is historical, that is to say, chronological, but we have paused only for the major figures. Indeed, eucharistic philosophies are elaborated in the dust of polemics, but not in such a way that they present a united front. On the side of Catholic theologians and spiritual authors, it seems that they unknowingly anticipate the brilliant intuition of Gabriel Marcel, for whom the mystery illuminates the problems rather than the other way around, and thus Christ's presence illuminates communion and the multiplication of the sacramental species.

In various aspects the philosophy (born of the theology) of the Eucharist persists today, where it takes on very beautiful formulations. It becomes quickly apparent that the eucharistic question par excellence concerns the treatment of the sacramental species. Questions concerning the eucharistic transmutation are bound up with this issue, and thus not just with the nature of the consecrated species. At issue is what happens to the species during their multiplication, multilocation, division, and destruction. The eucharistic miracle is certainly concerned with consecration, communion, and the reserved sacrament, but above all, with persistence and presence. But the condition of the sacramental species remains, and the real presence is attached to them.

These pages of historical analysis have been conceived according to this central thread. The core of the book is based on courses given at the Gregorian University of Rome and the Institut Catholique de Paris in 1980. The course in Rome was given in Italian and, thanks to the zeal of Giuliano Sansonetti, it will be published shortly in Italian. The present volume is not a translation from Italian but the original French version. Once again, the technical and dedicated assistance of Alain Pernet has been invaluable to me, but I dedicate this work of reflection and piety to two great Dominican friends who have departed, Fr. Liégé (1921–1979) and Fr. Dominique Dubarle (1907–1987), the former dean of the faculty of philosophy of the Institut Catholique de Paris, who opened its doors to me in 1969.

Chapter 1

René Descartes and Eucharistic Physics

J ean-Luc Marion has nicely said that Descartes's theology, after his grey ontology, is a white theology, white as this page on which I begin writing. He explains: "We will qualify this theology as a white theology. White because it is anonymous and indeterminate, like a carte blanche that qualifies its beneficiary without specifying the enterprise, or as a blank check, which does not specify the amount of credit that it nevertheless grants. The theology of Cartesian metaphysics remains white first of all because its beneficiary (or its carrier) remains, ultimately, anonymous."[1] The theological discretion that Descartes has imposed on himself responds to his enigmatic motto: *larvatus prodeo*, I go forward, masked.[2] In fact, he has never developed the third of the divine wonders that the *Olympica* signaled by a meteoric line: *hominem Deum*. There is, however, an exception to this legendary prudence, and it is the Eucharist. For Henri Gouhier, the Eucharist served as a "sample" of Cartesian theology[3] and it permitted Jean-Robert Armogathe to entitle his learned thesis *Theologia cartesiana: L'explication physique de l'Eucharistie chez Descartes et dom Desgabets*.[4] But this sample is unique. Why? Is it because Descartes decided to take leave from his normal reservations, albeit with precaution? The meaning of the Cartesian revolution and the emancipation of philosophy should not be misunderstood. Descartes, a student and friend of Jesuits, is a sincere believer, a good Catholic, an obedient son of the Church. He is convinced that he possesses the truth, that he has invented the true Christian philosophy that is capable of supporting the faith; and the question of the Eucharist offers an incomparable

---

[1] *Sur la théologie blanche de Descartes* (Paris: Presses Universitaires de France, 1982), 450.

[2] See the explanation of this motto by Henri Gouhier, *Essais sur Descartes* (Paris: Vrin, 1937), 292–94. For the sentence about the *Olympica*, see Gouhier, *Les Premières Pensées de Descartes* (Paris: Vrin, 1958), 84–85.

[3] Henri Gouhier, *La Pensée religieuse de Descartes* (Paris: Vrin, 1924), 248–58.

[4] Jean-Robert Armogathe, *Theologia cartesiana: L'explication physique de l'Eucharistie chez Descartes et dom Desgabets* (La Haye: Nijhoff, 1977).

solution. Descartes, remarkably, desires to help the theologians in their embarrassment, for their doctrine of real accidents leads to absurdities. He never renounced this great apologetic intention. Gouhier recalls the mystical origins of Cartesian philosophy, the pilgrimage to Loretto, the friendship with Cardinal Bérulle, the condemnation of Galileo, which did not particularly move Descartes. . . . The fact remains, according to Gouhier, that Cartesian Christianity lacks warmth; the good intentions "express themselves in a system where religious objects take such little space, and where the essential problems of the Christian life are not even posed."[5] Descartes's piety is certainly not feigned, but it is also not ablaze. Nevertheless, Maurice Blondel is without doubt too severe when he portrays Descartes as cunning and evasive in his "Le christianisme de Descartes."[6] Maritain and Laberthonnière have more balanced analyses.

If, contrary to his customary disposition, Descartes responded with so much availability to the eucharistic difficulties of "some theologians," it is because he thinks he has in hand a solution that is "extremely clear and easy for *his* principles." It successively counters the problem of real accidents without substance and a substantial change without a change of appearance. It is this marvelously appropriate solution that we will examine here. The main texts are "Reply to the Fourth Set of Objections" (to Arnauld)[7] and the "Reply to the Sixth Set of Objections" (number 2),[8] the letters to Fr. Denis Mesland on May 2, 1644, and especially on February 6, 1645, to Clerselier in March 1646, another to an unknown correspondent, also without a date, and finally the farewell letter to Fr. Mesland in 1646.[9] We will also add the passage from the *Principles of Philosophy* on surfaces (II 13, 15).[10]

---

5 Armogathe, 196.

6 *Revue de métaphysique et de morale*, 1896, reproduced in *Dialogue avec les philosophes* (56–67).

7 "Reply to the Fourth Set of Objections," in *Meditations, Objections, and Replies* (Hackett, 2006).

8 "Reply to the Sixth Set of Objections," in *Meditations, Objections, and Replies* (Hackett, 2006).

9 Besides the letter to Clerselier, English translations of the letters are collected in *Selected Correspondence of Descartes*, trans. Jonathan Bennett. Available online at https://www.early moderntexts.com/assets/pdfs/descartes1619_4.pdf.

10 Also see II § 4: extension alone constitutes the nature of the body—its nature consists in the fact that it alone is a substance which has extension.

THE THEORY OF ACCIDENTS

Descartes's eucharistic theory is a theory of physics, in short, the first that tries to render physically plausible the physical transformation of the consecrated bread and wine, whereas scholasticism remains entangled in a metaphysical conception of matter, namely, hylomorphism. Descartes, "going up on the rampart" as Gouhier says, is convinced that his physics is a Christian physics (!) and that it explains the miracle of the permanence of the species. However, the new physics seems quite clearly to be in disagreement with the formulations of the Council of Trent, and it is the objection of the "theologians" that the young Arnauld relays to him (he was not yet *le Grand* Arnauld). Indeed, in Cartesian physics the substance of bodies is extended, things are reduced to shape and movements, while "sensible qualities" or secondary qualities are only "some different movements of small bodies that are around us. . . ." There is no more than extension, shape, and motion. Extension is identified with substance and the modifications of extension are the modifications of the substance: how could a change of substance be able, in these conditions, to leave the extension and the shape intact? The problem of eucharistic accidents seems aggravated, for, as Arnauld states, "we believe on faith that once the substance of the bread has been removed from the Eucharistic bread only the accidents remain there."[11]

However, the objection does not surprise an unprepared author, who, on the contrary, is accustomed to not trusting the "vision of the eyes."[12] With Descartes everything begins with a piece of wax that smells like honey, brought fresh from the hive and submitted to a metamorphosis: it melts in fire, it is liquid, it cools down, hardens, and is malleable; kneaded into a ball and struck, it makes a thud. . . . It changes, but under its various manifestations it remains the same piece of wax. What then constitutes its identity? It is an "inspection of the mind" that assures the permanence of the object through the diversity and the dissolution of its appearances. The judgment or intuition of the intellect establishes the identity of what is perceived. Just as the thing that thinks, as seen in the Cogito, returns to the thing that doubts, that recalls, that feels, that imagines . . . so the vision of thought recovers the wax that is yellow, liquid, solid, soft, round, square. . . . This substance of wax that is only accessible to the view of the mind is not, however, a mental thing, and the

---

11 "Reply to the Fourth Set of Objections," 149.

12 See the end of *Seconde Méditation Métaphysique*.

changes that modify the substance do not constitute it, as phenomenalism believes (Hume). Extension belongs to the corporeal substance, to which the intelligence links the appearances, which one should not trust.

The eucharistic question presents the inverse situation and so is like a counter-test: the permanence of accidents in the alteration and even the substitution of the substance. But the terms of the solution are the same, which is about detaching, in a matter of speaking, the accidents and transferring them to something else for support: thus, there is no contradiction in the fact that they persist while their original substance (bread and wine) are replaced. The persistence of the accidents will require some explanation. But Descartes, in his *Reply*, begins with a *captatio benevolentiae*: if we are not able to conceive, he says, the separation of the substance and its forms, the all-powerful divinity is able to separate them by consequently maintaining absolute accidents, accidents of a substance that is no longer! Conceding this in order to be safe, one does not have to turn toward this desperate solution, since one can propose a much more economic hypothesis. It consists in a word used to define a median term, which functions, so to say, as the joint between the exchanged substances and the unchanged accidents.

This "median term" is the surface, which he also calls "intermediate" in the long letter to Mesland. It is the crux and the key of the argument, just as the substantial bond will be for Leibniz's theory. Nevertheless, it afflicts the worthy editor of the article "Descartes" of the *Dictionnaire de théologie catholique*, Mgr. Chollet, who cannot find enough groans to complain about the "obscurity" of these Cartesian claims: "All of this eucharistic theory of Descartes is very difficult to understand." Incidentally, he is not entirely wrong, as the champion of French clarity has his obscurities. Descartes, however, does not fail to explain himself. The senses are reached or *touched* only by the surface of bodies, sensible knowledge is produced by a "touching," a contact (Berkeley will later say that vision is a "touching at a distance"), and contact happens solely on the surface or the area. To put it otherwise, the surface is the area of contact. Philosophy compares it to intentional species. It is the area, and it alone, that is touched by the sense organs, whether immediately or through the mediation of the air or other bodies. Surface is, in any event, an extremity and a median term, of the sort that belongs neither to one nor to another, it is *between* (the body and the contiguous body, which is most often air), as an impalpable shared wall.

But Descartes holds a surprise. The surface is more than the (simple) surface! It is not reduced to "the sole exterior shape of bodies" or to the "small circuit," the perimeter, which entirely surrounds them. It is everywhere, in the interstices and intervals of matter. The exterior surface therefore doubles as the corpuscular surface. For every body is a collection of material particles, leaving intervals between them. These miniscule intervals multiply the surfaces, and there are as many surfaces as corpuscles. The body is porous, perforated; its intervals are "full of air or some material," and the particles continually move about: in the case of bread, they are the flour, in the case of wine, they are "alcohol, water, vinegar, and dregs of tartar."[13] Consequently, the species do not risk being assimilated to merely external physiognomy. Further, the summary analysis of the elements of bread and wine begins a sketch of eucharistic physics, in the sense that the substance of bread is made from a plurality of substances, of particles, which are themselves composite ingredients and are even contaminated by intrusive materials that are not a part of the substance. It is then impossible to be content with an overall view of the bread under its external whiteness (this was already implicit in Mersenne's early question and the response on November 25, 1630). Transubstantiation, which must be taken in the stronger and the more active sense and not as a mere spatial transfer, involves a closer analysis. An analogous problem will reappear with the animalcules of Leibniz.

It is not first of all a question of the eucharistic conversion and the physico-ontological mutation that happens to the bread and wine, but of the persistence of the accidents. They remain intact after the Consecration, while the substance has changed. How is this possible, how ought one to understand it? By assimilating the species with the intermediate surface: "*the species of bread* . . . [is] that surface which is in between the individual particles of the bread and the bodies surrounding them."[14] The theorem that governs the argument is the following: "a given surface must always act and be acted upon in the same way, even though the substance that was beneath it is changed."[15] The surface, in fact, is definitely not the corporeal thing that it surrounds, for it is only the localization in space, the extended mode, and as such it does not belong more to one body than another, since it is only

13 "Reply to the Fourth Set of Objections," 149.
14 "Reply to the Fourth Set of Objections," 151.
15 "Reply to the Fourth Set of Objections," 153.

the common place—the position—that they occupy. Its "only being is purely modal."[16] The "Reply to the Sixth Set of Objections" brings some precision to this notion. One can consider the surface of a body to be either its flat surface, length and width, like its thin film (leaving aside the depth that is not denied)—or like a mode or a manner of the body (in this case one can play on the geometric sense of "surface area" [*superficie*]). This modal surface is the question. It is dimensional and does not differ from the "external place" (*Principles of Philosophy* II, 15) that can be attributed to the "surface of a surrounding body" (changing appearance with the body). In sum, the surface, or, if it is applied to the "surface area in general," is always identical as long as it has the "same size and shape."[17] These distinctions are only differences of perspective, made by abstraction; and the long letter to Mesland, which mentions three surfaces (that of the bread, that of the air that touches the bread, and the intermediate surface), clearly articulates that they are "the same thing" and that only thought separates and distinguishes them, as, conversely, thought perceives the piece of wax under its mutations. Therefore, they do not really differ. The tenet of the "Reply to the Sixth Set of Objections" conforms to that of the *Principles of Philosophy*, except that it only envisages the intermediate surface, the "same mode" of two conjoined bodies, like that of a body and the surrounding air. But the result of three surfaces contracted into one or a surface decomposed into three is identical. The benefit of involving the intermediate surface consists in bringing out the surface of the bread, the mode of the substance of the bread. Nevertheless, as there is no real distinction, it requires that the substance of the body of Christ must be exactly isomorphic, imperceptible, covering the same place and the same location.

This ingenious theory is clarified by a few examples, each with differing reach and relevance. The examples aim to show that whatever changes and mutations happen to affect the substances, their surface—their shape—can remain intact and numerically identical; for it is the surface alone that impresses the senses. The example of the tower (from the "Reply to the Sixth Set of Objections") is the simplest: in effect, the air is ceaselessly mixed and replaced, and this replacement by an "object" (of the same dimensions) leaves the place of the tower intact. To put it otherwise, the same silhouette is outlined on the horizon. More specious is the alleged example in the letter

16 "Reply to the Fourth Set of Objections," 150.
17 "Reply to the Sixth Set of Objections," 173.

to Clerselier on March 2, 1646: suppose, Descartes writes, that a purely corporeal substance takes the place of another equally corporeal substance, a piece of gold in the place of a piece of bread, or more simply, a piece of bread A takes the place of another piece of bread B. Only the numerical, material unity changes: the matter of the gold receives the accidents of the bread, the matter of the bread A that of B. Of these two situations, the second is hardly compelling, for it is only a permutation, a translation, as the piece of bread blends with the other piece of bread. The first is more deceitful. It is the reverse of Midas's misfortune, for this miracle transforms metal into bread. Except that the bread, in order to be converted into a golden substance, is already there, and the piece of gold is, as it were, withdrawn. Besides, the operation is reversible, and the ambiguity of the "piece of gold *in the place of* the piece of bread" is only eased arbitrarily. In any case, the example is instructive, as is the continuation of the letter ("there is something more in the Blessed Sacrament: the matter of the body of Jesus Christ is put under the dimensions or the state of bread—but the soul of Jesus Christ that informs this matter is also there"). This suggests that Descartes's theory has the tendency to *bring about* the body of Christ by substituting it for the bread and by its assumption of the accidents, rather than in a conversion of the substance of the bread into the substance of the body of Christ. A tendency that could be a temptation to consubstantiation.

The example of the boat immobilized by the contrary forces of the wind and the current (*Principles of Philosophy* II, 15) demonstrates stability within an environmental instability: according to a mark on the shoreline, the surface area (the occupation of the place) does not move. But this image only adds a moving support (the river) to the previous image of the tower, and it even loses the benefit of the substitution, since here the change is only the alteration of an environment whose effect is neutralized. But, because the vessel cannot roam in this tumult, it suffices to eliminate it and to conserve only the bank of the river and the current in order to obtain the intermediate surface in all its clarity. This is what Descartes does in his missive to Mesland, with the Loire turned into a Heraclitan river. The water constantly flows and changes, the shoreline is replacing itself, but the "blonde Loire"[18] is one and the same in the changing of the container and its contents, thanks to "the identity or similarity of the dimensions."[19] The matter is lost and the

18 Baudelaire, however, calls it the green Loire.
19 *Selected Correspondence of Descartes*, 173.

form remains. Pascal was presumably thinking of this comparison in a hastily written fragment (*Br.* 512), to which we will return in the next chapter. But he connects it, and not without some injustice, to the subsequent explanation of transubstantiation. In any case, one arrives again at the mind's judgment of identity that, inversely, perceived the permanence of the piece of wax under the plurality of its aspects (the matter remains and the form is lost).

The major endeavor of Descartes, the eucharistic believer, focused on the permanence of the species, which he attempted to render plausible by equating them with the intermediate surface. Whatever the alterations of the substance, the surface cannot be affected at all, even if, in our extreme case, the alteration of the substance becomes a change of substance. The theorem justifies the non-mutability of the species; it does not make a pronouncement on transubstantiation itself, which is, incidentally, somewhat compromised to the extent that the corporeal material is in continual movement and agitation. If Descartes proves too much in rendering the persistence of accidents quasi-natural, then he proves too little in minimizing the substitution of one substance for another (because of the continual change, the *perpetuum mobile*, that his examples assume). Moreover, as ingenious as the appeal to the exterior place and the intermediate surface area may be, it is vulnerable to the following objection: the intermediate surface may well take its identity solely from "the identity or similarity of the dimensions," but it is nonetheless a shape of the extension and, as it happens, a mode of the substance (of the bread). Because the shape or the extension does not change, how can one say that the substance changes, and in fact changes radically? The supposed benefit of the theory is then called into question. Descartes understood this difficulty, just as he internalized the surface and attached it to each particle. But in an undated letter to an anonymous recipient, though likely from 1646, he pours out this confession from his heart: "Thus one may ask all theologians as well as myself: 'When one corporeal substance is changed into another and all the accidents of the former remain, what is it that has changed?' And they must reply, as I do, that there is no change that the senses could detect, and hence no change in any basis for giving different names to these substances."[20] And yet the faith tells us that the body of Christ has taken the place of the bread. How can he be exactly under the dimensions of the bread when the extension

---

20 *Selected Correspondence of Descartes*, 182.

has not changed? This is the question of real presence and of the "how" of transubstantiation. It obliged Descartes to break his silence once again. The letters to Clerselier and to an anonymous person allude to a solution, namely, that now it is the soul of Jesus Christ that, in the Blessed Sacrament, "informs the matter." That is to suggest the close relationship of the doctrine of accidents and the interpretation of real presence. But the first to hear of the explanation was a young Jesuit from La Flèche, Fr. Denis Mesland.

THE "HOW" OF TRANSUBSTANTIATION
AND REAL PRESENCE

First of all, a word on Fr. Denis Mesland, correspondent and confidant of Descartes, who is not to be confused with the older, homonymous, Fr. Pierre Mesland, to whom he is perhaps related. The scarce documents concerning him do not always agree. He was born on March 3 (or 30), 1615, in Orleans; he entered the Jesuits at the age of 15 (November 12, 1630); he was a "regent" and teacher in La Flèche. He began his contact with the philosopher during his years of theology (1641–1645); as a young teacher he had written a summary of the *Meditations*. He was a generous soul and decided in the Tertianship (1645–1646) to dedicate himself to the missions. It seems improbable that he was "exiled" on account of his Cartesian sympathies, especially since Descartes counted a good number of supporters and friends among the Jesuits. Bridoux and even Alquié say that his punishment was to be sent "among the Iroquois." In fact, Denis Mesland went to the Antilles (1646) and, despite the desire of his illustrious friend, he moved forward. He made his profession on April 25, 1649. As a missionary to the Caribbean and to Martinique, with zeal and an indefatigable energy, he went to Guyana in 1651, living in a hut in a Galibi village, coming from the island of Granada. He founded the mission of Cayenne in 1653 with Fr. Ignace Pelleprat. The hard worker followed the Orinoco River and disappeared in 1653; he was believed to have died, killed by the Spanish. But in 1657 he was found living among the natives, nearly naked as well. Exhausted, he later retired to the college of Santa Fe in Bogotá, where he died at an uncertain date, either January 18, 1672 or December 7, 1674.

Such is the man to whom Descartes, on February 9, 1645, expresses his eucharistic theory concerning the mode of real presence, after having taken refuge many times in the Council of Trent's prudence clause: *ea existendi ratione, quam etsi verbis exprimere vix possumus*. He begins by recalling and completing his explanation of the continuity of the species, beginning with the intermediate, median, and unaltered surface between the body of Christ that replaces the bread and the other breathable, surrounding "air." The median surface remains *eadem numero*, because it takes its numerical identity uniquely from the *quantitas dimensiva*, from the identity or similitude of dimensions we have already mentioned (it is here that the example of the Loire comes into play).

Then Descartes takes on the question of real presence, obviously closely connected to the doctrine of the accidents (as the letters of 1646 to Clerselier and to an anonymous recipient suggest). The heart of the explanation is the substantial unity of soul and body. The soul is the form of the body, and— here is the fundamental theorem—all that is substantially united to a human soul is a human body. It is the soul that confers on the body its identity and its indivisibility, no matter the extension of the body, from embryo to adult, no matter the incessant development of the cells. The use of the analogy of digestion or of assimilation for the eucharistic conversion (foods "*naturally* transubstantiate"[21]) could make one believe that Descartes understands the miracle in the same way as does Saint Thomas. It is not so: the infinitesimal particles of the bread and the wine remain as such in the darkness of the organs, and it is only with regard to their union with the soul that they are said to be transubstantiated. So while the commentary of Armogathe,[22] which presents a double operation of conversion of the substances and of the union of the soul of Christ with the substance (of the body), comes from a good intention, it seems too benign for Descartes. By the power of the words of consecration, therefore, the soul of Jesus Christ *informs* the host, informs the particles of bread and wine, and "remains supernaturally attached to each one of them, even if one separates them." For, again, quantity has nothing to do with it, and all that which is informed by the same human soul is "a whole and entire human body." From this proposition Pascal derives his joke that the Loire rolls its lazy waves simultaneously in France and in China![23] Malebranche, for his part, clung desperately to the explanation concerning the bond to any kind of body, before he capitulated. But for Descartes, the solution is illuminating. When questioned by Mes-

---

21 *Selected Correspondence of Descartes*, 182.

22 Armogathe, *Theologia cartesiana*, 73.

23 Blaise Pascal, *Pensées et Opuscules*, ed. Léon Brunschvicg (Paris: Hachette, 1909), 561–62, fragment 512.

land about the Eucharist during the *Triduum Mortis* (according to St. Thomas, the apostle would have only consecrated the body without the soul), Descartes responds without embarrassment saying that, unless the Church pronounces otherwise on this point, the matter of the Eucharist "would be as strongly disposed to be united to the soul of Jesus Christ as was the matter of his body lying in the sepulchre."[24] Likewise, the matter of this fictional host on the evening of Good Friday would have the dispositions of the body without blood (poured out), and the wine would have the dispositions of blood without flesh (exsanguinated); the body would have been alone in the host, the precious blood alone in the chalice. The soul being the entelechy of the body that it animates, the solution is correct if the "predisposition" of the host is enough to make it the body of Christ, with or without a soul. Nevertheless, can one say that a cadaver is awaiting a soul, and that transubstantiation is about the body alone?

The difficulties are, in fact, difficult to ignore, and Mesland had to draw attention to them. The soul of Christ is in the Blessed Sacrament *by concomitance*, while transubstantiation directly concerns the substance of the body, not the transforming infusion of a soul. On the other hand, even if the soul is the *forma corporis*, it is less convincing to say that it suffices to transform the body that it inhabits. The Cartesian dualism does not leave any room for an alternative to the following: that the body before the soul is only matter and inert extension (the mechanistic hypothesis). But the soul does not inform any body whatsoever. This is Fr. Fabri's perplexity: what if God attached my soul to a rock?[25] This makes one think of the Husserlian fiction of a consciousness grafted onto a locomotive. It is true that Descartes would not be lacking in arguments to defend himself on this issue, and Blondel in this case comes to his defense (in insisting on the *substantial* union of the body and soul).

As a matter of fact, what is more serious is the suspicion that, by the operation of the words of consecration, the bread becomes the body of Christ while remaining bread, just as in his explanation of accidents the body became bread by anticipation and reversibility. For the holy Body is held precisely under the intermediate surface, external and internal, which is to say under the shape and all the dimensions of the bread; and it is not at all necessary that the body be there in its integrity, with its exterior members, its

---

24 *Selected Correspondence of Descartes*, 181.
25 Cf. Armogathe, *Theologia cartesiana*, 75 and note.

arms, its hands, with extension, an exterior figure, its normal use. . . . Pascal's fragment *Br.* 512 is forceful on this subject and it would appear impossible that he had not read the letter to Fr. Mesland (though perhaps without knowing the author). On the original copy of the letter there is this crossed-out passage: "it is impossible to attribute to the body of Jesus Christ another extension or another quantity than that of the bread."[26] It also attests to the fact that Descartes changed his mind, that he stopped short on the path of impanation, and that he understood the permanence of the species in the strongest sense, despite the surface's character as a modal entity. Transubstantiation is a miracle, certainly, but it would be a "new miracle" for the preservation of the species to cease, as when "in place of the consecrated bread, flesh or a child appeared in the hands of the priest."[27] Descartes probably knew the tradition of the eucharistic miracle of Lanciano (eighth century).[28] Rosmini, the great eucharistic theologian, also stumbled on this question of the dimensions. He noticed the slight divergence at the heart of the formulation of the dogma of transubstantiation, which perhaps did not have a decisive significance: "*conversionem fieri totius substantiae panis in substantiam corporis Christi.*"[29] He is right that the declarations of the canons speak, again and again, of the *totus Christus.*[30]

Blondel, however, pleaded for the Cartesian theory, in the name of Descartes's claim of "the close union that the soul has with the body."[31] He saw a sketch of the idea of assimilation (a traditional hypothesis) as singularly fruitful in these eucharistic remarks, and perhaps also this new substance of the *Vinculum* that, according to Leibniz, is born of several substances. Is this enough to ward off the dualism? Does this safeguard the numerical identity of the body born of the Virgin Mary (*Ave verum corpus natum*) and

---

26 Cf. Armogathe.

27 "Reply to the Fourth Set of Objections," 153.

28 In the province of Chieti. See the *L'Osservatore Romano* from April 23, 1982, p. 5. Note also the "eucharistic miracle of Ferrara" (in the church of Santa Maria in Vado), on Easter Sunday, March 28, 1171: blood that spurted from the broken host and sprayed the vault of the small church; the brown spots are still visible.

29 Catholic Church, Peter Hünermann, Helmut Hoping, Robert L. Fastiggi, Anne Englund Nash, and Heinrich Denzinger, *Compendium of Creeds, Definitions, and Declarations on Matters of Faith and Morals*, 43rd ed. (San Francisco: Ignatius Press, 2012), 1642. Henceforth cited as Denz. All numbers correspond to the 43rd ed.

30 Denz. 1639–1641, 1651–1661.

31 René Descartes, *Principles of Philosophy*, trans. Valentine Rodger Miller and Reese P. Miller (Dordrecht, Holland: Reidel, 1983), II.3.

the glorious body? The difficulty is not resolved, and Descartes put his hypothesis on the shelf. He was silent, a "sign of a religious life perhaps more profound than has been previously noted."[32]

CARTESIANS

Yet, that which Descartes wrote in confidence to the missionary was promptly distributed, under the care of Clerselier: copies were circulated by the dozens, and because of them, a eucharistic debate was soon ignited after the death of Descartes (†1650), which was complicated by a posthumous confessional quarrel. On January 6, 1672, Clerselier relates to Dom Robert Desgabets a conversation he had with the archbishop of Paris, François Harlay de Chanvalon, who requested, on behalf of the king, that Clerselier and his son-in-law Jacques Rohault "contain it." Then, at a second audience, the overly zealous propagandist provided a "very faithful copy" of the missives to Mesland to the fastidious prelate. There was another untimely supporter: Antoine-Paul Le Gal (Le Gallois). The risk of heresy was not chimerical. At Saint-Wandrille, where Le Gallois taught, on the day of Corpus Christi, as they read the readings of the Second Nocturn of Matins, which are drawn from St. Thomas, they "were booed by some students."[33]

The Cartesian Benedictine of Verdun, Dom Robert Desgabets,[34] who has been shown to be a very relevant figure,[35] attempted above all to defend Descartes against the reproaches concerning the subsistence of bread ("impanation," of which the Lutheran version is rather a coexistence of substance, consubstantiation, Denz. 1652). This is modeled on the Incarnation, a sort of hypostatic union of Christ and the bread: "he is impanated" (the error envisaged in Denz. 3121–3124 concerns a simple conjecture of Fr. Joseph Bayma, SJ, from his articles in the *Catholic World*). The insertion of the soul of Christ makes it so that the bread is no longer bread. But the problem is in knowing if this bread becomes *a* body of Christ, bodies of Christ, or else *the* body of Christ, *idem numero*! However, Dom Robert, who would

---

32 Gouhier, *La Pensée religieuse de Descartes*, 258.

33 "Descartes" in *Dictionnaire de théologie catholique*. On this whole quarrel, besides Armogathe, see Francisque Bouillier, *Histoire de la philosophie cartésienne*, vol. I (Durand, 1854), 409–97.

34 Armogathe, *Theologia cartesiana*; Paul Lemaire, *Le cartésianisme chez les Bénédictins: Dom Robert Desgabets* (Paris: Alcan, 1901).

35 Note the study group from the Sorbonne with Geneviève Rodis-Lewis (†August 25, 2004), Joseph Beaude, and J.-R. Armogathe.

later submit to the ban on this subject by his superiors, develops his own eucharistic philosophy. In the line of St. John of Damascus, Rupert of Deutz, Durand, and of course, Descartes, he forges a theory of eucharistic assimilation (using analogies from the Wedding at Cana and from ordinary eating), which is a trans-elementation, a transubstantiation (without *meta-ousia*), *sit venia verbis*. His axiom is: *Forma dat esse rei*, it is the form that confers the being of a thing. The unity of Christ is not a unicity—for every body is extended, *partes extra partes*, and therefore impenetrable; every portion of matter occupies only one place at a time. Rejecting the solutions of St. Thomas and Duns Scotus, Desgabets conceives of a "perfective substantial conjunction," a perfective conversion of substance to substance. The soul—the form—of Christ is united to what is substantial in the bread and thus the substance of a body of man is created. The divinity of Christ (the second Person of the Trinity) is united simultaneously to the Body and the Soul, thus assuring identity with the Body in Heaven, as well as with the fraction and the multiplication of hosts. The eucharistic body of Christ is extended—a commonplace for Cartesians—but without formal organs, which does not give rise to any difficulties (Descartes did not exclude this possibility, because he admitted the possibility of eucharistic apparitions that are, so to speak, "organic," though he had some reservations). According to the Council of Trent (Denz. 1639–1641) the divinity is eucharistically united to the body and blood in virtue of the hypostatic union.

Because the soul confers being, the argument concerning the Eucharist during the *Triduum Mortis* is rejected by Desgabets: there is in this case no consecration at all. On the other hand, Desgabets is orthodox with regard to the question of the presence of the body in the chalice by nature of concomitance. The problem that brought him under suspicion of heresy is the idea that the soul of Christ is the essential form of the substance, such that the accidental form is the visible aspect of the bread. Desgabets retracted his "errors"—Jansen calls them his "eucharistic daydreams"—with submission and humility.[36]

Jacques-Bénigne Bossuet, an admirer of Descartes, discouraged the dissemination of the long letter to Mesland, and he feigned to not believe in its authenticity. This permitted him to save Descartes while condemning the so-called Cartesian exhibitions on the Eucharist. He sticks with the *Meditations on First Philosophy* (the replies to the fourth and sixth objections),

---

36 "Accidents eucharistiques" in *Dictionnaire de théologie catholique*.

whose orthodoxy appears to him as guaranteed. Indeed, the rapprochement, which is otherwise ambiguous, with the intentional species seems to him to leave no doubt about the substantial change. But inasmuch as Bossuet is mild and indulgent for Descartes's Cartesianism, he vituperates against Malebranche's.

Nicolas Malebranche, the pious Oratorian and intrepid thinker, found himself caught in a web of polemics with the Jesuit Louis Le Valois (1639–1700), who wrote *Les sentiments de Descartes conformes à ceux de Calvin* with the pseudonym Louis de la Ville. Then a fervent Cartesian, Malebranche rebelled in a short "memoir to explain the possibility of transubstantiation."[37] Malebranche opposes Fr. Le Valois, who strongly contested the necessity of a substance being extended. The body of Christ is always extended. "A body without extension is a body that is annihilated!" "The head, the feet, and all the parts of this sacred body are restricted to a mathematical point!" How is this possible? "De la Ville speaks like the heretics who say that the body of Jesus Christ is in the Eucharist, but without his substance or his extension!" "An infinity of mathematical points does not make a body, nor even a physical point, and is far from being able to make a human or organic body, such as that of Jesus Christ."

The argument consequently gravitates around the notion of extension. The quantity of extension does not matter, provided that it is there, and the particular extension does not matter provided that there is general extension! This is under the premise that "God is able to will all that is conceived clearly and distinctly." God "by his infinite power can make it so that the whole Christ can be [in the host] under the smallest quantity." It is not at all inconceivable that God could reduce the body of Jesus Christ in his essence to an insensible (that is, imperceptible) point, for "a point is also the essence of the extension—that is, a physical point, for a mathematical point does not make a body" (see above). The extension of the human body can be reduced to a miniscule space (as in the embryo, "as small as a bean," the head of a pin!). Very little suffices for the essentials: the massive and considerable pain of a severed arm corresponds to a part, perhaps smaller than a grain of sand, "of the brain to which the soul is immediately united." Once more, the size, the volume, the mode and the provenance of the growth . . . does not matter for the essentials: "when I was only one year old," Malebranche sighs, "I was destined to be two meters tall. It does not

---

37 In *Oeuvres complètes de Malebranche* XVII, 1.

matter whether the bread that made me grow—o how!—came from this baker or that"; "if I would have eaten less, if I were smaller or shorter, I would not have the same extension, but I would have the same body of a man." Material extension, being infinitely divisible, permits the existence of extremely small bodies that only the microscope can see, organized bodies smaller than a grain of sand (like Pascal's mite).

But the perpetuation of untenable propositions, like the reduction to a (mathematical) point, or the penetration or interlocking of parts or accidents without a subject (that is to say, modifications without anything being modified), is unnecessary and only serves "to harden" the Calvinists. Malebranche returns to the stipulation of the relativity of the corporeal extension, which obsessed him: the stature is indifferent, the pygmies are men just as are giants; if the earth were no bigger than an orange, and everything was proportionate, no one would notice it (J. Lequier states the same thing). An infant who grows from one foot to six feet: would he not also be able to return from six feet to only one? The body "dissipates" and is therefore renewed. It is the soul that assures identity and continuity. Several bodies affected by the same soul make "only one body, only one self." At the Resurrection, the cannibal will recover his body made up of other humans' consumed bodies, but not as a plurality of bodies, whereas the bodies that he formerly consumed will be recuperated by their respective souls.

The legendary intrepidity of this thinker makes one smile. But after all this heroic, pro-Cartesian polemics, he recovers his spirits in order to construct a sentence worthy to serve as a motto for a treatise on the Eucharist: the Eucharist, being a mystery, should not be explained. This also reflects his feeling of desperation.

Chapter 2

Blaise Pascal:
The Most Hidden God

I f one were to rely solely on the indexes of the *Pensées*, for example in the Brunschvicg or Lafuma editions, and look for the word "Eucharist," the findings would be meager and one would miss some of Pascal's most significant suggestions. His devotion to the Blessed Sacrament is demonstrated during his final sickness and at the moment of his death. During that time of Jansenist austerity, one needed grave reasons in order to receive Communion, and the doctors did not consider him to be in a state to keep the eucharistic fast, nor to be sick enough to receive the Eucharist as Viaticum. Gilberte Périer recounts:

> He very much desired to receive Communion; but the doctors opposed it, saying that he would not be able to keep the fast, unless it was at night, which they did not want to do without necessity. And in order to receive the Viaticum, it would be necessary to be in danger of death, which they did not consider to be the case, so they could not advise it. This resistance angered him, but he was forced to surrender to it.

His sickness, however, worsens, and Gilberte secretly "prepares the candles" and everything that was necessary for Communion the next morning. During the night the sickness caused violent convulsions and his loved ones feared "that they would see him die without the sacraments after having asked for them so often and with such insistence." But Pascal recovered calm and lucidity. Thus, the priest of Saint-Étienne-du-Mont, Fr. Beurier, could say, "Behold our Lord, whom I bring to you, behold him whom you have so desired." "He made an effort, and he stood up only halfway, in order to receive him [the priest] with more respect. Questioned on the principal mysteries of the faith, he responded clearly: 'Yes, sir, I believe all of it, and with all of my heart.' He then received the Holy Viaticum and the Extreme Unction while crying. He thanked the priest, who blessed him with the holy ciborium, and he said, 'May God never abandon me!'" These were his final words. After his thanksgiving, the convulsions resumed and he died twenty-four hours later, August 19, 1662, at one in the morning. He was thirty-nine years old.

Thus Pascal had accomplished in his person that which he wrote about a while before concerning the death of his father, Étienne Pascal, in a long, pious letter to his sister on October 17, 1651: the union of the Eucharist and death. "In sacrifices the principal part is the death of the host . . . the achievement is the death."

Such an admirable devotion forms a part not only of Pascal's soul, but also of his thought. This thought is, in a single movement, an original apologetic, a critique of knowledge, and a spiritual meditation or a mysticism. Mystery, for Pascal, is the source of intelligibility, and the eucharistic mystery especially is the most enlightening for the eyes of the heart. It is simultaneously an apotheosis of the hidden God and the touchstone of Catholic truth. The formulations from the important letter to Charlotte de Roannez (October 1656) are well known:

> This strange secrecy, in which God is impenetrably withdrawn from the sight of men, is a great lesson to betake ourselves to solitude far from the sight of men. He remained concealed under the veil of the nature that covers him till the Incarnation; and when it was necessary that he should appear, he concealed himself still the more in covering himself with humanity. He was much more recognizable when he was invisible than when he rendered himself visible. And in fine, when he wished to fulfill the promise that he made to his apostles to remain with men until his final coming, he chose to remain in the strangest and most obscure secret of all, which are the species of the Eucharist. It is this sacrament that St. John calls in the Apocalypse *a concealed manna*; and I believe that Isaiah saw it in that state, when he said in the spirit of prophecy: *Truly thou art a God concealed.*[1] This is the last secrecy wherein he can be. The veil of nature that covers God has been penetrated by some of the unbelieving, who, as St. Paul says, have recognized an invisible God through the visible nature. Heretical Christians have recognized him through his humanity and adored Jesus Christ God and man. But to recognize him under the species of bread is peculiar to Catholics alone: none but us are thus enlightened

---

[1] *Vere tu es Deus absconditus.* Modern exegetes tend to interpret this to mean that God is hidden in his people, sheltered in Israel. Kaplan remarks that this would actually compromise Pascal's meaning. See Henri Gouhier, *Blaise Pascal: Commentaires* (Paris: Vrin, 1966), 187–243. The book by Lucien Goldmann, *Le Dieu Caché: Étude sur la vision tragique dans les Pensées de Pascal et dans le Théâtre de Racine* (Paris: Gallimard, 1955), which had its fifteen minutes of fame, is completely wrong on this point.

by God . . . . the heretics, seeing the perfect appearances of bread in the Eucharist, do not think to see in it another substance. All things cover some mystery; all things are veils that cover God. Christians ought to recognize him in every thing.[2]

It is a memorable text, which places the Eucharist at the center of the Catholic faith, at the heart of the obscurity where God himself desired to be submerged in order to be more ardently searched for. In a way, he comments on the *Adoro te devote, latens Deitas,* the *hic latet simul et humanitas,* and the *Jesum quem velatum nunc aspicio.* It is an adorable mystery that invites contemplation and not the subtleties of the intellect. Yet, Pascal prepares an "apology" and his first movement is to vigorously attach eucharistic belief to a totally naked faith.

How I hate these follies of not believing in the Eucharist, etc.! If the Gospel be true, if Jesus Christ be God, what difficulty is there?[3]

Impiety, not to believe in the Eucharist, because it is not seen.[4]

Nevertheless, he neither ignores nor disregards the theological controversies. And although he did not intervene in the post-Cartesian eucharistic debate, one can perceive a trace of it (which is, in my opinion, irrefutable) in fragment 512, which demands a brief analysis:

It [the host] is, in peculiar phraseology, wholly the body of Jesus Christ, but it cannot be said to be the whole body of Jesus Christ. The union of two things without change does not enable us to say that one becomes the other; the soul thus being united to the body, the fire to the timber, without change. But change is necessary to make the form of the one become the form of the other; thus the union of the Word to man.

Because my body without my soul would not make the body of a man; therefore my soul united to any matter whatsoever will make my body. It does not distinguish the necessary condition from the sufficient condition; the union is necessary, but not sufficient. The left arm is not the right. Impenetrability is a property of the body.

---

2 *Thoughts, Letters, Minor Works* (New York: P.F. Collier and Son Co., 1910), 354–55. Translation slightly altered.

3 *Pensées,* 224. Translation slightly altered. Citations of *Pensées* refer to the paragraph numbers from *Thoughts, Letters, Minor Works,* which uses the Brunschvicg numbering.

4 *Pensées,* 255.

> Identity *de numero* in regard to the same time requires the identity
> of matter. Thus if God united my soul to a body in China, the same body,
> *idem numero*, would be in China. The same river which runs there is *idem
> numero* as that which runs at the same time in China.[5]

The fragment does not belong to the preparatory bundle of the *Pensées*. Was
it intended for the *Provincial Letters*? This is doubtful. But, despite the
authority of Armogathe,[6] it seems uncontestable that he is thinking of Descartes and specifically the letter to Mesland on February 9, 1645. Léonce
Couture, Henri Gouhier, Michel Le Guern, Francis Kaplan all think this.[7]
Armogathe's argument is quite specious, and incidentally he hesitates in his
view, but he argues that the fragment goes against the letter. His argument
is not topical, for, to state it quickly, having read the contentious points, one
can very easily provide the opposite interpretation.

It is not clear whether Pascal knew the name of the author of the letter.
He does not provide it. The beginning makes an allusion to the *totus Christus* of the Council of Trent (Canons 1 and 3; Denz. 1651 and 1653). It
expresses Clerselier's fear and the content of the statement that was crossed
out on the original copy. Pascal's complaint is that the author inclines toward
consubstantiation, the association of substances, rather than towards conversion. But, union is not conversion, the soul united to the body does not
become the body, the fire does not become the wood. If there is not a prior
change of bread into the body the soul is not sufficient. The hypostatic union
(where the divine person is the subject, the *hypokeimenon*, of the man), on
the contrary, makes Christ a divine man, whereby all his actions are attributed to the Person (according to the communication of idioms, the peri-
choresis). However, the example applied to the Eucharist is not *ad rem*, for
there is not a substantial union, but a transubstantiation, a conversion. The
eucharistic equivalent to the hypostatic union would be impanation.

---

5 *Pensées*, 512. Translation slightly altered.

6 Jean-Robert Armogathe, review of *Pascal et Descartes*, by M. Le Guern, *Archives de Philosophie*
36, no. 3 (1973): 460–61. Jean-Robert Armogathe, "Dom Desgabets et Port-Royal," *Chroniques de
Port-Royal* 17–18 (1969): 70–72. Armogathe clearly dismisses Desgabets as the author; he would
admit Descartes, if need be, not as the author of the letter to Mesland, but as the interlocutor of
Wallon de Beaupuis.

7 Léonce Couture, "Commentaire d'un fragment de Pascal sur l'Eucharistie," *Bulletin théolo-
gique, scientifique et littéraire de l'Institut catholique de Toulouse* (Paris: Lecoffre, 1898); Henri
Gouhier, *Cartésianisme et Augustinisme au XVIIe siècle* (Paris: Vrin, 1978), 221–22; Michel Le
Guern, *Pascal et Descartes* (Paris, Nizet, 1971), 54–58; Francis Kaplan, *Les Pensées de Pascal*
(Paris: Éditions du Cerf, 1982), 580–81. The fragment is enumerated as 959 by Lafuma.

The second paragraph does not present difficulties. It is the soul that determines a human body (a Cartesian thesis), but not just any body. The condition of the union of the soul to a corporeal matter is necessary, though it is not sufficient. The bread must have become the body. And the body is not just any body. Today, one would say that it is a structure. Impenetrability (antitype) is a general property of bodies. Moreover, this does not contradict Descartes, who refused the interpenetration of the parts. But he tends to reduce the body to the dimensive quantity of the bread. Yet it is the body of Christ that is in the Eucharist, with his flesh, his limbs, his blood, etc. . . . and this is not an impanated body.

The final paragraph, a rather enigmatic one, treats the numeric or material identity.[8] One would suppose that if one is in Paris, while one's soul is united to a body in China, this body in exile would be the same identical body, as in the phenomena of bilocation or of duplication of the body. How can we understand the last phrase, which resumes [Descartes'] example of the Loire? It should be understood with an exclamation mark that brings out the irony and the absurdity of the statement. Pascal pushes to its absurd conclusion the fact that the matter of the river (water and the earth of the riverbed), though channeled, is in constant flux. Thus, every river that flows would be the same as any other. But simultaneity does not create identity, the required material identity. Pascal's example therefore builds on the bond between the *hic et nunc* of the conservation of the species and transubstantiation, whereas Descartes tended to disjoin them in making the species the median surface. The objection, however, is not very relevant to the extent that the river appears transportable like the integral soul, and because Pascal transposes simultaneously that which coincides locally for Descartes.

It is not that Pascal mocks the explanations, but that he simply does not care about them. He prefers to place the Eucharist back in its natural milieu, which is Catholic doctrine. It is appropriate that it retain its character as a test of faith: "As Jesus Christ remained unknown among men, so His truth remains among common opinions without external difference. Thus the Eucharist among ordinary bread."[9] It is a lapidary remark with great significance. The exquisite soundness of Pascal's spiritual theology appears again in fragment 554: "At the Last Supper He gave Himself in communion

8 [In two brief sentences that were removed here, Tilliette originally notes a peculiarity of Pascal's use of French, writing "'À la Chine' veut dire 'en Chine.' Pascal emploie des formules qui ont l'air prélevées à l'avance de Malebranche." —Trans.]

9 *Pensées*, 789.

as about to die; to the disciples at Emmaus as risen from the dead; to the whole Church as ascended into heaven." And in the laconic fragment 666: "The Eucharist. *Comedes panem tuum. Panem nostrum.*" The parallel here is striking.

Besides these traces of his meditation, the Eucharist, just as Christ himself, enters in the prophetic and symbolic view of Revelation and is a part of the Pascalian apologetic. The Eucharist, "after the Lord's Supper" is the "truth after the type,"[10] which does not stop it from remaining a type itself, *panis angelorum, panis viatorum.* "Christians take even the Eucharist as a type of the glory at which they aim."[11] Indeed, it is peculiar to the sacraments, and to a preeminent degree to the Eucharist, that they be simultaneously truth, reality, as well as figurative: *res et sacramentum.* This indissoluble duality allows the eucharistic faith to avoid vanishing into symbolism or getting bogged down in a crass material signification. "The subject of the Holy Sacrament" is, with the Incarnation and indulgences, a cornerstone of the Christian and Catholic truth, as seen in the beautiful fragment 862 on heresies ("The source of all heresies is the exclusion of some of these truths"):

> 2nd example: On the subject of the Holy Sacrament.
> We believe that, the substance of the bread being changed, and being consubstantial with that of the body of our Lord, Jesus Christ is therein really present. That is one truth. Another is that this Sacrament is also a type of the cross and of glory, and a commemoration of the two. That is the Catholic faith, which comprehends these two truths which seem opposed. The heresy of to-day, not conceiving that this Sacrament contains at the same time both the presence of Jesus Christ and a type of Him, and that it is a sacrifice and a commemoration of a sacrifice, believes that neither of these truths can be admitted without excluding the other for this reason. They fasten to this point alone, that this Sacrament is emblematic; and in this they are not heretics. They think that we exclude this truth; hence it comes that they raise so many objections to us out of the passages of the Fathers which assert it. Finally, they deny the presence; and in this they are heretics.[12]

---

10 *Pensées*, 654. Also see the latent duality of the *Agnus occisus ab origine mundi* of fragment 685.

11 *Pensées*, 670.

12 *Pensées*, 862. Translation slightly altered.

Chapter 3

The Protestant Counterattack: Pierre Bayle and Pierre Jurieu

The climate of controversy, which is both deleterious and stimulating, that surrounds the majority of Catholic writing on the Eucharist in the seventeenth century is also experienced by the Protestants. Protestants stiffen their opposition just as the Catholic realism remains insistent. There is a passage of the *Leviathan* where Thomas Hobbes, with his cold ferocity, takes up the Catholic belief and submits it to ridicule. Hobbes anticipates the mockery of the philosophers of the Enlightenment and is obsessed by the "kingdom of darkness" (that is, Catholicism). Pierre Bayle is much more loyal to his former coreligionists. He is panicked and terrified of hell, a relentless scholar, and, because he relapses from Catholicism back to Protestantism, he occupies a liminal space between the confessions and between the epochs. He is a representative symbol of the lively Catholic-Protestant dialogue where swords cross with contrary opinions.

The deceased Descartes had been surreptitiously brought into the Protestant camp, and Louis de la Ville pushed him there with his perfidious anti-Malebranchean libel. But Pierre Bayle (1647–1706), a Protestant neophyte, formed in Sedan by the famous Pierre Jurieu, also jumped at the opportunity, and in a *Recueil de quelques pièces curieuses* he brought together some writings from the quarrel (which A. Robinet made use of in his edition of Malebranche). Intervening personally, and under the erroneous guise of ecumenism, he makes a stand diametrically opposed to the Cartesian arguments of Malebranche. He urges the Catholic Church to abandon an error: in decreeing that "all the parts of his Body are penetrated by one another," "the Council of Trent decided on an error."[1] The Roman Church should imagine a "new manner of the real presence" and promise

---

1 This is a deduction, for the Tridentine Canons (1 and 3) enunciate no such thing (Denz. 1651 and 1653). This is a theological interpretation of the text that declares, "in virtue of the natural connection and concomitance by which the parts of Christ the Lord, who has already risen from the dead to die no more [cf. Rom. 6:9], are united together. Moreover the divinity is present because of its admirable hypostatic union with the body and the soul" (Denz. 1640).

"to irrevocably rescind the Canon that decided that the Body of Jesus Christ has all of its parts penetrated by the others under the species of bread and wine." He refers to a text by a professor in Sedan (it is himself) who said: "it is just as impossible that the matter [of the body of Christ] be preserved as it is that two things be equal while one is larger than the other." The Reformers are much more correct when they give a figurative sense to the words "this is my body." They are right, and in as much as the Catholic Church believes itself to be infallible, we will see "volumes upon volumes pile up in order to prove the literal sense," while "two pages will suffice to refute it," which makes him say that the Council of Trent said something impossible. But Bayle would not wish to "embitter the Roman Catholics against the Cartesians in their communion." Rather, he is concerned to search along with Descartes for "another manner of reality," for an agreement would be possible provided that Catholics renounce the "interpenetrated and transubstantiated presence." Besides, Bayle remarks, Calvin has some "strong expressions" about "eating the body of Our Lord." One must leave the "dogma of the reality as a more general notion," and not wish to explain everything with the utmost precision, "which one must never do with mysterious things, if one wishes to avoid schisms." This is quite close to the wisdom that Malebranche achieved.

Bayle studied at a good school, that of his teacher Jurieu.[2] But before Jurieu, there was Louis Tronchin, the Cartesian theologian from Geneva. Bayle was born in Ariège and studied in Toulouse. He was first a Protestant, then a convert to Catholicism, then a recidivist, and then had to go into exile in Geneva. It was precisely the difficulties inherent in transubstantiation that brought him back into the Protestant fold.[3] In Geneva he experienced a sort of mystical awakening and rediscovered his Protestantism. He is all ears when Tronchin criticizes the eucharistic doctrine of the first Reformers and declares that the sublime "secret" is simplicity itself. The original manuscript of the course is lost, but there exists one that is equivalent.[4] The spiritual union is more real than the corporeal, and the Eucharist

---

2 See Walter Rex, *Essays on Pierre Bayle and Religious Controversy* (La Haye: Nijhoff, 1965), chapter 4: "The Eucharist: Geneva, Sedan, and Rotterdam," 121–52. Élisabeth Labrousse's summary in *Pierre Bayle*, 2 vols. (La Haye: Nijhoff, 1963) treats Jurieu and his relations with Bayle in detail. See vol. 1, 131–33, 143–47, 151–73, 193–96, 206–60.

3 Rex, *Essays on Pierre Bayle and Religious Controversy*, 126. See Labrousse, vol. 1, 80–81. Bayle spent only seventeen months as a Catholic.

4 Rex, *Essays on Pierre Bayle and Religious Controversy*, 131.

is incomprehensible just as the love of God is incomprehensible. Concerning divine omnipotence, which the Reformers intended to limit by denying transubstantiation, Tronchin makes an appeal to philosophical and rational criteria, inspired by Descartes.[5] The traces of Descartes are also perceptible in the treatment of the Eucharist, as evidenced by an interesting letter by Bayle.[6] Bayle here drafts his refutation of Le Valois (1680) in the spirit of Tronchin. Another Genevan professor, François Turrettini, though a conservative, clearly denies (De Transsubstantiatione) the real change, and he proves it by appeal to the senses, reason, and the faith. But Louis Tronchin is more important.

At the academy in Sedan (1675), Bayle was the colleague of the renowned Pierre Jurieu (1637–1713), the author of the Examen de l'Eucharistie (1682). An informed conservative, Jurieu was sympathetic to Descartes, but he directs his argument against the real presence quite otherwise, insofar as Descartes can be molded into a Protestant perspective. Suppose for fifteen minutes, he challenges Catholics, that Protestants were correct and that "this is my body" has a figurative meaning. If this is so, what are you doing? You are adoring bread. He shudders for them, for they are worse than the savages who adore the sun and the stars. The reply that their adoration is directed toward the Person of Christ, not at the bread, is no different than what anyone else could say, such as the Israelites before the Golden Calf or the Persians prostrating before the sun. The text that seems to support them (the institution narrative) is false or corrupt, or poorly interpreted. They do not have an excuse, for error is not an excuse and here their ignorance is voluntary, for they blind themselves and gouge out their eyes.[7] On the other hand, those who do not believe and adore the host, even when it is by constraint, are even more culpable and are "criminals twice over." "Were [Jesus Christ] there corporeally, he would be horrified by the forced cult. He does not desire a fake adoration." This remark is stated as a general maxim. To oblige adoration of the host without belief, no matter how adorable it may be, is to "join hypocrisy to profanation." To adore without belief is to commit a sin, for "all that one does without faith is a sin." To compel a Reformer to prostrate before a consecrated host is not an act of religion, it is an act of hostility.

---

5 Rex, 133.

6 Rex, 136.

7 This example is inspired by the story of Amphitryon.

There is nothing in scripture (the only source of *faith*) about the adoration of the Eucharist; and the *senses* and our *reason* dissuade us from it. One should therefore know that *Hoc est Corpus meum* is to be understood in the figurative sense. Like the theologians from Saumur (Daillé, Jean-Robert Choué, the uncle of Tronchin), Jurieu is attached to the rationalist tradition of Protestantism. In short, he employs the following arguments:

1. The first rule is that when a text says something absurd, one must understand it in a figurative sense (criterion of reason).
2. When a scriptural proposition is not only absurd, but also contradictory and impossible, one must explain it figuratively. This is the case for the *Hoc est Corpus meum* (again, the criterion of reason).
3. When a text commands a crime, for example, to gouge out one's eyes, one must take it figuratively; but to eat his (Christ's) flesh is a crime, so it therefore means "revisiting in spirit the memory of the passion" (ethical rule).[8]
4. When a text attributes something to God that is unworthy of him, one must not take it in the literal sense (ethical criterion).

The more or less fortuitous *rapprochement* between Bayle and Jurieu in the context of the eucharistic controversy should not make us forget that these friends will become irreconcilable enemies. Voltaire, forcing the issue a little, notes:

> The fiery Jurieu persecuted Bayle
> Who will ever be respected by good minds
> And the name of Jurieu, his fanatical rival,
> Is only known today by public horror.[9]

---

8 [It should be noted that these rules, including this particular example, come in large part from Augustine's *de doctrina christiana*, though, obviously, without suggesting modern rationalism. —Trans.]

9 Voltaire, *Oeuvres complètes de Voltaire*, vol. 9 (Paris: Garnier, 1877).

Chapter 4

G. W. Leibniz between the Confessions

Antoine Arnauld, now known as *le Grand*, functions as the hinge between Descartes and Leibniz, so to speak, as well as the hinge between two eras of eucharistic philosophy. Just as he invited Descartes to lay out his theory about the permanence of accidents, so he prompted Leibniz to formulate his ecumenical conception of the Blessed Sacrament. Leibniz, young and zealous, though he worked toward a rapprochement of the confessions and won over Bossuet, did not in fact believe that the dogma of transubstantiation could be preserved with the notion of an extended substance. Somewhat furtively hostile to Descartes and to Cartesianism, he does not mind using his influence to insult his illustrious predecessor. The theory that he laconically proposes to Arnauld in order to avoid the disadvantages of the Cartesian doctrine rests upon a different notion of substance.

Leibniz's personality, which was clever, conciliatory, flexible without breaking, and prudent, dwelled in a physical body that he described uncompromisingly in his "sketched self-portrait"[1]: he was of a small size, a fragile body, pale, with large feet and cold hands. He was never thirsty, he never sweated, but he had a voracious appetite and slept deeply. He had short, coarse, brown hair; poor, myopic, and nearsighted vision; a delicate voice that was high, distinct, and voluble; he was uncomfortable with gutturals and the hard "k" sound, he had weak lungs, a dry and warm liver, and entirely wrinkled hands. He sweetened his wine, loving sweets and fragrances. He ignored colds and never coughed or sneezed. Even though he was dominantly "bilious," he secreted little phlegm, though he did salivate and spit, especially after drinking. He was a night owl and would write into the night. He was self-taught, curious, solitary; sedentary, he avoided play and movement. He would quickly become agitated, but the mood would

---

1 Foucher de Careil, *Lettres et opuscules inédits de Leibniz* (Paris: Ladrange, 1854), 388–89.

not last. In general, he was even-tempered, neither sad nor happy. He complained of a weak imagination and a terrible memory. But his judgment was excellent, his brain dry and spiritual.

His new conception of substance is well expressed in some numbered *Remarks* "on the real and substantial perception of the body and blood of Our Lord."[2] The Church has always believed in a perception (real reception) of Our Lord in the Eucharist. Negating this would be an absurdity or an impossibility in the literal sense. But, if extension is constitutive of bodies, there would be the contradiction that a body or a substance was immediately united to some other elongated substance. Huygens said very well that the idea that some people (Cartesians) have of the body is exactly the same as that of the void! In fact, extension is not primary; it presupposes "something that must be multiplied, determined or extended," and it therefore encloses multitude, continuity, and diffusion. It is relative. But that which is continued and repeated is the resistance itself, a primitive *force* of passion and action, a first passivity that Leibniz calls the form, which is Aristotle's first entelechy. The essence of the body consists in force. God, who made everything *pondere, numero, mensura*, applied it to the dimensions. It is true that usually bodies do not operate at all *in distans* (Leibniz is opposed to Newton), that they do not occupy sometimes a greater and sometimes a smaller space. But that which God willed for the good order of things does not compel him, such that he could not change his established laws for reasons of a superior order.

Leibniz returned more than once to this dynamic notion of substance in the framework of his eucharistic theory. Thus, in his correspondence with the zealous Paul Pellisson, who was bothered by a substance that changes in force, that is by a real presence reduced to a presence of force and virtue,[3] Leibniz guards himself against these "quibbles" and distinguishes the same subject *in concreto*, or the substance, from the essence of the subject, or the primitive force, the substance *in abstracto*. Substance is force plus the subject.[4] Previously he had strongly defined the attribute of extension: "as whiteness is extended in the milk or hardness in the rock . . . so the corporeal nature or materiality (which envelops the force and that which depends

---

2 Gottfried Wilhelm von Leibniz, *Gothofredi Guillelmi Leibnitii: Opera Omnia*, ed. Louis Dutens. 6 vols. (Geneva, 1768). Vol. 1, 30–31. Hereafter cited as Dutens.

3 Foucher de Careil, *Lettres et opuscules inédits de Leibniz*, 291, December 30, 1691.

4 Foucher de Careil, 312–13, January 8–18, 1692.

upon it, namely, resistance, impenetrability, inertia) is found to be extended, that is to say spread out, repeated, continued in the body."[5]

These remarks are obviously subsequent to Leibniz's first attempts to write about the Eucharist. The preparations were earlier, just as was his anti-Cartesian path. The important letter to Arnauld (1671)[6] mentions reflections initiated twenty years earlier, and Paul Schrecker published a letter to his brother in October 1669, accompanied by "Remarks" by Simon Löffler.[7] The ecumenical concern is already evident there and is accompanied by Leibniz's discussions of the Eucharist, albeit with highs and lows. What exactly does he think, he who excels at entering into the point of view of the other? He almost seems to espouse the opposing faith, as it slips into his reasoning. A sample of this clever flexibility is a document related to a controversy about transubstantiation between Molanus, the Abbot of Lokkum, and some monks, a document whose emphasis arouses some suspicion:

> As to the *terminus a quo*, in order to know how much change to grant to the bread and the wine? I respond that what is at issue here is a great mystery that surpasses the capacity of men and perhaps also of angels. Who am I and what importance do I have, me, a tiny worm just crawling on the floor, in order to dare the gigantic effort of piling Pelion on top of Ossa? Who am I, a tiny, ignorant humanoid with the nature of worms and frogs, and how much like nocturnal bats blinded by the sun am I to attempt a sacrilegious glance, with the obscure light of my reason, at the full arch of the mysteries? Bringing my offering therefore to the altar of the Athenians, with the consent of the doctor of the Gentiles himself, I piously adore that which my simplicity does not know: and in my opinion the Council of Trent is not against us.[8]

In what follows he invokes the *audax Iapeti genus*, Aristotle, Hercules, Mars, Lynceus ("I am not a Lynceus capable of seeing what greater need there is of knowing that the *terminus a quo* rather than the *terminus ad quem* is changed"), in order to insist on real presence without much of a desire to be attached to the litigious term transubstantiation. It is this

---

5 Foucher de Careil, 399, November 19, 1682.

6 In Karl Immanuel Gerhardt's edition of Leibniz's *Philosophische Schriften* (Berlin: Weidmann, 1875–1890), t. I, 75. Hereafter cited as Gerhardt.

7 Or "Animadversions." Cf. Paul Schrecker, "G.-W. Leibniz. Lettres et fragments inédits," *Revue philosophique de la France et de l'Étranger* 118 (1934): 79.

8 Dutens, vol. 1, 674–75.

presence that he recognizes and adores in the Blessed Sacrament: "in this admirable mystery, with humility, fear, and supreme trembling." Bossuet blessed and applauded these declarations of faith and fervor.[9] Perhaps he had not guessed, due to the excess of his reverence, the pointed ear of the bat in the fable,[10] which would serve nicely as Leibniz's emblem. His attempt at arbitration is like a deposit; it gives credit to the efforts of the informal peacemaker, the expert in compromise, who thinks he has found the way to diffuse the disputation between Catholics and Protestants, three centuries before the ecumenical conversations at Les Dombes, which recently sketched an important rapprochement.

But Leibniz's personal eucharistic faith is not easy to penetrate, and it was undoubtedly subject to some vicissitudes after the disappointment of the failure of his negotiations. The *Systema theologicum* is irreproachable from the point of view of Catholic orthodoxy, but Baruzi remarks that it is really a diplomatic text. Similarly, the *Confessio orthodoxiae Hungaricarum Ecclesiarum*, with the remarks for Christoval de Rojas y Spinola,[11] and the correspondence with Landgraf Ernst von Hessen, comprising a "Demonstratio possibilitatis mysteriorum Eucharistiae" in a *Demonstrationum catholicarum conceptus*, leaves nothing to be desired with regard to orthodoxy. But Leibniz adapts! When he returns to his convictions he is afraid that the adoration of the host would be misunderstood; he even has an aversion and a phobia of the alleged worship of this "album et rotundum, minutum et paniforme, rem fragilem, rotundam, tenuem, albicantem," this "white and round something," this "white and this round [thing] that they [the Catholics] carry" in procession. ... The Lamy-Toinard discussion (1694) about "whether or not our Lord ate the Paschal Lamb" (a discussion that even occupies the exegetes) provided him (from Lorenz Hertel) with a piece of information that must have delighted him: in a panel of the Last Supper in Soest in Westphalia, "the painter placed a nice ham on the table where, according to the vulgar opinion, Jesus Christ is seated in order to eat the paschal lamb; does it not seem to you, sir, that this is effectively to bury the synagogue?"[12]

---

9 Dutens, vol. 1, 676–77.

10 [Perhaps Tilliette is referring to the fable in which the bats pretend to be either beasts or birds, in order to avoid conflict. —Trans.]

11 A Franciscan bishop, whose biographical notes appeared in *Leibniziana*.

12 Leibniz, *Sämtliche Schriften und Briefe*, vol. 10: *Allgemeiner Politischer und Historischer Briefwechsel* (Berlin: Akademie Verlag, 1979), 89. Should we add that, in the face of certain deviations of eucharistic devotion, Leibniz is not wrong in his aversion to the worship of the species?

Nevertheless, the ecumenical preoccupation is predominant and constant. He says numerous times that "Eucharistiae Sacramentum est tesserae Christianae unitatis," and it is in this ecumenical context that his statements on the Eucharist should be explored.

TRANSUBSTANTIATION AND REAL PRESENCE

Jean Baruzi created a valuable collection of Leibniz's eucharistic texts in his anthology, although he does not offer much commentary on them.[13] But the essential part of the controversial points is expressed in an early letter to Arnauld, previously mentioned at the beginning of this chapter.

The principal objection is about transubstantiation. Leibniz tries to minimize it by showing that transubstantiation and a real multipresence are mutually implicating, that they are two sides of the same coin. Thus it would "unlock the deadbolt" and "open the door" to unity. For an "ultimate and intimate analysis," transubstantiation and multilocation of the body of Christ go together. How is this to be understood? Evidently it is not about presence *sub diversis speciebus*, which is not a veritable multiplicity (one does not consecrate the bread without the wine, and vice versa). What Leibniz means is that the multiple, local presence is linked to the multiplication of the species, and it is multiple because it is multiplied by the *species*, which involves transubstantiation—that is to say that the substances of the bread and wine give way to their species. For if it is impossible that one substance (the body of Christ), whose nature is to be extended, is found *idem numero* in many places at the same time, it is not at all unthinkable that a corporeal substance (the body of Christ), which is not extended in itself, by its dynamism (*conatus ad existendum*) acts in many places at the same time. A unique substance is communicated in various locations by the species. Transubstantiation and multipresence "amount to the same thing" in the sense that, having become simple species, the former substances of bread and wine multiply, repeat, and diffuse (exactly according to the natural mode of the substantial force) the presence of the unique substance of the Body and Blood: transubstantiation is the supernatural operation by which the bread and wine convert into (the simple species of) the substance of Christ. Real presence presupposes and has as its condition transubstantiation. Leibniz, who does not accept the *actio in distans* in his physics, allows it in celestial physics.

---

13 Jean Baruzi, ed., *Leibniz* (Paris: Bloud, 1909), 72–74, 248–62.

As we have seen, this is not precisely a theory of transubstantiation: we still have, like in Descartes's first hypothesis, the persistence of the accidents. While claiming to be loyal to the Augsburg Confession, he is glad to not be a Cartesian, and he declares this to Pellisson as well as to Fr. Isensehe. Pellisson is euphoric: "You permit Luther himself to believe like we do. I count the difference between you and us as almost nothing" (October 23, 1696). Leibniz, for his part, being pleased with himself and his explanation, expands on it to Christoph de Rojas (1694), where he seems to adopt the Scotistic point of view:

> Caeterum explicatio transsubstantiationis per solam multiplicationem praesentiae corporis Christi in locum panis annihilati, egregia est, et incommoda prae ceteris optime tollit. [Moreover, the explanation of transubstantiation by the unique multiplication of the presence of the body of Christ in place of the annihilated bread is remarkable and does away with the disadvantages of all the others.]

But he adds honestly:

> Interim multi putant verba Tridentini ubi dicitur substantiam panis et vini converti in substantiam corporis et sanguinis Christi aliquid amplius velle, et longissime differre conversionem unius in aliud a successione simplici in alterius locum. [However, many think that the words of the Council of Trent, where it says that the substance of the bread and the wine are converted into the substance of the body and blood of Christ, are more significant and that the conversion from the one to the other differs enormously from the simple succession by translation.][14]

This scruple honors him. In fact, even so, the explanation is unsatisfactory to the extent that it is somewhat theurgic. It tends to reverse the terms: *Corpus meum est hoc* (or, *hic*). Multipresence is the index of transubstantiation, and is its condition, with the implied Leibnizian conception of the dynamism of substance. Malebranche "had hoped" in vain "for a conciliation of the multipresence with the notion of the pure and simple extension." The notion of force is much better. But aporias remain: the *how* of transubstantiation, what it consists of, and how the miraculous operation

---

14 Leibniz, *Politischer und Historischer Briefwechsel*, 112.

is carried out. He himself was not occupied with this, and would wait for the opportunity, which will come in the following century.

Notwithstanding its inadequacy, however, it is through his dynamic theory of transubstantiation in view of the multipresence that he influenced Catholic theology, even more than Descartes.[15] He could boast about a certain caution in the Council of Trent, where it binds unity and multiplicity: "et ut multis nihilominus aliis in locis sacramentaliter praesens sua substantia nobis adsit" (Denz. 1636); "Totus enim et integer Christus sub panis specie et sub quavis ipsius speciei parte, totus item sub vini specie et sub eius partibus existit" (Denz. 1641, 1653). This was also used as a reference for some recent theologians, such as Leray and Véronnet, who, to be honest, are a bit extravagant. The illustrious Cardinal Franzelin himself had utilized the dynamic hypothesis as a philosophical hypothesis. Though, for the sake of honesty, we should say that in a note he declares not to have seen the similarity of his position with that of Leibniz's *Systema theologicum* until after the fact. He implements a dynamic conception of matter, he distinguishes the *energeia* of the substance from its *energema*, that is to say from the drive or the resistance. It is a nonimmanent transitional act (a parameter) of the substance and distinct from it. Therefore, nothing prevents God from keeping it intact, in the absence of the substance. The weight, the density, the sound, the color, the temperature, the taste and even the smell (all phenomena conveyed by the vibrations of ether) will remain. Thus, the conservation of the species adapts quite well to the theory of the emanation of force. Of course, the miracle only happens for a time and the species become corrupt. One sees that Franzelin's "possible hypothesis" is less philosophical than physical. It opens the way to Leray's rantings, but also to the praiseworthy attempt, even if filled with pitfalls, of Selvaggi's notion of the physico-chemical parallelism of transubstantiation. This will be a question farther along.

THE SUBSTANTIAL BOND

During the ecumenical discussion Leibniz essentially acknowledged transubstantiation. But how does transubstantiation fit into his system? What is the aptitude, the capacity of the Leibnizian system to shape an adequate theory? The same problem was posed to Descartes. And initially he was not

---

15 Besides Franzelin, note also Palmieri, Tongiorgi, and Leray. Leibniz's *Systema theologicum* is published in Fouchier de Careil, *Lettres et opuscules inédits de Leibniz*, 607–28.

pressed to respond any more than Descartes was. It was necessary that the occasion present itself: such was the exchange of letters with the Jesuit Barthélemy Des Bosses, who will be his Mesland, albeit more loquacious. The particular interest in this issue posed a question to the monadological system because the intrusion of the eucharistic problem constrained Leibniz to modify or to complete a key point, at least hypothetically: his teaching on organized bodies. In other words, it led him to establish the theory of the substantial bond.

After the failure of his negotiations, which consumed him at the turn of the century, Leibniz retired somewhat into his own corner, disappointed. This did not prevent him from producing some occasional interventions concerning the Eucharist, which are scattered in his correspondence. When he is at the Court of Austria he tends to take on the color of the milieu that he is in, and thus to catholicize. But, failing to convince the Catholics, he addresses the divided sects of his own confession. For them as well, the eucharistic body is the *tesserae unitatis*. The "Preface" to the *Theodicy*, "on the harmony between reason and faith," contains two paragraphs (§18 and 19) that are intended for his coreligionists. The Reformed (above all Zwinglians) and the "evangelicals" disagree on the subject of the Eucharist, as the latter at least admit a concomitance of the two substances during the reception of the sacrament, while the former are content with representation. The Lutherans, on the other hand, propose the "ubiquitous diffusion" of the "body of our Savior," as well as the "multiplied reduplication" (or, replication), but not ordinary presence. Calvin perhaps only differs from those who subscribe to the Augsburg Confession in that he requires faith in addition to "oral reception" in order to "participate in the substance." This real participation is explained by the analogy of the immediate operation and presence (§19). This is active, dynamic. According to Newton's theory, a body can act at a distance on several others, and Locke (as well as Leibniz) retracted his earlier opinion on this point, having read Newton. In any case, nothing is impossible for God; the author of nature surpasses the power of nature and is able to abrogate his own laws (the iron that floats, the fire that does not burn). This type of reasoning is well known to us.

None of this is a question of transubstantiation, and, let us repeat, Leibniz's eucharistic zeal has cooled by this point. In the correspondence with Des Bosses he speaks of "*your* transubstantiation," which, it seems, he has nothing to do with. The fortuitous circumstance of a discussion on composed bodies—amidst other problems—forces him, however, to envisage a compatible explanation with the system of universal harmony. He had the chance to have an exchange with a partner sufficiently acute and intelligent to permit him to push himself to the limit.

The Jesuit Barthélemy Des Bosses (Bossaeus), born in Herve, Holland in 1663, entered the Society of Jesus in 1686 and taught literature, mathematics, philosophy, and theology in Hildesheim, Paderborn, and in Cologne. He died in Cologne in 1738, without having accomplished the great career that Leibniz had predicted for him. He also corresponded with Wolff. His translation of the *Theodicy* was reviewed and corrected by Leibniz. Their epistolary exchange, which began in 1706 and lasted until 1716, the year of Leibniz's death, has been almost entirely preserved. It has been published by Gerhardt.[16]

This was the object of Maurice Blondel's Latin thesis, *De vincula substantiali et de substantia composita apud Leibnitium* (1893), which has been translated into French and skillfully introduced by Fr. Claude Troisfontaines.[17] Blondel had other motives as well, which we will discuss later. Afterward, in 1930, at the instigation of Fr. Auguste Valensin, Blondel resumed his Latin dissertation by transforming it into another book, with material assistance from Fr. Gaston Fessard. His change of attitude is very instructive, but this time he forsakes an analysis of the texts for a more critical discussion, reproaching Leibniz for his "timidity," his maneuvering. Fr. Marc Leclerc's excellent study from Louvain in 1982 deals with the two works and their respective issues.[18] Some earlier contributions, such as H. Joly and É. Boutroux, who inspired Blondel, and A. Boehm and V. Mathieu, treat the substantial bond as it functions in Leibniz, while J. Flamand follows Blondel's perspective.[19] Vittorio Mathieu gives homage to his illustrious predecessor before providing a magisterial commentary on the correspondence, in which he underlines its interest and its aporetic tenor. Finally, Christiane Frémont provided (in 1981) an annotated translation of thirty-five of Leibniz's letters, with an introduction that exaggerates the possible

---

16 Gerhardt, vol. 2.

17 Claude Troisfontaines, ed., *Maurice Blondel: Le lien substantial et la substance composée d'après Leibniz* (Louvain-Paris: Nauwelaerts, 1972). The introduction is 140 pages long.

18 Marc Leclerc, *La Finalité chez Leibniz. Introduction à l'interprétation blondélienne* (unpublished), Catholic University of Louvain.

19 Alfred Boehm, *Le "Vinculum substantiale" chez Leibniz. Ses origenes historiques* (Paris: Vrin, 1962); Vittorio Mathieu, *Leibniz e Des Bosses (1706–1716)* (Turin: Giappichelli, 1960); J. Flamand, *L'Idée de méditation chez Maurice Blondel* (Louvain: Nauwelaerts, 1969).

importance of the Vinculum.[20] Blondel's own reworking of his Latin thesis is entitled *Une énigme historique: le "Vinculum substantiale" d'après Leibniz et l'ébauche d'un realisme supérieur.*[21] It has been revised and edited by Fr. Gaston Fessard, as we have just noted.

A useful presentation would include a whole summary of Leibnizian philosophy as a system of monads and of universal harmony. Instead, we will content ourselves with returning to some canonical texts, such as the *Discourse on Metaphysics*, the *Monadology*, the *Principles of Nature and Grace*, as well as the work of the best interpreters, such as Yvon Belaval.

It is within a system that only accepts metaphysical units or points as ultimate reality (such as the soul or the self) that the question of compound and particularly organic bodies, and their effective unity, is posed. And, in fact, this occupied Leibniz many times without his having recourse to the hypothesis of the Vinculum. What about bodies that are not simple and, in particular, organisms? Leibniz debated this for a long time in his early correspondence with Arnauld. The correspondence with the Franciscan Fardella also directly addresses the question.[22] There is also quite a lot to glean from the letters to Rémond de Montmort, Bourguet, Des Maizeaux, the Queen Sophia Charlotte, and Lady Masham (daughter of Cudworth), among others. But it is only in his correspondence with Des Bosses that he advances the hypothesis of a substantial bond of the monads, and this is in order to respond directly to the objection of transubstantiation, obliquely touching on the constitution of organisms.

Arnauld, who does not easily admit defeat, adduces some examples of massive objects, such as marble tiles, or elaborate objects, such as a watch, in order to call for a unity more solid than the simple aggregate (of substances). He is bothered by the fate of the "ram of Abraham" reduced to ashes: what happens to the incinerated animal according to a philosophy in which destruction is only a metamorphosis and there is no possible death? What about its substantial form? Leibniz retorts that the unfortunate ram always subsists under a minimal body, in some nook on Mount Moriah.

---

20 Leibniz, *L'Être et la Relation. Avec Trente-Sept Lettres de Leibniz au R.P. Des Bosses* (Paris: Vrin, 1981).

21 Maurice Blondel, *Une énigme historique: Le "Vinculum substantiale" d'après Leibniz et l'ébauche d'un realisme supérieur* (Paris: Beauchesne, 1930).

22 Michelangelo Fardella taught in Padoue, Quebec, and was a mathematician. These Latin letters are found in Foucher de Careil, *Nouvelles lettres et opuscules inédits de Leibniz* (Paris: Auguste Durand, 1857).

The result of their disagreement is that Leibniz, at this time, tends to assimilate organized bodies to inorganic bodies. But these actually contain some imperceptible microorganisms; and the gradual and accidental unity of these aggregates proceed from (1) the representation of the monad, which contains all that follows after it, and (2) the working together and harmony of the monads, that is to say, of the substances. His constant goal is to reduce what is composite, even the organic, to simplicity.

The axiom that drives Leibnizian ontology is "that which is not truly *one*, is then not truly a *being*," as well as the corollary: "where there are only beings by aggregation, there would not even be real beings." Unity is the monad, the *unum per se*; the universe is its representation, but it is immured alive. However, besides God, the great Monad, there are no monads in a pure state; they are not without some body or matter of which they are the entelechy. Consequently, the universe is not made of atoms of substance, but of a multitude of souls, of an infinity of animated bodies. There is nothing uncultivated, nothing sterile, nothing of death in nature. A quiver of life in an indefinite gradation runs up to the borders of matter, vibrates and reactivates the feeble respiration of lethargic monads even at the most buried extremities. Even more than the garden full of plants, Leibniz's favorite comparison is the fish tank, a fishpond, teeming and shimmering with scales; in the most tenuous folds of the material world, life throbs or grows numb. The other example, addressed to Arnauld, is drawn from the smallest animals: "One finds that there is a prodigious quantity of animals in a drop of water imbued with pepper; and one can make millions of them die all at once, and both the frogs of the Egyptians and the quails of the Israelites of which you speak, sir, do not come close."

But the solipsism of the monads very much complicates the status of the compound body. The monad is enclosed and even precluded. To say that "the compounds symbolize with the simple" is a verbal solution. What does "symbolize" mean? An accord, a consensus. The monads, in fact, are not some ingredients of bodies or of matter, but are required and demanded. In the monadic universe harmony marries finality. The corporeal *phenomenon* is certainly founded by its relation with the central or dominant monad that subjects the subordinate monads. But the body is in a perpetual flux, and can one be satisfied with representations of the monad in order to secure the unity of the compound?

It would take too long to follow the vicissitudes of compound bodies and the formation of the theory of organisms in these letters, which is the most notable impetus for the correspondence with Des Bosses. But Arnauld had stubbornly set the stage.[23] These are the occasions that obligated Leibniz to differentiate, if not the substances, at least the "substantiated." At first, he had the tendency to reserve substance for only simple elements, for monads, conceived on the model of the soul or of the ego, even if this concerned "totally nude monads" (not clothed) in a stunned state.

Should one jumble together, under the rubric of unities *per accidens*, or aggregates (like a pile of sand), unities as heterogenous as a rainbow (a simple phenomenon), a pile of rocks, the earth, a tree, a horse, milk, a machine? Leibniz separates the case of humans and animals (his treatment of animals is only in a rough draft). For the rest, he considers as aggregates all that does not have a soul, particularly groups, collective beings, moral entities. . . . This follows for a people, an army, a frozen pond with all its fish, as well as a herd of sheep: "even if these sheep would be so linked that they could only walk with an equal step and that one could not be touched without all the others crying out." Arnauld insists on the diversity of "unsuitable units" and Leibniz, without withdrawing the exclusivity that he granted to substances, like the ego, agrees that a bag and a heap are more aggregates than natural or artificial machines endowed with corporeal unity. Certain beings are only beings of reason, phenomena (a pair of diamonds, an army, a machine), their unity being mental. And yet, apart from being settled thoughts, there is something real and substantial in these beings, even in a rainbow and a pile of rocks. And Leibniz multiplies substances, for underlying inanimate objects are living, imperceptible substances. But in fact he only makes small concessions. No form of unity other than the mental is suitable for aggregates, for officers of the East India Company as well as for a heap of sand, *arena sine calce*. A rejoinder by Arnauld incites him to explain himself on the *expression* or the *inter-expression* [*entr'expression*]: what is dispersed in several beings is expressed or is represented in "a single indivisible being," and like all sympathizing substances, it is a gradual mutual correspondence, a concert and a harmony; everything conspires. . . . Finally the substantial forms are everywhere, "everything is full of animated bodies"; it is therefore necessary that everywhere in the body there are indivisible, ingenerable, and incorruptible substances, having something

---

23 The correspondence with Arnauld has been translated into French and is presented by Geneviève Rodis-Lewis. [The correspondence has also been translated into English as *The Leibniz-Arnauld Correspondence: With Selections from Correspondence with Ernst, Landgrave of Heesn-Rheinfels* (New Haven, CT: Yale University Press, 2016) —Trans.]

that responds to souls. And this goes as far as the eye can see: "one body is several bodies" (to Fardella); "Bodies are multitudes" (to Des Maizeaux).

The above doctrine remains more or less intact up to the pressing entreaties of Des Bosses: organisms are aggregates, substantives. Without hesitation Leibniz lines up his taxonomies, his lists of stereotypical examples: army, herd, pond, watch—stack of logs, pile of rocks, herd, army, pool—machine, pool, herd. And so on. In the correspondence with Des Bosses, we can read all these in one breath: choir of angels, army, herd, fishpond, house, stone, corpse. . . . It does not matter what it is since bodies are not substances, but phenomena in perpetual flux.

However, under pressure from Des Bosses, Leibniz did not maintain the equivalence of compound substances until the end. Nevertheless, both on this problem and concerning transubstantiation, he stubbornly kept two irons in the fire. First, he is forced to accept the non-accidental *Unum per se* of the organic body, man or animal. What then constitutes the unity or union of a compound substance? It is here that the famous hypothesis of the substantial bond, *Vinculum substantiale*, comes in. Leibniz expressly says that he only spoke of it to Des Bosses (indeed, *Monadology* does not breathe a word of it).

Vittorio Mathieu has provided a masterful commentary on this correspondence. After having followed all the twists and turns of the discussion on compound bodies (itself intertwined with many other questions), he concludes that Leibniz remained hesitant and that he did not achieve a real theory of the organism, out of fear of affecting the monads. Monads are untouchable, self-sufficient. They do not descend into organisms, they do not enter into their modifications. Leibniz's system remains a "system of individuality." Admittedly, the theory of the substantial bond comes very close to a biological philosophy, and it is a meeting point with Aristotelian philosophy. But, according to Mathieu, it is more of a means of evading the problem than of solving it. This aporetic conclusion, which perhaps gives too much weight to the monadology, is not shared by Claude Troisfontaines. It is nonetheless a plausible thesis, insofar as the substantial bond interferes or alternates with the monad, without a real mediation of the schemas.

Leibniz, in his conversation with Des Bosses, keeps several solutions in his sights: if bodies are aggregates (and certain bodies are undoubtedly only aggregates), their unity is entirely extrinsic, resulting from representations of the monad. They flow like a river, they are restored like the ship of Theseus, so often repaired that all its parts have been replaced. The subordinate monads that constitute the moving body *consent* to the dominant monad. That is not much. Or if the bodies are pure phenomena (and some are, like a rainbow or a parhelion), they are also well established in the representations of the monad. This hypothesis of phenomenal bodies, consonant with the monadology, persists until the end of the letter, even in the explanation of transubstantiation. But Leibniz oscillates between aggregates of monads and simple phenomena. Obviously, reducing the body invariably to an *Unum per accidens* raises some difficulties. Leibniz either resigns himself or simply decides to attribute to the organic body the *Unum per se*. This is quite literally why he brings up in this debate the idea of the *Vinculum substantiale*, the substantial bond, which he also calls a unifying reality, realizer of phenomena, substantiating, substantial superaddition, compound substance. . . . Although the bond is immediately adopted by Des Bosses, it is considered by Leibniz as *his* bond, the bond *quod urgeo*. He does not speak of it elsewhere, as we have already said, but he seems to hold onto it.

But does he really hold onto it? There is a letter to Pfaff, reproduced in the Dutens edition of Leibniz's works,[24] to which Blondel draws attention. Leibniz seems to apologize for his theological incursions and to consider the doctrine of the substantial bond as a *lusus ingenii*. On the other hand, one should not take this retraction too seriously. He adapts to his surroundings, like a chameleon, and Pfaff did not deserve the trouble of a battle. On the other hand it remains true—and it must be taken into account—that the substantial bond is a hypothesis, a conjecture. As such it creates a problem for the interpreters of the monadological system. But Leibniz presented it only when considering the Eucharist. He himself did not need the idea, and he stressed that he did not adhere to *your* transubstantiation. It is therefore, in the words of Fr. Fessard, a "volunteered suggestion." Moreover, he retains the solution, which does not involve substances, the solution by another means, with simple phenomena.

However, the nonspecialist reader still has the impression that the substantial bond of the monads interests him and is close to his heart. He finds more and more reasons, beyond the eucharistic ones, to attach himself to it. If he is concerned that in all circumstances the monads are preserved, he also resolutely advocates for the bond. Being at first generatable and corruptible, the bonds become in the course of the correspondence ingenerable

---

24 Dutens, vol. 1, 32: "De consecratione Eucharistiae, occasione Dissertationis Pfaffi." See also 78, note.

and imperishable. Nothing undermines the self-sufficiency and solipsism of the monads, which draw all *ex propria penu* (from their own funds), but the realizing bond, even if it is only an echo of the monads that it links together, is an "originary echo," a principle of action and source of modifications: "My substantial bond is in the subject not as an accident, but as the substantial form or the source of modifications, albeit in the mode of an echo."[25] Without it there is no real connection, either physical or metaphysical. Only it guarantees a real continuity, because the monads are solitary, secluded. The relationship postulates a real, substantial bond. What are commonly called substances are only substantiated, but when one poses the question of the absolute substance that realizes phenomena, we immediately have the compound substance or the compound, comprising the entelechy. And compound substances are the only living, the only natural organic machines. It therefore seems that Leibniz has traded the preference he previously displayed for reduction to phenomena for substantial bonds. Nevertheless, he did not choose definitively.

There is a mysterious aura around the substantial bond in Leibniz's philosophy. What does it mean exactly? Does it arise to meet certain needs? Does it break the closure of the monads and initiate a higher realism? It enters the system at a slant, but does it manage to straighten it? The nature of the bond and its role give rise to a problem of interpretation that goes beyond the eucharistic framework. It has been examined by Blondel and others, most recently in Fr. Marc Leclerc's dissertation. Blondel's constructive criticism in 1930 will bring us back to this.

The *Vinculum* arrives unexpectedly in the Leibnizian meditation, and the occasion was an almost point-blank question by Des Bosses concerning real presence and transubstantiation. Invited to give his opinion on a point that tests the ecumenical capacity of the system, Leibniz responds immediately, slightly stunned, without proposing the hypothesis of substance-bonds. Henceforth, the question of eucharistic transubstantiation goes hand in hand with the problem of organisms and real unity; it follows the vicissitudes, that is to say the fate, of compound substances, since Leibniz acts very quickly to disconnect and protect simple substances, the monads ("monads excluded from the miracle," which is the title of a paragraph from Mathieu). But the discussion involves many hazards, a movement back and

---

25 *Die philosophischen Schriften von Gottfried Wilhelm Leibniz*, vol. 2, ed. Karl Immanuel Gerhardt (Berlin: Weidmann, 1879), 503–4.

forth, trial and error, because faith in transubstantiation implies faith in substance and it obliges Leibniz to revise his doctrine of compound bodies. Questioned therefore by Des Bosses on September 6, 1709, Leibniz, a bit taken aback and speaking off the cuff, replied on September 8 that the case required an "altior disquisitio," an in-depth investigation. While awaiting this examination, which he will undertake only with reluctance, he proposes a hasty solution, which transposes the idea of the substitution of substances, at the level of the monads—provided that the problem does not concern him, does not reform him:

> Remove the constituent monads of the bread, their active and passive primitive forces, and in their place [*substituta*] the presence of the constituent monads of the body of Christ, there remain only the forces derived from the bread, displaying the same phenomena as the bread monads would have shown.[26]

The derived forces are the accidents, the appearances. Leibniz admits a transfer of the monads; he engages them in the supernatural operation. What follows will show that he did not do it without repugnance and, moreover, there is a small "with respect to" (*quoad*) which can be taken in the restrictive meaning. In fact, he does not provide an explanation but rather outlines a formulation.

But Des Bosses has put himself in a Leibnizian frame of mind and he is not satisfied. How do the derived forces break out, these so-called accidents, which are in fact modes of primitive forces? Suddenly Leibniz backtracks; he removes the monads from the operation and resorts to a "superadded union," which is already a sketch of the *Vinculum*: the bread is substantiated, made of countless substances or monads, thanks to a superadded union which substantializes and produces a new being (the being of bread). It is therefore not necessary to destroy or to change the monads, it suffices to replace their substantial union with a divine equivalent.[27] It is still vague, and at least the monads are put out of play, disconnected. Transubstantiation does not bring about, if I dare say, a disturbance. But Des Bosses is still not satisfied, as we can understand. He would like to see the monads of bread destroyed, replaced by the monads of the body of Christ.

---

26 Gerhardt, vol. 2, 390–91.
27 Gerhardt, 399–403.

A long break of eighteen months intervenes in the eucharistic debate, without a single letter exchanged. It is resumed at the beginning of 1712. The hypothesis of a superadded real union comes into clearer focus. If faith requires bodily substances (*si fides nos ad corporeas substantias adigit*) (it is not faith [*belief*][28] in the existence of bodies, as Fr. Marc Leclerc suggests, who corrects himself in a note; it is the Catholic faith), the bodily substance consists of this unitive reality which adds an *absolutum aliquid*, a substantial though fluent unity, to phenomena. It is therefore in the mutation of this unifying reality that "your" transubstantiation would take place. Neither the monads nor the sensible phenomena based in them are involved in the supernatural change. This seems to confirm Catholic dogma itself, since it also excludes the idea of the soul of Christ changing in transubstantiation: "I would say the same of all the other monads of the Most Holy Body."[29] The substantial bond, which now is called by name, *adds* something to bodies, a reality that surpasses the firmly grounded phenomenon. Leibniz even anticipates Des Bosses' desires, admitting "absolute accidents" resulting from the absolute nature of the union. But, for his part, he would prefer to explain the eucharistic accidents by phenomena alone. He does not develop how.

The editor adds a supplement to this major letter (from February 5), which contains the sentence that made Maurice Blondel rejoice: *ex pluribus substantiis oritur una nova.*[30] This is the birth certificate of the *Vinculum*. The formula immediately sets off insights and perspectives, which are not repeated:

> It will not be a simple result ... but in addition it will add a new substantiality or a substantial bond that will not be the effect of the divine intellect alone, but also of the will [an invaluable notation that has not escaped the attention of Blondel or Fessard]. ... And in this consists the metaphysical bond of the soul and the body, which constitute a single subject [*suppositum*], and the union of natures in Christ himself is an analog.

Here again the mystery of the Bond is clarified. This is what Blondel called Leibniz's "secret meditation."

---

28 [Tilliette writes *belief* in English —Trans.]

29 Gerhardt, 435–36.

30 Gerhardt, 438.

But, let us repeat, this christological insight exists only in a draft. And further, Mathieu is justified in observing that the *Vinculum* does not have the desired coherence, as the monads are only elements of the bond: it requires them, they are not the ingredients. Leibniz is charged with "avarice," and it is not surprising that Des Bosses was not delighted with the contribution (*offa*, in Italian) that he was offered.[31] This bond binds poorly and is easily detached. Like nutmeg, we do not know whether or not it is there. Many problems are pending regarding the unifying reality. Is there a bond of monads of bread and wine? It is obvious (thanks to the supplement) that it is the substantial bond of the Sacred Body which is at issue: does it assume a double role? Is the application of the *Vinculum substantiale Christi* to the intact bread monads with their phenomena sufficient for us to speak of transubstantiation? Descartes's immortal question begins again: what is there that has changed? Des Bosses finds it easy to throw fuel on the fire, as Mathieu says,[32] by insisting (on August 28, 1712) on the necessary destruction of the bread monads. But Leibniz definitively rejects this hypothesis, and he never returns to it again.

Mathieu said amusingly, concerning the discussion beginning on September 20, 1712, that it is not making much progress with regard to the meat in the oven, but rather what varies is the culinary art, according to the delicate palates of the correspondents. This is more true of the debate on organisms than of the eucharistic question itself.[33] Indeed, this missive of September 20 brings useful precisions. It envisages several conjectures to account for transubstantiation: (1) God can apply the bond (of bread) to other monads (the Body), while it ceases to unite what belongs to it; (2) he can also purely and simply (*plane*) remove this substantial bond and replace it with another (the Body), uniting the other monads; (3) in this case, either it ceases to unite these other monads and is transferred from monads to monads; (4) or, while retaining its natural monads it supernaturally unites new ones. It is obviously this last hypothesis that prevails and that accounts for transubstantiation as a "mutation of the whole substance of one body into the whole substance of another body, which however retains its first nature." The reference to the Tridentine definition readily suggests the conversion of the substance of bread into the substance of the body of Christ.

---

31 Mathieu, *Leibniz e Des Bosses*, 150–51.

32 Mathieu, 199.

33 Mathieu, 199.

Indeed, but let us emphasize that despite the apparent similarity of the two subjunctive verbs (*retineat*), the relative clause (*quod tamen suam priorem naturam retineat*) most likely relates to the first *corpus*, namely the nature of the bread. There is indeed a certain ambiguity, but the following clarifies the reasoning and undoubtedly allows us to attribute the transfer (adduction) to the Bond of the Body. The ambiguity is, in fact, removed: the first bond (the bread) is destroyed, and its accidents along with it (because they share the fate of the substance, though in fact they survive in phenomena, as Des Bosses mentions in the following letter), accidents being understood here as pure concrete states of the substance. The replacement is assured by the substantial bond of the body of Christ. A question arises concerning the bread and wine, which, not being substantives that constitute an *unum per se*, do not have a single substantial bond, but several, as aggregates of organic or substantiated bodies. It is therefore *many* substantial bonds that are removed, and thus the words of consecration fall on the compound of these substantial bonds.[34]

The entreaty of Des Bosses, who would like to involve only the monads and their phenomena, would require an attribution of perceptions corresponding to those of the destroyed monads (of bread and wine) to the monads of the body of Christ, and the accidents of bread and wine to the body of Christ. Pure monads and mere phenomena are not enough, one needs "something that realizes." Des Bosses grumbles. His long reply is a step-by-step, point-by-point, defense. In particular, he asserts that this form of transubstantiation is very meager and incomplete, as it brackets the monads, *magna, imo potissima pars substantiae*.[35] In addition, it should be the case that the bond of bread and wine be the *tota substantia* required by the council. But Leibniz is unwilling to be taken in, and the hypothesis involving the monads has been definitively relegated.

Yet another hypothesis emerges alongside the substitution of bonds, a hypothesis that is preferred in a letter dated October 10, 1712. Moreover, Leibniz had already pointed to it succinctly. This is the hypothesis of bodies reduced to mere phenomena, without bonds. This runs alongside the first hypothesis, and it will prevent the discussion from getting stuck, despite some stagnation. The letter of January 24, 1713, a response to a lengthy letter from Des Bosses, summarizes the three possible conjectures about the

---

34 Gerhardt, vol. 2, 458–59.

35 Gerhardt, 463.

metousiasmós (or *metousiôsis*). If bodies are simple phenomena, it must be said that their substances consist of true phenomena, which God perceives by the science of vision, like the angels and the elect, who therefore see the body of Christ where we perceive bread and wine.[36] As for the substantial bond, it can be made supernaturally independent of its monads; it can be transferred (or changed) and accommodated to other monads. Let us translate this: the monads of bread and wine remain without the substantial bond, thus reduced to the state of pure monads with their phenomena. This presentation contains an anomaly when compared to the letter of September 20 analyzed above. Here, in fact, it is the bond (or rather the bonds) of bread and wine that "adapts itself" to the monads of the body of Christ. In his haste, Leibniz chose the first part of the first hypothesis, without worrying too much about the bond of the body of Christ. The *mutari* can be interpreted as *converti*, and therefore render an orthodox sense of transubstantiation. But is the bond, having deserted its own monads and having become the bond of the eucharistic body, identical to the Bond of the monads of the body of Christ? Descartes's difficulty reappears, and the bond floats between monads which are not its own and phenomena of monads which are no longer its own. Obviously, Leibniz is groping around and he writes a little quickly. The fact remains that at the end of the paragraph, having hitherto allowed himself to be influenced by Des Bosses (the application to the monads of Christ), he changes his mind and declares his preference for the solution that destroys the bond (of bread) and keeps the monads. The discussion returns to the fourth part of the hypothesis.

There is another change of mind in the following letter (August 23, 1713). Leibniz had decided that the bonds, although absolute, were subject to birth and death, to generation and corruption. Although he could not find his notes, he now comes around to Des Bosses' opinion. Since the animal does not die, the bond is ingenerable and incorruptible, at least naturally.[37] We therefore speak of removal, suppression (*tolli*), or mutation (*mutari*), rather than destruction. To use Mathieu's term, the "unanchored" bond (of bread) is "accommodated" to monads that are not its own, after having been removed. It is stated in the form of a theorem, and one is again left with the difficulty of the Bond of the body of Christ. The tone is aporetic; the discussion stalls, even recedes. The bread and the wine form a collection

---

36 Gerhardt, 473–74.
37 Gerhardt, 474.

of substantial bonds, because it is packed with animalcules, or micro-organisms, while the body of Christ possesses a total substantial bond: and it is therefore on this side that "you" must seek the "possibility of transubstantiation."[38] But Leibniz is not willing to start again, and he repeats the hypothesis of the pure phenomena, which in their miraculous content are only accessible to the vision (*obversantur*) of the divine Spirit and those to whom God reveals them.[39] So he puts his second iron back into the fire.

The note on January 10, 1714 confirms in general the independence of the substantial bond, its perpetuity, its possible alteration, and the fact that supernaturally it can be "accommodated" to "others and other monads" *per saltum*, and that it can be produced and be taken away. The relative stagnation of the Leibnizian discourse is attenuated by the fact that it goes a little further into the relationship of the bond to the monads, its allocation to the only dominant monad, its natural dependence on the monads, and its (natural) character as an echo. Its modifications depend on the monads that it unites naturally, but, once again, God can, by a miracle, make it correspond to foreign monads, such that it is disjoined from its usual monads. He can attribute to the bond what is not provided by the monads, and take away from it what they do provide. It is clear that, by way of this distant language, Leibniz is heading not only toward the priority (*husteron proteron*), but toward the exclusivity of the *Vinculum substantiale Christi*. This is in the letter of April 29, 1715.[40]

Doubts, however, begin to work on him, since he goes over the whole question of the *Vinculum* the following August 17. This letter is one of the most difficult.[41] Leibniz again indicates his perplexity about absolute accidents, which certainly seem to be substantial. He prefers to back off from this and to speak, quite correctly, of species that are non-illusory real phenomena (like the rainbow, the parhelion).[42] The two alternative hypotheses are somehow synthesized. In the case of the miracle of the Eucharist, in the

---

38 Gerhardt, 482.

39 Note the theological soundness of this conclusion.

40 Gerhardt, vol. 2, 496.

41 Gerhardt, 503–5.

42 Leibniz mentions in passing the legend of Doctor Faust devouring a cartload of hay as a non-illusory phenomenon. This can already be found, attributed to a monk from Erfurt (with the coachman, the chariot, and the horse), in the magic pamphlet of Lercheimer von Steinfelden (1585), then by contamination attached to Faust from the "Popular Booklet" of 1587 (and a previous source would be the *Problemata theologica* of 1575, by the theologian Benedictus Aretius from Bern).

absence of substantive bonds (of bread and wine) removed by God, only the monads and the true phenomena remain, as if there were no substantial bonds in nature. The monads of bread and wine, once they are stripped of their substantial bonds, are the substantial bonds of the monads of the body of Christ which act (*influxum habere*)[43] in their place: thus the substance of the body and blood of Christ is perceived (or received). The substitution is perfect, the phenomena (species) of bread and wine are the phenomena of the Eucharistic Christ. How then can we understand the very enigmatic last sentence, where some (for example, Christiane Frémont) see only (*invita latinitate*) the repetition of the miracle of Consecration:

> Nam vincula substantialia earum monadum erunt sublata, et post cessa-tionem phaenomenorum, seu species destructas, restituenda non quidem qualia fuerant, sed qualia prodissent, si nulla fuisset facta destructio. [Because the substantial bonds of these monads will be removed, and after the cessation of the phenomena, or the destruction of the species, (they) will have to be restored not certainly as they had been, but as they would have appeared if there had been no destruction.][44]

It seems that for grammatical as well as for more substantive reasons, the redundant interpretation should be ruled out. Rather, this concerns (and this is new in Leibniz's writings) the fate of the substance (of bread) as soon as the species, consumed or corrupted, can no longer be the appearances of the body of Christ. The problem (incidentally attached to stercoranist opinion) occupied Catholic, scholastic, and other theologians. The most convincing opinion is that the subsistence of the "destroyed" species is pro-vided by a new substance, recreated or "returned"—but not as it was. The verb *prodissent* and the unreality that follow are likely to intrigue. They are, in fact, quite embarrassing. It is unlikely, since the bonds are immortal, that it will be the "destruction" (provisional, always possible) of the bonds of

---

43 *Influxus* is the prevalent theological term, and thus the surprise of Christiane Frémont is com-pletely out of place.

44 Gerhardt, vol. 2, 505. I take this opportunity to correct note 24 (on page 611) of my article in the *Gregorianum*, "Problèmes de philosophie eucharistique II," 65, 1985, 605–33, which was not without confusion. As a matter of fact, theologians, because of the heresy of stercoranism, have paid too little attention to the fate of the deserted species. These have followed the common fate of substances destined for disintegration and death. But as long as they remain, they are the object of worship. Fr. Maurice de La Taille (p. 638–42) recalls that there is no real relation of Christ to the species and that it is necessary to distinguish the meta-empirical nature of the bread from its empirical nature. See n. 39.

bread; Leibniz avoids this vocabulary. Following this, destruction should concern the species. These bonds which appear intact and new are not regulated by the formulation of a condition that has indeed been met (*si nulla . . . destructio*), but they come back unaltered and different as if there had been no species and their destruction.[45] For Leibniz as for Descartes, the miracle is indeed hidden, irremediably hidden.

The final letter (of May 29, 1716) is not free from obscurities either. Mathieu calls it a long swan song,[46] in reality a rather halting song, for which the philosopher apologizes (*saltatim scribo*). Leibniz defends his hypothesis one last time. If the compound substance, the *Vinculum*, is absent, and if the monads are not present, there is no compound. Yes, Leibniz answers, except by a miracle.[47] No one will say that the body of Christ is in the Eucharist if he were not told of the miracle. This miracle is the total and instantaneous separation of the substance and the ingredients in perpetual flux: all of the compound substance—the bond, the realizing of phenomena—is removed in the terrestrial thing, replaced by the realizing of phenomena in the celestial thing (*res terrena, res caelestis*, classical terms from St. Irenaeus). Until the end the simple substance is put aside, and until the end the alternative hypothesis is maintained. Chance wanted it to have the last word. The substance would then be made up of constitutive phenomena, as whiteness consists of unobservable bubbles, such as foam. The accident would be the view of white. God could substitute black for white, keeping the accidents of white, and only white would be seen. But the perception of the unobservable, the privilege of God and the blessed, would consist, not in

---

45 To me, communion also seems to be implied, which is why here I translate *percipere* more readily by "receive." But I would somewhat correct the unsubstantiated opinion that I expressed, following V. Mathieu, in my article in *Gregorianum* (1983, 2), in the sense that the problem now seems to me more eucharistic than Leibnizian. Leibniz has in mind the fate of the species when they are no longer species and when they follow the common path, "as if transubstantiation had not occurred," as the most reliable and the most anti-stercoranist theologians say. The cessation of the phenomena signals the destruction of the species. We must remember the strong sense of "species" for Leibniz, which is as a real vehicle for transubstantiation (see the letter to Arnauld). The phenomena of accidents disappear, the species are destroyed (the sacramental signs), substances reappear (a mass or vinegar for Franzelin, human blood or ashes for Billot). Leibniz basically completes its transposition. "Destruction" (of the species) in the unreal proposition would therefore be a prudent synonym for transubstantiation, but by means of eating or corruption, and not in the sense of annihilation as Frémont and Marion want.

46 Mathieu, *Leibniz e Des Bosses*, 196.

47 Gerhardt, vol. 2, 518. Another difficult text, where Mathieu's hypothesis is not satisfying. One should be sure of reading *abest* (which is also in the Dutens), instead of *adest*, which would be more logical.

foam and mounds, with the texture of white, but in valleys or the texture of black. Like the disciple of the *Spiritual Exercises*, the one devoted to the Eucharist is ready to believe as black what he sees as white, if the Church says that white is black.[48]

THE SUBSTANTIAL BOND AFTER LEIBNIZ

The substantial bond remained for Leibniz an attractive, seductive hypothesis, but a hypothesis nonetheless. This is what makes Christiane Frémont's recent and enthusiastic interpretation questionable. According to her book *L'Être et la Relation*, the *Vinculum*, far from being a more or less erratic and marginal suggestion, is in fact the key to the monadological system and what allows Leibniz to complete it triumphantly. Being is relational. The relations that intersect and multiply the immense game of Leibnizian mirrors produce by means of intensity the *kat'exochen* relation, the substantial union. Christ and the Trinity complete the system. It is almost too beautiful, and such a perfect unison of natural and supernatural harmony makes one fear that the triumph will be that of logical pantheism.

Blondel was much more timid in his Latin thesis, although he sensed, through the usage of "new substance" and the secret meditation, an extension and an aspiration of Leibniz's system towards a christological realism. The christological background is indisputable, and discreet signs show that Leibniz was quite aware of it. On the other hand, in the 1930 reworking of the Latin thesis, Blondel, so favorable to Descartes, shows little affection for Leibniz. In short, Blondel reproaches him for his pusillanimity. Leibniz allowed the magnificent intuition of the Substantial Bond, born of the eucharistic analogy and pointing toward Christ, to collapse. He had the possibility of accessing a "higher realism" of existent beings; the *Vinculum* was "this hole from above," this gap in the sky, which exploded the monadological closure and logical idealism. He was afraid, he retracted, and the hypothesis took refuge in "a disreputable corner" of the work, from which Blondel began to exhume it. This later severity of the philosopher from Aix is somewhat astonishing, but at a time when his own Catholic philosophy was frank and avowed, he wanted to cut sharply like a surgeon and denounce the cautious approach of the philosopher he once admired. We will see in chapter eight what he himself did with the *Vinculum* in his *L'Action*.

---

48 Gerhardt, 519–20.

Mathieu, espousing the point of view of Des Bosses, thinks that all the trouble and the failure of the philosophy of the organism, as well as the doctrine of transubstantiation, comes from that which Leibniz did not allow to touch the monads: the substantial bond, which functions like a cantilever. Between the bonds and the phenomena, which are the phenomena of the monads, the monads do not intervene, so to speak. The respective situation of the monads of bread and the monads of the body is all the less clear since they are not concerned with transubstantiation. There is no doubt that the bond (the substance) of the body of Christ replaces the bonds of bread, but these float in a kind of suspension if they are not destroyed; and sometimes Leibniz gives the impression that they are that which is transformed—unified—and attached to the "monads of the most holy Body." The remarkable intuition of the *Vinculum Christi* is lost in the concern of making the letter of dogma pass in Leibnizian language.

But perhaps, as Fr. Claude Troisfontaines suggests, Mathieu attaches an exaggerated importance to the monads. They constantly flow and renew themselves, they metamorphose; their nature is to pass on. They are vessels of Theseus, or the Loire River. And, as between natural transubstantiation and the supernatural, the difference of the eucharistic miracle, seen from the side of the monads, resides in the degree of suddenness (*per saltum*). Leibniz did not leave the Cartesian realm and, like the French philosopher whom he hardly admired, he respected dogma and was concerned to make it plausible, even intelligible. But even more clearly than with Descartes, the attempt is inserted into a system, and this is why a theological aporia gave the impetus to a philosophical development. For anyone who delves into a theological question encounters philosophy.

Nevertheless, Leibniz wants to be faithful to tradition. A. Boehm did well to show (even though his evidence is not exhaustive) that the bond or the problem of union was rooted in scholasticism, where Leibniz was able retrieve it. It would have been more convincing if Boehm had expanded the investigation to include the Platonic heritage of the *desmos* and the *Band* of Germanic Theosophy. But Leibniz's use of the bond is largely original and autonomous. However, it remained a private affair, and Fr. Des Bosses did not have, let us remember, the future that his illustrious friend had predicted for him.

Chapter 5

The Holy Communion of German Philosophers

LESSING: BERENGAR'S ADVOCATE

Ridicule and sarcasm generally accompany the eucharistic agnosticism of the Enlightenment, especially in France, and one could easily gather a sad anthology of mockery, of which Voltaire's in *The Ignorant Philosopher* would be the most benign:

> VIII. Substance: this very expression "substance which is beneath," sufficiently acquaints us that this thing beneath will ever be unknown to us; whatever we may discover of its appearance, there will always remain this beneath to discover.
>
> XXV. Nonsense: That pretends to communicate to me transubstantiation by the touch, by showing me according to the laws of motion, how an accident may exist without a subject, and how one single body may be in two places at the same time. I shut my ears, and retire with still greater precipitation.[1]

This is nothing compared to the sacrilegious articles on "Eucharist" and "Transubstantiation" in the *Dictionnaire philosophique*. They are abject and repugnant, the latter especially, and are attributed to a certain Guillaume, a Protestant minister. But all the *Aufklärer* are not inept and impious. Germany in particular produced, besides the obtuse Christoph Friedrich Nicolai, the line of Lessing, Mendelssohn, and Kant, which does honor to the age of philosophical reason. Gotthold Ephraim Lessing, the indefatigable and versatile seeker, passionate about the truth, admired by Kierkegaard, is the paragon of a truly enlightened and intelligent *Aufklärung*, and this is why he allured the young successors of Kant, Schelling, Hegel, and Friedrich Schlegel. His work is varied and circumstantial, composed of the most diverse writings, multidisciplinary *avant la lettre*, captivating due to the

---

1 Voltaire, *The Ignorant Philosopher* (Girard, KS: Haldeman-Julius Company, 1922), 10 and 36–37.

brilliance of his style, the irony, the liveliness, and the consistently dazzling intelligence, with a charm whose freshness remains intact. In controversy, his polemical writing is incomparable, and his "critico-theological" texts, all from the end of his life, are the most lively and the most famous.

The only writing that matters to us here is "Berengar of Tours," published in 1770. This is one of those rehabilitations or "rescues" (*Rettungsschriften*) that Lessing willingly undertook, moved by his taste for paradox, his native generosity, his sympathy for heretics and for the vanquished. In this case he defended the famous eleventh-century monk from Tours, whose extorted oath, dated February 11, 1079, can be found in Denzinger.[2] The text is, of course, occasional. An investigator with universal curiosity, fond of old manuscripts, Lessing was appointed curator of the famous library of Wolfenbüttel in the autumn of 1769, a position previously held by Leibniz. Rummaging through the reserve of manuscripts, he had the chance to put his hands on and identify a more or less altered copy of Berengar's reply to Lanfranc (Archbishop of Canterbury) concerning the sacrament of the Last Supper. He had been stimulated in this research by his very recent conversations with the theologian of Brunswick, Conrad Arnold Schmid, who discovered a text by a disciple of Berengar, Adelmann. It was to Schmid that he addressed, in epistolary form, his discreet apology for Berengar: after Jérôme Cardan, after the "Ineptus Religiosus" and Cochlaeus, and after Leibniz and Adam Neuser, he now took up the defense of the learned theologian and archdeacon of Angers, persecuted by Peter Damien, Lanfranc, Cardinal Humbert, and Durand of Troarn, then, after his death, by religious historiography, especially the Benedictines. Even Luther was not sympathetic to the adversary of the real presence (and Lessing's attempt to bring them together is not convincing).

In reality, the source of the debate, the conception of the Eucharist, is hardly addressed by the author. Supported by his documents and his prodigious erudition, Lessing highlights above all the historical aspect. He justifies the apparent cowardice of Berengar, he pinpoints the bad faith of Lanfranc and of the civil and clerical authorities. The personality of the heretic, however, only appears in halftone. "He had prepared reasons, but was not prepared for death," Lessing notes about a first abjuration in Rome in 1059 (which was written by Cardinal Humbert),[3] following several con-

2 Denz. 700.

3 Denz. 690.

victions. He finds his excuses touching ("I am a coward, I am like Aaron, and like Peter!"). All in all, the Church behaved with leniency and indulgence toward such a relapsed and repeat offender! In reality, it seems that there had been fewer councils and synods against Berengar than the hostile Benedictine literature wanted, and Berengar knew the sympathy for his teaching and the protection of Cardinal Hildebrand (the future Gregory VII). Berengar never held that the consecrated bread and wine were "simple signs," since he believed and taught "a true and essential presence of the Body and the Blood." He would have denied the notion of transubstantiation, but he accepts the language of "conversion." Transubstantiation implies destruction and recreation, regeneration: it is impossible (at least, this was the explanation in vogue among Scotists, although St. Thomas dismisses the idea of annihilation). The texts are striking: it is a "quibble" to "interrogate" him, to subject him to a trial of intentions for having challenged the subject.

That Lessing's favor leans toward Berengar is obvious. He is horrified by the crude formulations of Cardinal Humbert ("the sacramental body chewed by the teeth of the faithful," "the corruptible body of Christ"). The second unfortunate expression is inadmissible, the first, awkward, according to Louis Billot, though tolerable if need be (though Cardinal Humbert, in his reproaches to the Greeks, is not free from inconsistencies and contradictions!). In the end, while defending himself against "extending his hand toward the ark of an unbalanced alliance," Lessing goes up and places himself in the midst of this and offers a solution typical of his insinuating, dialectical manner, which recalls or anticipates his ideas on Revelation, the construction of the Gospels, the formation of the canon, dogmas, the relationship of faith and reason, etc. If the doctrine of simple signs is the oldest, is it not too brutal of a leap to move to the idea of transubstantiation? Is there not a transition from "pregnant" signs, to signs "changed into things"? This metamorphosis was accompanied by countless arguments and quarrels around transubstantiation. How is it possible that the transition from simple signs to pregnant signs took place in calm, notwithstanding its audacity, in fact its even more scandalous character? But if there were no quarrels, it is because there could not have been any. This transition did not take place for the reason that the doctrine of simple transient signs never existed. It is the idea of pregnant signs that is the primitive and the originary one.

HAMANN AND KANT

The lack of sacramental sensibility among Protestants of various stripes appears in these two great antagonists and companions, Hamann and Kant. Neither the hyper-realistic pietism of the former, with his thick and native religion, nor the rationalism of the latter were touched by the Eucharist. The Lord's Supper is not the subject of any of Hamann's dazzlingly elliptical texts, in which the density of the prose results in a theological and spiritual impact. This is all the more detrimental since the intrepid doctrine of the Incarnation displayed by the Magus of the North, as well as his original theory of language, which he called his bone to gnaw on, could prepare for a eucharistic development, at least an implicit one. And yet food, chewing, digestion, excretion, play a big role in the life and in the sensual theology of the Magus. His sense of corporeality postulated a goal of assimilation. And above all, does not language, which he persistently linked to the body and the sexual mystery, have its divine-human knot, its idiomatic coincidence, in the performative word of Consecration? Yet Hamann does not say so explicitly.

Nevertheless, a theologian of the former East Germany, one of the best experts on Hamann, Martin Seils, believes that one can find the Lutheran eucharistic schema deeply imbricated in the hamannian "metaschematism." He notes that the expression used at the end of the *Metacritique on the Purism of Reason* (against Kant), "the sacrament of language,"[4] is undoubtedly not accidental. But Hamann did not complete the connection to sacramental language. However, concerning the Bible, which is language par excellence, Hamann writes these remarkable lines to Herder on December 28, 1780:

> The passage from the divine to the human always seems to me exposed to such an abuse. The two extremes must be purely and simply conjoined in order to explain the whole, *ousía sômatos* and *exousia toû axiômatos*. It is by this union that the book is sacred, just as a prince is born from a man. A *koinônia* without transubstantiation, neither body nor shadow, but spirit. However, I must first make some progress in order to be able to explain myself on this matter.[5]

---

4 Hamann, *Sämtliche Werke*, ed. Josef Nadler, vol. 3, 289.

5 See Martin Seils, *Theologische Aspekte zur gegenwärtigen Hamann-Deutung* (Göttingen: Vandenhoeck & Ruprecht, 1957), 114.

"Substance of the body," "Communion without transubstantiation": Martin Seils did not fail to spot the sacramental allusion. The *koinônia* without transubstantiation "corresponds exactly to the idea of consubstantiation in the evangelical doctrine of the sacraments." We can conclude: at the place where Hamann embarked in his thoughts concerning the "passage from the divine to the human," he perceived a consubstantial "in, with, and under" of human *ousía* and divine *exousía*. But, above all, this means a real presence, in spirit, of the "divine" substance in, with, and under the real human "matter."[6] It is therefore a eucharistic schematism that would be underlying the corporeal and linguistic union of God and man; but it is less accentuated than the coincidence of opposites and the communication of idioms. Hamann did not take the opportunity that was before him; he was not struck by the Pauline texts which seem particularly suited to him, for example the astonishing parallel of the table of the Lord and the table of demons (1 Cor 10:16–22).

His Amphitryon and commensal from Königsberg, Immanuel Kant, had other reasons to be reluctant about the Eucharist. It forms a part of the *parerga* of religion, and its importance is entirely peripheral. He noted the following in the *Anthropology*, and not without a malignant intention:

> The word *Hexe* [witch], which has now become a German word, comes from the first words of the formula of the mass used at the Consecration of the Host, which the faithful see with *bodily* eyes as a small disc of bread but which, after the formula has been pronounced, they are obliged to see with *spiritual* eyes as the body of a human being. For the words *hoc est* were initially added to the word *corpus,* and in speaking *hoc est corpus* was changed to *hocuspocus,* presumably from pious timidity at saying and profaning the correct phrase. This is what superstitious people are in the habit of doing with unnatural objects, in order not to profane them.[7]

Another, less innocent, explanation is possible, when we know that *hocuspocus* means sleight of hand or magic.[8]

A religion reduced to its moral core has nothing to do with the sacrament of the eucharistic presence. However, a remark added to the second

---

6 Cf. Seils, *Theologische Aspekte*. "Substance of the body," "authority of the commandment."

7 Immanuel Kant, *Anthropology from a Pragmatic Point of View* (Cambridge: Cambridge University Press, 2006), para. 14, p. 42, note f.

8 The word dates from the end of the seventeenth century. The etymology comes from Tillotson.

edition of *Religion within the Boundaries of Mere Reason* gives some value to the memorial of the Last Supper. If Jesus had had a political goal, he would not have been able to recommend the commemoration of such a defeat on the night before his death. On the other hand, the memory could retain the failure of an excellent and purely moral intention, in order to instigate a religious revolution: "And we may indeed even now regret that the design did not succeed, even though it was not in vain, for after the Master's death it gave way to a religious transformation that quietly spread everywhere, though in the midst of many sufferings."[9]

The meaning of communion is ecclesial and religious by priority. Its purpose, as its name suggests, is to conserve the community as a stable "ethical body," the members of which are united under the rule of "the principle of the mutual equality of the members' rights and their sharing in all the fruits of moral goodness."[10] Communion means equality, democracy. It can include the eucharistic meal, but not if coupled with the notion of sacramental grace:

> The oft-repeated solemn ritual of *renewal, continuation,* and *propagation of this church-community* under the laws of *equality* (*communion*), which after the example of the founder of such a church (and at the same time in memory of him) may well assume the form of a ritual communal partaking at the same table, has in it something great which expands people's narrow, selfish and intolerant cast of mind, especially in religious matters, to the idea of a cosmopolitan *moral community,* and it is a good means of enlivening a community to the moral disposition of brotherly love which it represents. But to boast that God has attached special graces to the celebration of this solemn ritual, and to incorporate among the articles of faith the proposition that the ritual, through a purely ecclesiastical action, is in addition a *means of grace*—this is a delusion [*Wahn*] of religion which cannot but work counter to the spirit of religion.[11]

One could not state more clearly that communion, the Lord's Supper, is not sacramental. Thus Kant remains below the level of Luther's sacramentality. In fact, it is a complete refusal.

---

9 Immanuel Kant, *Religion within the Boundaries of Mere Reason* (Cambridge: Cambridge University Press, 1998), 96, note.

10 Kant, *Religion within the Boundaries of Mere Reason*, 184–85.

11 Kant, *Religion within the Boundaries of Mere Reason*, 188–89.

FICHTE: A MYSTIC WITHOUT SACRIFICE

Fichte is not a philosopher of the Eucharist, or rather of the Last Supper. It did not hold his attention, even if in his youth he gave a dialectical and vigorous sermon on the reasons for Christ's death. His Johannine philosophy, however, is evident in the popular lessons of *The Way towards the Blessed Life*, where the sixth lecture offers a unilateral and personal exegesis of John 6:53–55, from the discourse on the Bread of Life. If, up to this point, the eucharistic philosophies and physics were conceived in order to harmonize with doctrine or to establish a conciliation between the intention of the system and the givens of the faith, Fichte, encouraged to be sure by his Protestantism, does not have a cure for orthodoxy. He operates a speculative reworking, in a grand style, of the formulations of Revelation. That is to say, the new wine of thought is poured into and shatters the old wineskin of the words of the Gospel. Fichte appropriates John's message, transcribing it into his own language. Reading this text, it is clear that he is not offering a symbolic interpretation, but rather claims to state the literal meaning of the preaching of Christ. The radical distinction he makes between metaphysics and history allows him to avoid all exegetical and hermeneutical problems.

This is what he provides in his mystical rereading of the Eucharistic Discourse ("unless you eat the flesh of the Son of Man and drink his blood, you do not have life within you"): "Jesus declares (the identity of the disciples' Life with the Divine Life) in the most clear and forcible way, with absolute clearness, [but also as] the most completely unintelligible and offensive" (an allusion to the scandal caused to the Jewish audience).[12] It is about becoming totally and completely Jesus and about being metamorphosed into his person, without reservation or restriction, attempting only to reproduce him in his personality, being *transubstantiated* into him. For he is the Eternal Word become flesh and blood, and it is as if it were he himself who was thinking, not us; to live absolutely and totally like him (a *homoousias*), as if he lived in our place. The command is to become him entirely, for he did not set himself up as an inaccessible ideal, and his disciples imitated him perfectly, according to the words of Paul: "It is no longer I who live, but Christ who lives in me." It is an absolute requirement and an essential condition, so that his listeners arise from their tombs, an expression dear to Fichte, who is much more a philosopher of the Transfiguration and

---

12 Johann Gottlieb Fichte, *The Way towards the Blessed life; or, The Doctrine of Religion*, trans. W. Smith (London: Strand, 1849), 111. English translation slightly altered.

the Resurrection than of the Passion and the Cross. True, faith is required, but the ultimate and decisive proof is to do the Will of the One who sent him, or, said otherwise in the realistic and imaginary words of Christ, to eat his flesh and drink his blood.

The notion of sacrifice is absent from this mystical salvation. The Lamb takes away the sins of the world, but by no means does he atone for them for the sake of a wrathful God (Fichte criticizes the notion of satisfaction). How would a poor little nonexistent creature offend the majesty of God? And if we are in God, how would God sin against Himself? He who is united to God is impeccable. The representation of the Lamb slain from the foundation of the world does not occur in Fichte's theology. "[A]nd the blood of Jesus Christ the Son of God—not, in the metaphysical sense, his blood shed for the remission of our sins, but his blood and mind entered into us,—his Life in us—'cleanseth us from all sin' and raises us far above the possibility of sinning."[13] Not poured-out blood, but the divine blood that beats in our own arteries, regenerates us, and associates us with absolute Life. We can observe that even if sacrifice is left to the side, at least the schematism of the eucharistic sacrament and communion implicitly inspires a mysticism of active union with God.

Christological implications control this arbitrary interpretation of the eucharistic institution. We will refrain from explaining them in detail because they go beyond the scope of our purposes. We will simply note that this idea of perfect imitation endangers Jesus Christ's birthright, and not adoptive, divinity, *Filius unigenitus*: metaphysically he incarnates the Eternal Son of God neither more nor less than we do, even if, historically, he is clothed with the extraordinary merit of having known absolute metaphysical truth, and of doing so alone and without help. But is this any more than what is found in Spinoza?

HEGEL: THE EUCHARISTIC MEMORIAL

The *Phenomenology of Spirit* masterfully shows, in the dialectic between Enlightenment and belief, the error of those who constantly accuse faith of idolatry (God as a block of stone, God as a piece of bread). For faith does not feel itself to be justly accused, and rightly so, since it knows that its God is not this stone or this bread, but is rather signified by them:

---

13 Fichte, 115.

Accordingly, it says of faith that its absolute essence . . . is something made of bread-dough obtained from the field, which, when transformed by men, is then returned there. Or when it says in whatever other ways that faith anthropomorphizes the essence and makes it objective and presentable. . . . What faith reveres is, to faith, without question neither stone nor wood, nor bread-dough, nor any other sort of temporal, sensuous thing. . . . [F]aith is in part just as well acquainted with that "*also*" [*Jenes auch*], but, to itself, that "also" lies outside of its worship. However, to faith, things such as a stone, etc., are not the *in itself*, but rather, to faith, what is in itself is solely the essence of pure thinking.[14]

At this phase of the dialectic, at least, faith gets the better of understanding. Does this mean that Hegel agrees with an "orthodox" conception of the Eucharist? That would be asking too much. He objects to accusing believers of a superstitious representation, a coarse and idolatrous realism, but, on the other hand, he tends toward a religion of the sign, and even more toward an entirely spiritual signification that risks violating the *res sacramenti*.

In fact, *On Christianity: Early Theological Writings*, in which Hegel slowly developed his convictions, insists on the religious character of the meal, of the memorial, and therefore of the sacrament, and offers reservations only about sacrifice. The Last Supper is above all a farewell meal, in a melancholy atmosphere. This is how it appears, quite subdued, encrypted, embedded with pagan symbols, amalgamated with the mysteries of Bacchus, in Hölderlin's famous poem with the significant title "Bread and Wine." An allusive but still recognizable evangelical schematism runs through the admirable elegy, although the register of the melody has been transposed:

—Holy remembrance, too, prompting the watch in the night.

—Or he [the God] would come himself and take on human appearance, comforter at the end, closing the heavenly feast.

—When at last had appeared a quiet Genius, heavenly comforter, who proclaimed the end of days and was gone, then, as a sign they had been here, once, and again would come, the heavenly choir left a few of those gifts behind, which, as in older days, humanly we might rejoice in.

—Meanwhile, the sick earth lies, held by the god slow of thunder, who brings with him delight, mingling it into the dark.[15]

14 Georg Wilhelm Friedrich Hegel, *The Phenomenology of Spirit*, trans. Terry Pinkard (Cambridge: Cambridge University Press, 2018), 321–22, para. 553.

15 Holderlin, "Bread and Wine," trans. Susan Ranson: sites.google.com/site/germanliterature/ 19th-century/hoelderlin/brot-und-wein-bread-and-wine (online).

The eucharistic symbolism is consciously related to the god of light and thunder, but this syncretism, which Heidegger highlighted, is not, any more than for Gérard de Nerval, meant to the detriment of the Christian God.

This philhellenic climate also rubs off on the mentality of the young Hegel. However, the *Theological Writings* look more for contrasts rather than for an amalgam. *The Life of Jesus*, an evangelical collection dominated by Kantian moralism, evokes the Last Supper as a Paschal meal (with the Lamb), but by evading the institution. The meal is perpetuated only for the purposes of remembrance. This same note dominates in the fragments entitled "The Positivity of the Christian Religion": the Last Supper is a memorial (*Andenken*), memory, symbol. Its aesthetic presentation is much better than the statements and affirmations on the Bread of Life discourse (Jn 6:47–63), which "even the theologians have pronounced to be rather harsh."[16] When later the Mass (the Last Supper) became obligatory, a religious duty, it determined the end of fraternization. But, on the other hand, the fraternal meal became an *erhabener Genuss*, a sublime delight; mysticism had taken hold of it.

Hegel's early writings are not always easy to date. We should adhere to the chronology of Herman Nohl, as found in the first volume of the critical edition. There the development corresponds, among other things, to a deepening of insights into the Eucharist. Indeed, the later text, "The Spirit of Christianity and Its Fate," presents a more elaborate development. The Last Supper is a "love-feast."[17] In a magnificent passage Hegel evokes the legendary "cup of coffee with a stranger" among Arabs, the cup of friendship, or perhaps hospitality. If they were enemies, we would not see them sitting together around the kettle. At the Last Supper, the experience of friendship is further emphasized, since the disciples and Jesus eat the *same* bread, drink from the *same* cup. We are close to a religious action, and yet Hegel endeavors to show that (1) it is a mystical, symbolic action, and (2) it is not a divine action.

1. By means of Christ's gestures and words, the union, the unification of the disciples, is made visible, tangible, and objective. But the action still goes beyond the visible; it is mystical and symbolic. Indeed, there is more than a comparison and an analogy between the shared meal and the union

16 Georg Wilhelm Friedrich Hegel, *On Christianity: Early Theological Writings*, trans. T. M. Knox (New York: Harper, 1961), 90.

17 Hegel, *On Christianity*, 248.

of the disciples with Christ and among themselves (on the other hand, in bold texts like Jn 6:56, "whoever eats my flesh and drinks my blood has eternal life," or Jn 10:7, "I am the gate for the sheep," there is only a comparison). There is more here than bread and wine, that is, they are mystical objects, which Hegel translates with this abbreviation: wine is blood, and blood is spirit. This spirit is a spirit of love. The same feeling lives in the disciples, they are penetrated with the one spirit of love. The spirit of Jesus passed through them, has become something real, in the strongest sense, because it is incorporated into them. The objective (inert, external) becomes, or becomes again, subjective. Hegel uses this comparison (which evokes the Reformed thesis of the fruit of the sacrament in the act of communion): as thought becomes a thing in writing and becomes again subjective (from death, to something living) in the act of reading. . . . The comparison would be better if the text erased itself progressively as one read it. But while it remains fixed on the paper, it is a substantiation without transubstantiation. However, bread and wine disappear as objects; they retain only the appearance. Another analogy, suggested by his philhellenic enthusiasm: when lovers gather at the feet of the statue of the goddess of love, the stone fades in a way, and only the passion that unites them, aroused by Venus, remains. The body disappears, the vivid feeling persists.

2. It is a symbolic action, and not religious or divine, because the bread and wine that are absorbed cannot be anything divine. The divine is not food and drink. The thing and the reality do not mix, they are two different realities: faith and the thing (the object), piety and seeing it and tasting it. The unification of the two does not happen, intelligence and feeling contradict each other, and the imagination is powerless to unite them into a vision of beauty. As above, Hegel uses a plastic analogy. Just as the pulverized, crumbled statue of Apollo awakens only a nostalgic remembrance of its beauty, so after the Last Supper a painful feeling prevails; it leaves in the souls of the apostles an astonished devotion and a melancholy serenity (which anticipates Schleiermacher's *Heilige Wehmut*). The Eucharist is not a true religious action that satisfies and fulfills desire. It is accompanied by disappointment: something divine was promised, which then evaporated in the mouth.

There is another very striking passage that indirectly concerns the Eucharist, since it treats the sacrifice of the Cross. This engenders the desire and the nostalgia proper to death, followed by the apotheosis of the Resurrection. But in Christianity, this apotheosis is burdened with a stigma of finitude, in contrast to the glorious pyre of Hercules on which the hero is consumed and transfigured. Christianity, in fact, has preserved the image and the representation of the Crucified. It is as Crucified that Jesus is risen and glorified, and it is for the sake of this image that Christians throughout the centuries have been tortured and martyred. Hegel was still quite far away from the vigorous Lutheran synthesis of contradictions that would one day make an "immense staurology" of his system. They undergo the charm of Greek beauty, of reconciliation through the imagination, independent of understanding. But has this molting of the system changed his view of the Eucharist? To a certain extent, the gap has narrowed between the thing and the spirit, and Hegel would no longer say that the promised divinity has melted in the mouth and dissolved. But he firmly maintains a dichotomy: a refusal of reification, of idolatry, and an attachment to faith, to the spirit (the proof of strength and spirit).

If we put aside the incidental allusion from the dialectic of the Enlightenment, Hegel's interventions on the Eucharist are now few in number and framed in a historical or confessional context: in *The History of Philosophy* (which is very indirect), in *The Philosophy of History* (with a clear polemical intention), in the *Encyclopedia,* and finally in *The Philosophy of Religion.* In *The History of Philosophy* Paschasius Radbertus is denounced for his limited attachment to "sensuous determinations," his "utter irrationality," like Hans Sachs who "made a Nürnberg version of sacred history."[18] Hegel severely criticizes scholasticism: it is "thought that God has deserted (*gottverlassenes Denken*),"[19] its representatives "philosophized without conception, that is, without a concrete."[20] He also adopted prejudices about the Middle Ages (because he had long since abandoned the point of view of romanticism), such as the globalization of the Church and theocracy. The crusades symbolize this time of illusion, which, although generous, was barbaric. In the Holy Land, the crusaders found only their own downfall, their own tombs, and disappointment, unlike Bonaparte in Egypt, who was anxious to bring the spirit of modern times.

The Philosophy of History strives for more equity. The (Catholic) Mass reflects the consciousness of the unity of the community, it commemorates

---

18 Georg Wilhelm Friedrich Hegel, *The History of Philosophy,* vol. 3 (London: Routledge, 1896), 88–90.

19 Hegel, *The History of Philosophy,* vol. 3, page 97.

20 Hegel, *The History of Philosophy,* vol. 3, page 100.

a real and eternal event, the sacrifice of the individual divine Christ, whom the host represents as being present. Here is Luther's legitimate critique: it is only in and by *faith* in Christ that the host is his body. But Catholicism makes the sacred into a *thing*, and moreover a thing seized by the priests: hence the separation of the clergy from the laity, like a caste, the separation of the landowning and authoritarian Church from the laity cut off from it, who need only to obey.

There is the same criticism, but more detailed, in the *Encyclopedia* (§552) and in *The Philosophy of Religion*. Catholicism considers God, in the sacrament of the Last Supper, as a thing, an exteriority, of which the Church is the possessor and owner; the subject is passive, subjected to the "servitude of knowledge and action." On the contrary, Lutheranism places the eucharistic transubstantiation in faith alone, "*im Geist und Glauben.*" Exteriority is abolished, and apart from faith and eating (*Genuss*), the host is an ordinary thing. As for the Reformers, they keep only the lively, but despiritualized, memory of the past. It is therefore an infirm spirituality and a purely moral relationship, a decadence in "the prose of the *Aufklärung* and mere understanding." Hegel thus sketches, in this important section of the *Encyclopedia* (taken up by *The Philosophy of Religion*), starting from the conception of the Eucharist, the characteristic or the state of being of the three Churches. It is ultimately up to philosophy to bring back to the fullness of the present the religious representation which disperses the Now of communion into the three directions of the beyond, the past, and the future.

FEUERBACH: THE "CONTRADICTION IN THE SACRAMENT"

The recurring leitmotif of *The Essence of Christianity* is well-known: man is the god of man, anthropology is the key to theology. Faith and Revelation (which in this case is Christianity) therefore have a true face, anthropology, and an illusory and false one, theology. Antithesis or criticism would not be possible if this reductive thesis had not been affirmed from the beginning. It would have been more convincing to provide a preface to the criticism of theological reason, but this criticism only rests on the purely human essence of religion. This is why the first part is brazenly dogmatic. Marx's interpretation adds almost nothing to the atheistic humanism of Feuerbach. It is true that the (left) Hegelians were able to hold that the critical clearing work had been carried out by their master, who had returned speculation from heaven to earth (without, however, re-establishing it), and even before that by the *Aufklärung*, whose bloodless God, the vague Supreme Being, would collapse with only a flick.

Under these conditions, Feuerbach did not have to work too hard to demonstrate the inanity of the illusion of dogmatic Christianity. It suffices to put it in its own terms and to put it in parallel with empirical reality or "sense certainty," the infallible ground of truth, in order to shatter the illusion. This is the tactic followed by the second part of *The Essence of Christianity*. One chapter deals with baptism and the Lord's Supper (the only Protestant sacraments) and endeavors to show their "contradiction." We will only deal with the Eucharist here (see part II, chap. 25).

The Christian contradiction bursts into the open in the Eucharist. The bread that has become the body of Christ is assimilated bodily; it follows the path of the body. It is only my faith, my state of mind (*Gesinnung*), that attributes sanctifying, supernatural effects to it. One acts on oneself. He who is unworthy of communion is deprived of all grace. What good is an external object, then, if it is entirely about feeling? The difference, the effect, lies in the meaning that I give to it. But the meaning is imaginary, and the "precious distinction between substance and accidents" is a *trompe-l'œil*.[21] Bread and wine are divine substances only in the imagination. Faith is only imagination, the mystery of the Lord's Supper is the very mystery of faith, "hence the partaking of it is the highest, the most rapturous, blissful act of the believing soul."[22] The Lord's Supper is the pinnacle of faith and its imaginary operation, since it literally destroys the obvious, unmistakable object. Fanatics have even seen blood in place of the wine. The distinction between real and unreal, reason and unreason, has been lost.

At bottom, Protestantism and Catholicism, the former more clever and the latter naive, are in the same boat, except that the former hides God immediately and avoids painful problems like that of a mouse eating the host. But the problem of the digestion of the Sacred Body remains for both, and with it the threat of stercoranism.[23] The situation of the Catholic is nevertheless more contradictory. The body enclosed in the priest's pyx is not a body, but a signifier and nothing but a signifier (bread) of the flesh. The signifier is real, what is signified is imaginary. The purely subjective religious

---

21 Ludwig Feuerbach, *The Essence of Christianity*, 2nd ed. (London, 1890), 242.

22 Feuerbach, 242.

23 Which was crudely discussed in the dispute at Ansbach in 1783. Note the *Apology of Melanchthon*.

affect creates the aberrant signification. This is what Zwingli stated frankly, bluntly, and irrefutably. The Eucharist is a matter of religious sentiment; if it acts upon someone, it is because it comes from himself. It is only a "pious representation." Consequently, there is no need for bread, wine, or ceremony. A hymn that sings about the blood of Christ is just as good, the bloody Savior still appears there, the Sacred Blood streams before the eyes of the imagination without the interposition of "contradictory, material elements."[24] But faith reverses the priorities and privileges a "religious materialism."[25] As a consequence of this, superstition and immorality follow. Immorality because intelligence is abused and deceived and, as a result, the heart is corrupted. "[S]ophistry corrupts the whole man. And the doctrine of the Lord's Supper is sophistry."[26]

Let us move on to the contradiction that is to be valued, if only fleetingly, in the emotional virtue of a beautiful hymn about the Passion. Because, essentially, it is all religious feeling that is condemnable, all piety which is depraved and corrupting. . . . What emanates from the heart of man is not necessarily good and sacred, or even to be recommended, for there is a perversion that is like a morbidity of the imagination, which Feuerbach does not discuss at length. But we must wait until the conclusion to find what is irreproachable, what is true in the sensible, and that the indecent religious materialism can be replaced by a healthy and simple materialism. After his praise of water, Feuerbach sang a hymn (though quite unlike Hölderlin) to bread and wine, elements that need no consecration in order to be religious (with support from a quote by Luther, skewed considerably: "Before eating, no dancing, and / On a full stomach stands a merry head"):

> Think, therefore, with every morsel of bread which relieves thee from the pain of hunger, with every draught of wine which cheers thy heart, of the God who confers these beneficent gifts upon thee,—think of man! But in thy gratitude towards man forget not gratitude towards holy Nature! Forget not that wine is the blood of plants, and flour the flesh of plants, which are sacrificed for thy well-being! Forget not that the plant typifies to thee the essence of Nature, which lovingly surrenders itself [selbstlos] for thy enjoyment![27]

24 Feuerbach, *The Essence of Christianity*, 245.

25 Feuerbach, 246.

26 Feuerbach, 246.

27 Feuerbach, 277.

The most banal symbolism replaces eucharistic mysticism. However, it is here that certain contemporary theologians will seek their inspiration and nourish their atrophied thinking! The book that called for such an impact ends fairly flatly with a worldly parodic invocation: "Therefore let bread be sacred for us, let wine be sacred, and also let water be sacred! Amen."[28] The baptismal waters conveniently complete this triple *Sanctus*. . . .

SCHLEIERMACHER THE THEOLOGIAN

The sacrament of the Lord's Supper sheds light on Schleiermacher's inspirational death on February 12, 1834. As his wife (Henriette von Mühlenfels-Willich) recounted, he had her recite some hymns from his childhood friend Albertini and, feeling death approaching, summoned his family for the celebration of the Lord's Supper. He gave his wife, her friend Frau Fischer, and his son-in-law Lommatzsch bread and wine with the words of Institution from 1 Corinthians 11, adding: "I hold onto these words of Scripture. They are the foundation of my faith." After the blessing, he looked at each one again resolutely, and he made this profession: "Let us remain one in this love and this community." With these words, death overtook him. His children were then brought in and the eucharistic celebration ended by distributing the previously consecrated elements to the children kneeling near the funeral bed.

This devotion as well as the improvised liturgy which characterize this moving action correspond to a declaration in *The Christian Faith*:

> And while the Lord's Supper is not the only means of maintaining living fellowship with Christ—and provisionally we are not regarding it here as an isolable action which even in isolation has a specific effect—yet we take it as being the highest of its kind, and subsume under it every other enjoyment of Christ as either an approximation to it or a prolongation of it. Hence we here keep more to this underlying idea than to outward forms in which the idea is realized.[29]

The sacrament of the altar is viewed as a strengthening of the spiritual life with a view to community. Baptism leads into the sacrament of the ecclesial community, and it acts on society through the believing community. But the community of believers among themselves, and of everyone with

---

28 Feuerbach, 278.

29 Friedrich Schleiermacher, *The Christian Faith* (Edinburgh: T & T Clark, 1928), §127.2, 589. Citations of *The Christian Faith* are first of the paragraph number then of the page number.

Christ, is united above all in public worship, the Lord's Supper. The ceremony refers to the institution, to the gift of flesh and blood, and Schleiermacher offers an answer to two issues: communion with the Body and Blood in its relation to pure spiritual delight, and the situation and the particularity of the Lord's Supper within Christian worship. Now, to first consider the second issue, the Lord's Supper is the summit of liturgical life, because the ecclesial community and the intimate community (with Christ) are inextricably linked therein. It is "the whole redemptive love of Christ" which is the agent of this communion, and not a personal activity.[30] He protects the sacrament from vicissitudes and circumstances. As for the first issue, it implies above all that the spiritual life of union with Christ expressed by the Bread of Life discourse and the allegory of the vine, *are not references to the Lord's Supper*. Subsequently, the action that is blessed and sanctified by the word of Christ will symbolize very well this double union, and the union is an analogue to the memorial ceremonies. But Christ could have instituted another external form for the same object. Moreover, it is the diversity of eucharistic rites that divides believers. The minimum to maintain is the use of real bread and wine, a uniform distribution, and that the communion follows a devotional address and common prayer. It is not necessary for the Lord's Supper to take place in the evening or for communion to be at the conclusion of a more important ceremony. Attaching the Lord's Supper to the Jewish Passover has the disadvantage of weakening the idea of an institution by Christ, especially since the New Testament documents are not unanimous about Christ's commandment, and the apostles did not follow the foot-washing prescription. But the apostles (perhaps following an esoteric teaching of Christ) had their reasons for prescribing the liturgy of the memorial of the Last Supper.[31]

Schleiermacher's well-known suppleness gives free rein to his evaluation of eucharistic theories. At the outset, we have to admit an exegetical fluctuation and uncertainty. It is less transubstantiation opposed to consubstantiation which distinguishes Catholics, and more the permanence of the real presence: it is a hermeneutically untenable theory that inclines toward magic. On the contrary, the Sacramentarians and the Socinians depreciate the Lord's Supper and reduce the bread and wine to mere signs. But, within Protestantism, a certain dialectic prevails between confessions. Given the

---

30 Schleiermacher, §139.2, 640.

31 Schleiermacher, §139.3, 642–43.

exegetical difficulties, it is essential to maintain the relationship between act and effect. Explanations come afterward, and they should be continued, for clarity has not been achieved. At present, Lutherans believe in the real presence within the bread and wine, for the purpose of the communion, based on the decision of Christ. Zwinglians (along with Oecolampadius) admit the spiritual connection but exclude real presence; Calvinists locate real presence within the act of eating and drinking. The Zwinglian theory is the clearest, the one that most closely resembles baptism, but it does not take enough account of Christ's own words, to which the other theories adhere. Lutheranism, however, moves dangerously close to Catholicism, and it is difficult to make its idea of consubstantiation intelligible. Calvinism has the advantage of avoiding Zwinglian "bareness" and Lutheran "mysterious sensuality," but it clarifies neither the participation in the body and blood, nor the proper distinction or relationship between the body and blood, nor, in general, the relationship among the sacraments (which makes difficulties for Zwinglians). The appeal of Calvinism does not therefore seem to be able to extend to all opposing factions. Ecumenism (intercommunion) is only to be hoped for by progress in hermeneutics.[32]

This agreement, however, takes place in the effects, the consolidation of the living community with Christ and in Christ. This fruit is a true rebirth and a forgiveness of sins, which makes preliminary absolution superfluous, if it was understood as a sacrament (and it still is, even for Melanchthon), and not as a simple anticipation, a "shadow" of the eucharistic reconciliation. Then there follow some conditions for a worthy and legitimate reception of the sacrament. For instance, no matter how small a community may be, an entirely private celebration is prohibited. Schleiermacher insists that this sacrament is not a sacrifice, and that therefore it is not a magical and superstitious transaction like the sacrifice of the Mass, which claims to repeat the unrepeatable sacrifice of the cross (and forgets the sacrifice of an entire life of obedience).[33] There are also quite specious arguments, like those which touch on unworthy reception, for unworthiness is not necessarily due to sin, but rather to apathy and distraction, therefore to a lack of faith that inevitably leads to inertia and falsehood (whence the anathemas of the ancient Church). But to involve an eternal damnation is exaggerated![34]

---

32 Schleiermacher, § 140, 648–51.

33 Schleiermacher, § 141, 651–55.

34 Schleiermacher, §142, 655–57.

Ultimately, the difference between Lutheranism and Calvinism is not such that it should threaten ecclesial communion. In Lutheranism, the sacrament is consumed by both the worthy and the unworthy, while one is filled and the other judged. In Calvinism, the unworthy do not enjoy the sacrament. The less there is of unworthy reception of communion, therefore, the more the differences will be erased. Progress in perfection is associated with doctrinal agreement, and unworthiness testifies to the imperfection in the Church. For a Church making progress, instances that involve theoretical dissent will disappear. It is clear that Schleiermacher wanted to minimize the differences.

A NOTE ON JOSEPH DE MAISTRE

This note is intended to provide a counterbalance to the absence of sacrifice in Protestant eucharistic theology. The potent work of Joseph de Maistre, the anti-Voltaire, traditionalism's great thinker, condemns what remains of the impious Enlightenment and its myth of progress. In the wake of the ninth dialogue in *The Saint Petersburg Dialogues*, he writes a long and very erudite text, the "Elucidations on Sacrifices."[35] It notes, with a large number of examples and citations, the universality and permanence of sacrifices, that is to say, the regeneration or atonement by blood, including the horrible practice of human sacrifice (as in Iphigenia), which also preoccupied Schelling in his *Philosophy of Mythology*. Such a barbarism must have "some secret and very powerful cause":[36] the irresistible idea of rebirth, or redemption, by blood. Indeed, "paganism . . . sparkles with truths, but all distorted and out of place," and is even in a state of "putrefaction."[37] Now, *"wherever the true God is not known and served by virtue of an express revelation, man will always slaughter men, and often eat them."*[38] Voltaire can sneer all he likes. A constant testimony of humanity proclaims the "expiatory power in the shedding of blood,"[39] which is the essence of sacrifice (referring to Cudworth's "De vera notione coenae Domini," at the end of the *Systema intellectuale universum*) and the raison d'être of the scourge of

---

35 Joseph de Maistre, *St Petersburg Dialogues: Or Conversations on the Temporal Government of Providence*, ed. Richard Lebrun (Montreal: McGill-Queen's University Press, 1993).

36 De Maistre, 359.

37 De Maistre, 366–67.

38 De Maistre, 371.

39 De Maistre, 358.

war. Redemption by blood, an idea as fundamental and as universal as that of sacrifice, could only be taken up and rectified by the Christian tradition: "sine sanguine non fit remissio" (Heb 9:22). Christianity has come to justify the prophetic cry of humanity in antiquity (see the Ninth Dialogue), adding a communion in blood to absolution by blood, which was also corrupted by paganism. Christian communion gives a privileged nourishment and secures a transforming union: like a word, the corporeal essence of the one who is called *Word*, "radiating from the centre of the All-Powerful, who is everywhere, and who enters wholly entire into each mouth, and who multiplies himself to infinity without dividing himself. More rapid than lightning, more active than thunder, this *theandric* blood penetrates the *guilty entrails* to devour the defilements within them."[40] A wonder that is simultaneously inconceivable and plausible, "which satisfies reason by crushing it."[41] Let us add a very beautiful passage from the Tenth Dialogue[42] on the holy altar: as every meal was a communion, religion wanted communion to be a meal. . . . De Maistre recalls the patristic comparison of the ear of wheat and the (crushed) bunch of grapes, "materials of the mystery;" the mystical bread and wine, presented at the holy altar, "break the SELF and absorb us into their inconceivable unity."[43]

40 De Maistre, 385.

41 De Maistre, 385. The footnote cites a eucharistic hymn.

42 In the camp of those opposed to de Maistre, we could point out the socialist banquets of 1848, with their more or less parodic reference to the Eucharistic Supper. See Frank Paul Bowman, *Le Christ romantique* (Geneva: Droz, 1973), 104–5 (and 61–62 for the revolutionary banquet of 1789, where the memory of the agape was only just perceptible). Bowman announced that a third volume would study "socialist eucharistic thought, which endowed the Lord's Supper or the Mass with a revolutionary content" (104). Mystical Socialism created an ersatz of worship and religion.

43 De Maistre, *St Petersburg Dialogues*, 295.

Chapter 6

The Celestial Physics of Franz von Baader

We are not simply inserting a mere *curiosum* between Hegel and Rosmini. Franz von Baader's dense little opuscule "On the Eucharist," written in French and translated into German by Therese Edel (née Hoffmann), is rich in precious insights. Above all, it advances down a spiritual path that for too long had been lacking in writings on the Eucharist.[1] We cannot let its unusual form and its pugnacious tone baffle us! Baader (1765–1841) is a theosophist, a prophet, and a visionary, in fact a second-hand one, and one inclined to exaggerate. But a genius bursts forth in his intuitions and shakes up the mystery of language. Here we can give an analysis of his theme, which takes root in faith, on the borders of gnosis. "If the author of this little Treatise tries to give some new insights into the mystery of the Eucharist, it is not from a desire to deepen or profane this *mystery of love*, but to give one *more* reason for believing in its existence."[2]

1. Food is necessary for life; it sustains and secures "within the Region (Element) from which it comes out," that is to say, from the Earth, from which we take leave by abstinence (the Cross). Primitive man, on the contrary, subsisted on "food from paradise." But, succumbing to temptation, he fell "from an upper region into a lower region," a fall that Baader says causes a "dislocation." And the upper world has become only "an image or something perceived by him." The man took "narcotics," he sank into sleep; he became a sleepwalker. The mixed world materialized him.[3]

2. The Lord's Supper has the opposite effect: it forms a single Body, communion, an agape feast, a "meal of love." Theologians have failed to develop this aspect of food, of the "hidden mystery in the nutritional process in general." Conversely, the principle of sustenance awaits a reaction from the creature in return. The "superior nourishing principle," becoming matter and

---

1 Franz Xaver von Baader, *Sämtliche Werke*, vol. 7 (Aalen: Scientia Verlag, 1963), 1–28.

2 Von Baader, *Sämtliche Werke*, vol. 7, 3.

3 Von Baader, *Sämtliche Werke*, vol. 7, 4–5.

food, *sustains* like a maternal love: love *descends,* "gives itself"; it is a fire that descends into light.[4] And inversely, or "vice versa," descending, condescending, "smoldering" love, which awakens life, waits for its *re-ascension,* the elevation, the rise from "the germ state" to that of "flowering." The word that becomes flesh, at its own risk and peril, wants to *need* to resurrect, to become spirit again by the creature (man).

3. Man can squander love. "If we are literally what we eat, we only eat what we are." Judas eats his condemnation, "the vicious receive communion every day, similar to the toad which sucks poison, even from honey," lilies and hemlock both gather from the earth, but one takes in perfume and the other poison. This beautiful image pulls Baader's thought to an analogy of a plant: the sun *communes* the plant, which incorporates and heightens the power of the sun, and in the same way each Christian allows "Christ to put on nature in him," incorporating and sensitizing his powers.

4. Man is the true microcosm; his regeneration, therefore, does not occur without repairing the two worlds, and "the repairer of man must also be the repairer of the two worlds." Now the *mixed* world below is better at displaying substances as ordered to this work of regeneration. The external nourishment must make one think of the interior, the impalpable, of the hidden and very effective presence of Christ, "the invisible center." The absorption of bread and wine must make one think of his earthly death.

5. Then he turns to the invisible and sensible relationship of conviviality, which joins the table companions, and which is experienced by all peoples. The host is sacred. From another point of view, given that man after the fall is forced to reproduce like animals, in his shame and bitterness he wants at least "the meal and the marriage to be sacred." This is, Baader adds, the key to the mystery of the Eucharist, the mystery of love.

There follows a long note which tortuously explains this relationship between the Eucharist and eros. Christ is like the *absent* magnetizer who would have left us substances (perhaps a piece of glass) capable of maintaining a *real* and integral relationship with him. He is a universal *Electrum.*[5] The union of husband and wife occurs "in the Lord's Supper," the "nutrition and the secret growth of the new man." In one and the same function is both the good of the individual and that of the species. To broaden the perspective: Christ and his Church must form "a Whole." He is the Bridegroom

4 Von Baader, 8, note.

5 Von Baader, *Sämtliche Werke,* vol. 9 (Aalen: Scientia Verlag, 1963), 403.

before whom all men "should have stood like a bride": the separation of the sexes or "the appearance of another spouse" must be attributed to the primitive adultery of the man who has detached himself from the uncreated image of the Father (Christ). Therefore, this division of the sexes "will be extinguished." The manifestation of this Image in a creature elevates it above the Region of visible fathers and mothers. Hence the dignity of women: she who caused us to be lost is the only one who can save us: Eva → Ave.[6]

Let us leave behind this fragment of erotic theology to emphasize the modernity and the density of some of Baader's eucharistic insights. He restores a significant meaning to transubstantiation. He articulates the Eucharist along with other dogmas (Incarnation, Redemption, the Fall, the Mystical Body), he links it to conviviality, and he rediscovers its meaning as a meal of love, as well as a symbol of the union of Christ and men, the true communion. Finally, he insists on nourishment. The Eucharist is the food of the soul.

Ten years later (1826), Baader gathered ideas that bolstered his views from the learned work of Ignaz von Döllinger.[7] Baader first utters his dissatisfaction with the new historians of dogma, neologists, and Protestants (Johann August Nösselt, August Hermann Niemeyer), who diminished the Church Fathers. This applies to Philip Marheineke as well, and he dedicated a booklet to him! Döllinger includes ten patristic authors in support of the bodily presence of Christ in the Eucharist. Baader chooses three: Ignatius of Antioch, Justin Martyr, and Irenaeus of Lyon. Justin compares the Eucharist to the Incarnation (*Fleischwerdung des Brodes*), and highlights the analogy of nutritional assimilation. Irenaeus, arguing against the Gnostics, underlines the realistic, "physiological" interpretation of the Eucharist: the true and substantial transmutation, the grain of wheat that dies, like the body blessed by the Eucharist that, decayed in the earth, is resurrected. He concludes with a quotation from the Maronite liturgy, which was probably "requested" by Baader (he read *qui* instead of *quae*).[8]

The paragraph of Hegel's *Encyclopedia* dedicated to the Eucharist,[9] so averse to the Catholic conception, had not escaped Baader's notice, who

---

6 *Sämtliche Werke*, vol. 7, 13–14, note.

7 Ignaz von Döllinger, *Die Eucharistie in den drei ersten Jahrhunderten* (Mainz, 1826).

8 Von Baader, *Sämtliche Werke*, vol. 7, "Recension der Schrift: Die Eucharistie in den drei ersten Jahrhunderten," 59–70.

9 See chapter five.

issued him a firm rebuke in the *Bayerische Annalen*.[10] Hegel made himself
an easy target with his view of the Catholic Eucharist as a "pure, inert putrefaction." Far from mortifying faith and spirit, Catholicism declares that the
exterior is a "nonessential appearance" and establishes the *faith* of the communicant as the *sine qua non* condition for real nourishment, which does
not mean that consecration is an unnecessary ceremony, as it is for Hegel.[11]
Furthermore, the Hegelian "Geist" is affected by a phobia of the body and
of nature, and if Hegel had consulted St. Thomas he would have seen that
communion is communication of nature (tincture, *tinctur*), and nature is
in the smallest part as well as in the largest. There is, in Hegel, a fear and a
contempt of nature, "irreconciled Spirit." Catholicism thinks differently:
baptism initiates a new and superior (vegetal, so to speak) incorporation,
which the Eucharist "pursues, maintains, restores, and completes."[12] And,
to repeat, it does not appeal to *faith* less than does Protestantism: only the
believing contact attracts or welcomes the healing power of Christ.[13] This is
not to the detriment of what is objectivity established by consecration,
which is confirmed by the judgment of worthy or unworthy reception.[14] A
nice quote from Paracelsus closes the debate, where we see that the phrase
"man eats what he is (*ist* / *isst*, see Feuerbach), and he himself is what he
eats" was suggested rather than copied.[15]

Baader alludes in this text to the previously published note in the same
review concerning a "Matter for Reflection (*Etwas zum Nachdenken*) on the
occasion of Corpus Christi in Munich."[16] The occasion was the reluctance
of a spectator about this display of public worship. This was therefore an
opportunity for Baader to vituperate further against "abstract representation, empty of spirit and meaning, a formless *Unding* without sensation and
therefore ineffective and unreal."[17] Against the abstract spiritualists and new
Gnostic Cerinthians, he elevates the testimony of John (what we have seen,

---

10 "Über eine Aeusserung Hegels über die Eucharistie," *Bayerische Annalen*, 1833, in *Sämtliche Werke*, vol. 7, 245–58.

11 *Sämtliche Werke*, vol. 7, 254–55.

12 *Sämtliche Werke*, vol. 7, 250.

13 *Sämtliche Werke*, vol. 7, 252–53.

14 *Sämtliche Werke*, vol. 7, 254.

15 *Sämtliche Werke*, vol. 7, 258, citing *Philosophiae sagacis seu Astronomiae magnae*, book one, chapter two.

16 In *Sämtliche Werke*, vol. 7, 241–46.

17 *Sämtliche Werke*, vol. 7, 244.

heard, touched) and that of doubting Thomas. Using a beautiful image, he asks them "why the One who was Incarnate and Resurrected, and who remained Man, would not manifest his reality and his presence every-where"—rather than reaching us and passing into view only, so to speak, in scattered places through an obscure curtain, "like a Christmas tree lit with innumerable lights, which is already present to us, although still hidden behind the curtain."

Toward the end of the "Lectures on a Future Theory of Sacrifice or Wor-ship" of 1836,[18] at the beginning of the fifteenth lecture, Baader provides a theory of the Eucharist that develops ideas that we have already seen: the analogy of magnetic attraction, the food chain (food and what is fed) like the "descent and ascent of Jacob's ladder." Hegel's fault is to see in the nutritional process only the act of removing food and not the subjection of the eater to the true host who becomes alive in him by the destruction of the food. The process of eating is a real absorption, a disclosure or dema-terialization of the food that enters into the internal principle of the one fed. Saint-Martin has already condemned the "Capharnite error" ("feeding on the debris of another"), which results from the Aristotelian-Cartesian conception of substance, which is entirely material (for whom two pounds of spoiled flour should provide more than half a pound of intact flour!). Transubstantiation is to be understood as a transmutation of food, "the entry of a higher nutritive force," to which the internal force of nutrition serves as a carrier. To an ascending transmutation a descending transmuta-tion responds, which ensures an effective presence (the opposition of being, becoming, and meaning is nonexistent in the eucharistic doctrine). In addition, the Eucharist ensures the persistence of the Savior, and thus the choice of substances must suit our substance: the bread that purifies our matter, the wine that awakens our celestial body, the spirit that illuminates the intelligence, the Word that penetrates our word, and Life that penetrates our divine essence.

The Eucharist, which announces the death and resurrection of Christ, is a commemoration, a presence, and a foreshadowing ("I will no longer drink this fruit of the vine"). It is this institution that binds and associates the members organically with their Head, and that incites them to carry out in society the work of liberation and the work of "restoring eternal life

---

18 "Vorlesungen über eine künstige Theorie des Opfers oder des Cultus," in *Sämtliche Werke*, vol. 7, 271–416. This text is dedicated to Eschenmayer.

and corporatization (*Leiben*)." Christ "speaks of the Eucharist as a nourishment for the eternal inner man, which is absorbed by him, and yet through this absorption there corresponds a vital extra-production of a future and fruitful implantation of an eternal inner man."[19] The Jews understood nothing of this "hard word," nor of the secret food of submission to the Father. They did not understand that the singular person of Christ was the means of subsistence for all, the "strength of the heart." For all men are, in fact, "anthropophagous" in the sense that they live in their interior being from a food of the heart and of the word (speech from the heart, a word coming from the heart).

The third eucharistic conference (lecture 17), after real presence and transubstantiation, deals with adoration, which implies the localization of Christ in the host. How absurd is the "shredding" or the *itio in partes* of the body of Christ, torn to pieces or located nowhere! Kant, with his play on real presence (the magical *hocuspocus* derived from *hoc est corpus*),[20] is closer to the truth than he knows. A person is only present to another person, and Christ is permanently present to the inner man: the one who believes in this will not be disoriented by the temporary exteriorization of this presence in the Eucharist (because the more includes the less). Consecration is a recognition and a naming of the hidden presence of the giver, his transformation into an effective, personal presence (not as "coming back," but as "not-going"). Conversely, contempt for this gift turns the blessing into a curse, solicits the concealed presence of the Destroyer.

The Eucharist gives the phase *Jovis omnia plena* [all things are full of Jove] a deeper meaning. The gift enters into me along with the giver, and I enter him, I incorporate myself into him. This is just like how fire is its own *pabulum—Alimentum in igne, Ignis in alimentante.* It is not a material change, which would only be a displacement or a movement (and therefore a dead addition or subtraction), but an ab-sorbtion, an intus-susception ("take up within") and an *ab intus productio.* The Eucharist binds food from within to food without, without fastening to it exclusively. The concept of *donatio ab intus* also applies to every sacrament.

In conclusion, Baader wants to express himself on two controversial points: 1) the double form, solid and fluid, of the sacrament, signifies "the

---

19 Vorlesungen, *Sämtliche Werke*, vol. 7, 391.
20 See chapter five.

two forms of organic corporeality," which consists, in its integrity, in the real union of the coherence of solid matter and the penetration of liquid matter; that is to say, the natural body implies a spiritual body, and that is enough to reassure the *Kelchlers*[21] (their scruples of making due with the bloodless body of the Savior); 2) the evolution of worship! But every form of worship evolves, and the eucharistic worship very quickly passes from its first form to the agape meals (where it is quickly troubled by disorder) and from these to the separation of the profane and the sacred. Baader refers to a book by David-Augustin de Brueys, *Défense du culte extérieur de l'Église catholique* (1686).

I would not want to give too much importance to an isolated note "on the Eucharist,"[22] where Baader declares that the distinction between man-as-individual and "man-as-principle" sheds "light on the doctrine of the Eucharist, which has not been sufficiently clarified." Christ does not hand over his individual body in the Eucharist, but his substance and his nature: hence the secret in which he hides, the absence of a visible figure, the ubiquity. His substance is the seed and the leaven of the body of the Resurrection. It is the same for food and for sexual union. We can distinguish between a primitive or central food and a secondary or peripheral one. Baader illustrates what he means by central food with the parable of the sun. The sun, without breaking its own body, *communes* animals and plants (see above), in a secret and primitive way, with its solar substance, and it raises them to the solar body. "Take and eat," the sun says to the inhabitants of the earth. Then, the analogy of the union of lovers, according to Ruysbroeck: it is a reciprocity of eating and being eaten, burning and cooling, acting and resting, consuming and nourishing—while deceitful and bad love is characterized by abstraction, lack of reciprocity, and the *horror et dolor vacui*. Food conditions and mediates the active (magnetic) relationship with that from which it comes, with its higher and deeper powers. Likewise, consecration (and other blessings) is also shown to be primitive and secondary.

The *Lectures on Speculative Dogmatics*,[23] which are also late (1836–1838) and are a brilliant example of Christian theosophy, only touches on the Eucharist in passing and in order to confirm the theology of celestial

---

21 The laity who were asking for communion under both species. See Denz, 1466.

22 "Über die Eucharistie," in *Sämtliche Werke*, vol. 10 (Aalen: Scientia Verlag, 1963), 290–92.

23 Franz von Baader, *Fortsetzung der Vorlesungen über speculative Dogmatik* in *Sämtliche Werke*, vol. 9, 1–288.

foods developed elsewhere. A bold shortcut from the eleventh lecture in the fifth book (1838) brings us closer to the trinitarian revelation of food: a reciprocal nourishment (*substanter*) and the food "which effects the body or the image." The note says: "Whoever eats me, says Christ, which is to say whoever rests in me, makes me work in him, is in me, and I am in the one who works through me. We are, says Paracelsus, what we eat and we eat what we are. Now, as Christ defines the Bread of Life of the world, likewise, He says that the Father nourishes him, or that he rests in the work of the Father in him, as the Father rests in his work."[24]

The idea of transubstantiation and consecration is close to that of absorption, in the sense already indicated of a transfer of one substance (*Verwesen*)[25] to another substance (*Wesen-Werden, Entstehen, Substantirt-werden, Bleiben or Beleiben*) that is higher, more subtle, more spiritual, where the thing is still present (there is also a descent into the material and the infra-spiritual). When I recognize the giver in the gift, he is present to me, and the opposite is the case if I do not recognize him. Later in this volume Baader writes about "the one who does not understand anything about baptism and the Eucharist [and Baader notes that the institution of the Eucharist precedes 'the spiritual baptism' of Pentecost], the one who does not know the (trinitarian) triplicity (natural regeneration, outpouring of Fire, true charity [love of the Father]) of the action or the effect of a bond with the Messiah, by which comes the triplicity of his effective presence of the giver in the gift." One thinks here of the analyses of Jean-Luc Marion.

This link between baptism and the Eucharist is not only ecumenical, but it is the beginning of a sacramental theology (and Holy Orders, Penance, and Marriage are implied) that rests on the great and unique sacrament of the dead and risen Body, the Mystical Body of Jesus Christ.

---

24 Von Baader, *Sämtliche Werke*, vol. 9, 234 and note. This was perhaps a reminiscence of Feuerbach.

25 *Verwesen* originally means "corruption."

Chapter 7

Antonio Rosmini:
The Eucharistic Life

Antonio Rosmini-Serbati's very beautiful eucharistic doctrine is regrettably incomplete, whether it is found in his *Supernatural Anthropology* (the second volume) or in the admirable *A Commentary on the Introduction to the Gospel According to John*.[1] These are the principal sources, but other clarifying writings are scattered in *Theosophy, Psychology,* and *Anthropology as an Aid to Moral Science,* which pertains to the constitution of matter, of universal animation, of the elementary life, and of the vital instinct. Rosmini is integrally both a theologian and a philosopher, and as he himself expresses it, he occupies the "borders of philosophical doctrine and theological doctrine." Thus, his eucharistic theory joins a literal fidelity to the dogmatic letter and to scholastic explanations (particularly those of Bellarmine) to his original speculation that is rich with new views, some of which have yet to bear fruit.

A dark shadow hovers over the memory of Rosmini, namely the shadow of forty condemned propositions by the Holy Office (decreed on December 14, 1887, Denz. 3201–3241). But Rosmini is not the object of the preceding decree on July 7, 1875 (Denz. 3121–3124). Rather, this is aimed at Fr. Joseph Bayma, SJ, for his articles in *The Catholic World,* concerning the support of the accidents of the bread and wine. Of those directed at Rosmini, four propositions (29–32) condemn "errors" concerning the Eucharist: the bread and the wine are or become the food of Christ; transubstantiation adds to the glorious body of Christ a part that is incorporated into him, which is equally undivided and glorious; it achieves *vi verborum* [by the power of the words] the quantity or the measure of the

---

1 As contained in the *Opere edite ed inedite di Antonio Rosmini*, ed. Enrico Castelli and Michele Federico Sciacca (Rome: Stresa, 1966), vols. 38 and 33 respectively. *Supernatural Anthropology*, vol. 38, will be cited here as *Antropologia sopranaturale*, and *A Commentary on the Introduction to the Gospel According to John,* vol. 33, will be cited as *Introduzione*. [There are now a great many translations of Rosmini's work in English, many of which are available at rosminipublications. com/library/. —Trans.]

body of Christ that corresponds to the quantity of the substance of bread and wine, the rest of the body being there *per concomitantiam*; those who die without receiving the Eucharist in this life, if they are baptized, commune at the moment of their death; Christ, descended into hell, could give himself in communion to the saints of the Old Testament under the species of bread and wine.

Cardinal Billot does not look kindly on Rosmini's elucubrations, in which Rosmini treats of things "ineffable." However, the alleged "errors,"[2] which greatly sorrowed the Rosminians, deserve to be analyzed a bit closer, which is helped by the work of Giuseppe Muzio.[3] The alleged errors are taken from *A Commentary on the Introduction to the Gospel According to John*. Muzio explains Rosmini's predilection for the image of a nutritive transubstantiation, the least inadequate of the theories. He highlights that it is the "subjective body" of Christ (the extra-subjective body was only present by concomitance) that appropriates the new substance. Rosmini lifts up the fact, on which he places much importance, that the conciliar text says "all" the substance of bread, the "whole" Christ, but only *the* substance of the body of Christ.[4] Muzio wonders what can be opposed to these statements. As to his original (one could say rash) conjectures (e.g., the glorious body of Christ, in each consecration, sits at table with the faithful; the miraculous viaticum administered to the dying who still have never communed), these are to be understood as an expression of Rosmini's piety and of his desire to explain the divine promises.[5]

We already remarked upon this theme of Rosmini's eucharistic reflections: at the Last Supper Christ himself communed, he is the first communicant, the communicant *par excellence*, and joining the actions to the word, he showed the model of transubstantiation to be like digestion, nutrition. The Eucharist is the food of his body and his blood, in the double sense of the objective and subjective genitive. Furthermore, the words, as beautiful as an incantation, "I will no longer drink of this fruit of the vine until I drink it anew in the kingdom of heaven," suggest the eschatological destination and eternity of the eucharistic sacrament.

---

2 Louis Billot, *De Eucharistia* (Spellani, 1890), 319, note; cf. 331.

3 Giuseppe Muzio, "Il senso ortodosso e tomistico delle quaranta proposizioni rosminiane. Testi di Rosmini e di S. Tommaso," *Sodalitas thomistica* 6–7 (1963): 70–81 on the Eucharist.

4 Rosmini, *Antropologia sopranaturale*, vol. 2, 299; *Introduzione*, 241.

5 Muzio, "Il senso ortodosso e tomistico delle quaranta proposizioni rosminiane," 71.

The first three suspect propositions are extracts from *A Commentary on the Introduction to the Gospel According to John*, lesson 87. The passage from the *Supernatural Anthropology* corresponds to proposition 29 concerning a *perfect* nutrition. The one that corresponds to proposition 30 envisages "an accession and a recession of a foreign matter" to the intact, immutable, and impassible body of the glorious Christ. The substance of the body of Christ, neither extra-subjective nor dimensional, is unscathed. For proposition 31, the author argues that the condemnation attributes to Christ that which is said of man. This is true, but the offending and obscure phrase is this: "the rest of the body and blood of Christ [in relation to the transubstantiated quantity] is only present by concomitance." The corresponding discussion from the *Supernatural Anthropology* does not leave a single doubt on this subject.[6] The fourth proposition (number 32) is taken from readings 72, 73, and 74. The eucharistic being of Christ confers a mysterious life in Christ. But the suspected hypothesis (the first communion of the moribund and of the saints of the Old Testament) excludes that which the condemnation makes him say, namely, "under the species of bread and wine." Rosmini only says "sotto la forma di pane et di vino" or "in forma di pane e di vino,"[7] which is not to be deliberately obscured (we will return to this) and therefore partially excuses the condemnation.

Concerning the endorsement of an eschatological communion that makes the Eucharist into an eternal institution, Giuseppe Muzio alleges that the Council of Trent (XIII, 8; Denz. 1649) speaks of a supersubstantial bread, a bread of angels that the *viatores*, after having eaten "under the sacred veils," "will eat without any veil," alluding to a passage of the *De Coena Domini* of St. Cyprian.[8] This concerns a spiritual eating, but Rosmini said nothing contrary to this.

THEOLOGY

The patristic idea of digestion or nutrition governs Rosmini's eucharistic theology. It fills many pages of the *Supernatural Anthropology*.[9] It is accompanied

---

6 *Antropologia sopranaturale*, 298–302. See *Introduzione*, 240–41.

7 *Antropologia sopranaturale*, 198–99.

8 [*De Coena Domini* is likely falsely attributed to St. Cyprian, beginning in the Reformation period. More likely, it is from the work of Ernaldus Bonaevallis (1156). See Robert J. H. Mayes, "The Lord's Supper in the Theology of Cyprian of Carthage," *Concordia Theological Quarterly* 74 (2010): 307–24, esp. 311, note 9. —Trans.]

9 *Antropologia sopranaturale*, 331–50.

by a profuse polemic against some unspecified adversaries, as well as against his mentor Bellarmine, in order to discard the thesis of annihilation-adduction. His polemic is divided into seven major difficulties, in which his chapters simply begin with "next," and is filled with patristic, scholastic, and liturgical citations. Though not flowery, Rosmini's thought is quite arborescent.

According to Rosmini, the eucharistic conversion is an "ineffable assumption and incorporation of the substance of bread and wine into the body of Christ," with the ambiguity of the word *nel* ("into" or "in") which is the key for the "nourishing," nutritive, interpretation of transubstantiation. "My flesh is true food, my blood is true drink" (Jn 6:56). Christ "intensifies the bread and wine by his life, just as he arrives in the nutrition." Unique, tremendous, and inconceivable as this may be, transubstantiation also involves some analogies, such as the transformation of the mortal body into an immortal one; the formation of the first man; the multiplication of the human race; the production of wheat, of a tree, of spring water; the burning bush; the wedding at Cana; and the staff of Moses changed into a serpent. It is a rather strange list that is actually copied from the texts of the Fathers and other religious writers.[10]

With the help of Bellarmine, though sometimes against him, Rosmini clarifies his notion of "transmutation." Because the end of conversion is complex, the individual, that which is changed, is not simply added up (like one plus one) but is rather supplemented, just like growth or nutrition. The Rosminian conception of the distinction between the subjective body and the extrasubjective or objective body is fundamental here. The "fundamental feeling" of Christ's own body, in effect, extends also to the adjacent spaces of the bread and the wine, in such a manner that it increases. The body of Christ is enlarged and distended in the host, for in heaven he acquired a sacramental nature, and it was Bellarmine who said this. For the body is able to lose the extrasubjective extension while conserving the subjective—which proceeds from the fundamental feeling. And this is what happens to the glorious body. This can help us understand the presence *per modum substantiae* according to St. Thomas. But, by reason of real concomitance, the entire dimensive quantity of the body of Christ is found in the sacrament. From this emerges the difficulty of the discordance between the dimensions, which holds true also when considering concomitance. One may allege that this concerns a dimensive quantity that is entirely internal, and that this can remain miraculously virtual and potential, or even convey that it is only this determined

---

10 *Antropologia sopranaturale*, 344–50.

portion that is measured by the quantity of the sacrament. But even then other aporias appear, for if the body of Christ is deprived of all objective extension, it no longer has relations with other bodies, and thus how can it be under the species? How is it limited, circumscribed, by the objective extension of the bread and wine? How can we explain, under these conditions, the relation of the body of Christ to the sensible extension of the bread?[11]

Then the manuscript stops, and Rosmini has not yet approached the important questions mentioned in the 36th article on the extension of the body of Christ and the origin of the new matter and of the extension that is thereby added. The tricky and contentious proposition 31—taken from *A Commentary on the Introduction to the Gospel According to John*—shows that he chose the solution of the determined portion of quantity. For "where one finds a part, one finds all."[12] Under every part of air or of bread there is the entire nature of air or bread. This is the thought of St. Thomas. The body remains identical, even if its particles change.[13] This altogether laudable rejection of multiple transubstantiations is, according to Rosmini, consistent with his theory of the subjective body and that of the eucharistic assimilation. But it entails a certain indecision at the level of quantity. In effect, the consecrated bread, which becomes the body of Christ, is an augmentation, an added portion,[14] but one in which all the body is present, because the fundamental feeling reaches to the limits of the body. Further: by transubstantiation a part that is incorporated, a part that is likewise undivided and glorious, is added to the glorious body of Christ, being one with the glorious Christ.[15] Nevertheless, if the sensitive principle, which is the driving force of Christ, has for its term the entire body of Christ, the communicant receives the entire body, but the entire body does not become the term of the communicant's sensitive principle. The communicant's sensitive principle shares in common with Christ's sensitive principle that part that is transubstantiated, which serves for nutrition, and not that which is corrupted. For it thereby ceases to be the veil of the body and blood of Christ, and, as rematerialized, follows another path inside the faithful![16] This last

---

11 *Antropologia soprannaturale*, 371.

12 *Introduzione*, 240.

13 *Antropologia soprannaturale*, 305.

14 *Introduzione*, 240.

15 *Introduzione*, cf. 243.

16 *Introduzione*, 241.

phrase makes an allusion to the classic problem concerning the fate of the species. Rosmini remains intrepidly faithful to his conception of the eucharistic nourishment (of Christ and the communicant), his somewhat reckless logic always proceeding from a profound eucharistic spirituality.

SPIRITUALITY

Rosmini's eucharistic spirituality is essentially contained in his commentary on *In ipso vita erat*, which surges in rushing waves from the unfinished commentary on the Johannine Prologue, which has been called a "work of sublime philosophy and theology" (F. Paoli). But our point of departure may be taken from the *Supernatural Anthropology*: the Eucharist as mystical food. It is, he repeats, the food of Christ, in the double sense of the objective and subjective genitive. The Rosminian intuition is that the Eucharist is the very life of Christ, that he lives from a mysterious eucharistic life, that he is nourished by the bread of angels, shared with the elect at the eternal banquet. And he is their food. He is nourished and he nourishes. The image of the natural transubstantiation in Christ calls for the supernatural transubstantiation in view of the divine nourishment that feeds souls. Christ gives the food that he is, his own food, he communes his own with the bread assimilated in and to him, to which he communicates his life.

At the Last Supper Jesus communed, and he gave communion to the apostles. Rosmini focuses on the introduction of the Last Supper in Luke's Gospel: "I have desired with a great desire to eat this Passover with you before I suffer: for I tell you, I will no longer drink of this fruit of the vine until the coming of the kingdom of God" (Lk 22:15–16). But he has a preference for the Matthean version: "I will no longer drink of this fruit of the vine until I drink it anew in the Kingdom of God" (Mt 26:29). This could not be a figurative wine, Rosmini continues, for that would render the wine "that he was drinking then," "the consecrated wine," into an allegory. Christ is saying that after his resurrection he will drink anew of this wine, and this wine as new, that is to say, an impassible and immortal blood, an inextinguishably powerful life, at the eternal banquet of his Glory, where he "intensifies the bread and wine by his divine life, converting them into himself."[17] He nourishes them from the wheat flower and the wine, which make the barren fruitful.

---

17 *Antropologia sopranaturale*, 277. The flare of (divine) life in Rosmini anticipates the modern philosophy of Michel Henry.

The eucharistic meal makes the participants into guests and table com-panions of Christ—*tuos ibi commensales*—in a very strict sense, for Christ is the host and the food. The Greeks said *homotrophoi*, "those who are nour-ished by the same food," and the Eucharist is "a nourishment for Christ and for us," whereby Christ is "a mother who nourishes her children with her milk."[18] Nothing is attenuated from the words of the hymn: *Cibum turbae duodenae—Se dat suis manibus*. The image of Christ eating the bread and giving communion demands the concomitant transformation of the bread distributed to the disciples. Rosmini collected numerous patristic refer-ences: Gregory of Nyssa, Cyril of Alexandria, John of Damascus, Theophy-lact, Elias of Crete, Alcuin, Simon of Gaza (thirteenth century, the Holy Spirit communes from his fire . . . , like liver from food), Gerson, etc.[19] To the objection that a glorious body is not nourished, Rosmini easily responds with the resurrection narratives.

However, nutrition as applied to Christ is susceptible to having a more grandiose sense, for it signifies the assimilation and incorporation, the vital-ization, of matter. For the body of the comprehensor can assimilate all, vital-ize all. This is a profound vision, pre-Blondelian, pre-Teilhardian, on the sanctification of matter. The Pascalian idea of the hidden and silent God represents another direction, which is also that of Blondel. Specific to Ros-mini, at least regarding his level of insistence, is the idea that the original Eucharist is the nourishment that Christ consumes, the food that he assimi-lates and ignites from his life, his immortal ambrosia. The Eucharist is made subjective, transferred to the eucharistic life of the Word "in whom was life." This life that was in him did not abandon him, even during his death.[20] Ros-mini raises the question of the *Triduum mortis* and of the Eucharist that the disciples "have preserved in themselves": "This Christ who was in them was dead; during the triduum of the death of Christ, Christ was dead in his dis-ciples; the disciples of Jesus Christ had in themselves during that time the dead Jesus Christ; in the same Eucharist that they received the night before Christ's death, if they indeed preserved it in them, there was the dead Christ, the body separated from the soul."[21] Nevertheless, the dead Christ continued to live not only insofar as he is God (preventing his cadaver from seeing

---

18 *Antropologia sopranaturale*, 281 and note.

19 *Antropologia sopranaturale*, 281–84.

20 *Introduzione*, 186, cf. 206.

21 *Introduzione*, 186.

corruption), but his soul continued to live from a mysterious, eucharistic life.[22] This divine and eucharistic life, communicated to the humanity of Christ, had never ceased, had never been "dead bread" like the death of his body.[23] His natural life disappeared, the spiritual life of the *viator* that was bound to the theandric union (which is also a life most often hidden) was extinguished, the glorious life was on hold: what subsisted was the divine, mysterious, eucharistic life.[24] The sacramental being of Christ was given as an "end" to the separated soul. "The bread that I will give is my flesh for the life of the world," the flesh of Christ under the form of food takes the place of his life in the world. Christ in the tomb was living from a eucharistic life, for the eucharistic nourishment remains for eternal life (Jn 6:27). This subjective and communicable life is his own: Jesus in his eucharistic life is the heavenly manna.

The Rosminian idea of Christ's survival by the Eucharist goes into largely uncharted territory. The Eucharist restores the Tree of Life that gave immortality: "The life of Jesus hidden in food is the fruit of this tree." Mysterious and occult by nature, it not only sustains the soul of the dead Christ, but it is communicated to the souls awaiting the Resurrection.[25] The loss of natural life does not impede the bestowal of "another better and eternal life." The soul deprived of the body, reduced to the intuition of being and to some inherited habitus, would not be alive, indeed, without the mysterious life that keeps it united to Christ.[26] The glorious being of Christ is therefore always coupled with his sacramental being.

This is the life that God provided when Christ was abandoned to death, and for which Christ gave thanks at the Last Supper.[27] Rosmini dives into the mysteries of the death of Christ and of human death, but not in the extravagant manner reproached by the author of the article on "Rosmini" in the *Dictionnaire de théologie catholique*. For Rosmini never removes the conjectural nature of his hypotheses. He seeks to fill the theological void of Holy Saturday and Purgatory. If he did not explain the eucharistic life of Christ and of believers in a better manner, it is because it is mysterious, "miraculous," and because it corresponds to a spiritual intuition. This "essential,"

22 *Introduzione*, 188.

23 *Introduzione*, 242.

24 *Introduzione*, 187.

25 *Introduzione*, 193.

26 *Introduzione*, 212.

27 *Introduzione*, 206.

"indissoluble" life results in a persistence beyond the grave for the sacrament and for the sacramental life, a prolongation of faith. For the life of faith is not incompatible with eternal life, which is itself faith with a greater light.[28] Faith is made sufficient for eternal life when Christ declares the necessity of "eating the flesh of the Son of Man." "Here is hidden a great mystery."

But this mystery is exactly the persistence of the sacrament of living bread that gives life to the world. It is the *pharmacum immortalitatis*.[29] The Eucharistic Blood is the blood *pro piaculo animae* of Leviticus, the new wine drunk in the kingdom of heaven. "The eucharistic being of Christ"—his immortal eucharistic life—"under the form of bread and wine, operates beyond this life, and gives to the separated soul, like the soul united to the body, a mysterious, indestructible life in Christ."[30] The dead Christ himself, we have seen, experiences in his soul the support of the eucharistic life, the sacramental bread and wine served him, somehow, as a sort of substitute body and life. The flesh that was delivered over persevered in the Eucharist. And on the model of the *Triduum mortis*, this supernatural and sacramental life, this eucharistic body, keeps the separated souls of the faithful afloat. It prevents them from sinking into the night of Tartarus and the "life of shadows and inanimation."[31] Finally, the descent into hell becomes for Rosmini the communion distributed to captive souls.

This is a strange and beautiful spirituality of Holy Saturday sketched in the light of Good Friday. In limbo, Christ gave communion to the just and to the saints of the Old Testament in order to open them to the vision of God. And so, in whatever mode, those who have only been baptized will be administered the Eucharist at the moment of their death, like a talisman or eye wash that will unseal their eyes. The epiclesis *"Jube haec perferri"* of the Roman Canon, glossed by Innocent III after St. Gregory, attests to the association of the triumphant Church with the sacrifice of the Mass. The life-giving food is also given to both the "heavenly comprehensors" and to the suffering Church of purgatory.[32] The eucharistic life, indeed, is supernatural; it augments and heightens the state of grace.[33] That is why whoever

---

28 *Introduzione*, 197.

29 *Introduzione*, 242.

30 *Introduzione*, 199.

31 *Introduzione*, 209, 215.

32 *Introduzione*, 203.

33 *Introduzione*, 208.

desired but failed to arrive at eating and drinking the body and blood of Jesus, will thereby participate in his death. At death the life that was hidden lights up, it is the soul that arises, and the same thing can be said about the last day of a man's life as the last day of the entire world.[34] From this we can see the importance of viaticum (but Rosmini did not comment on the unusual verse concerning "those who are baptized for the dead" [1 Cor 15:29, which does not mention the Eucharist]. The Eucharist is the viaticum for the dying, "the germ for the sudden resurrection of their souls"[35]). The Council of Trent speaks explicitly about the heavenly banquet of separated souls: "eumdem panem angelorum, quem modo sub sacris velaminibus edunt, absque ullo velamine manducaturi" (Denz. 1649).[36]

The fact that communicants receive a portion of the body and blood of Christ as the term of their sensible principle makes of this sacrament a *Signum unitatis*, efficacious for unity. Indeed, Christ and the faithful "feel the same eucharistic body to be like portions of their own proper bodies."[37] Thus is sealed the real union. But the eucharistic bread is not only a bond of love between Christ and the disciple; it is that also for the faithful among themselves,[38] as it forms the mystical body, that is to say the hidden body, which is an object of faith. Christ "keeps all the faithful who commune united to their own real and proper bodies, as it is with a bundle of cords, with the diverse portions of the eucharistic bread that he shares with them."[39] That is what the "fraction of the bread" signifies. The body of Christ is not divisible, but nothing prevents one part of his eucharistic body from being more closely connected to the communicant, corresponding to the host that he has consumed. The parts, albeit undivided from the identical body of Christ, are diverse in communicants and fructify diversely, as represented by the parable of the sower.[40] Rosmini's eucharistic theory, when it came to an end or was interrupted, regains those familiar and traditional topics of devotion.

34 *Introduzione*, 213.

35 *Introduzione*, 215.

36 *Introduzione*, 216–17.

37 *Introduzione*, 243.

38 *Introduzione*, 248.

39 *Introduzione*, 250.

40 *Introduzione*, 250–51.

Chapter 8

Maurice Blondel:
A Eucharistic Synthesis

t will be seen that the Eucharist is the inmost and ultimate key to Blondel's thought, but some premises are necessary in order to recall the intention and structure of this original, even if erratic, philosophy of action. The fundamental intention, which was discussed substantially in the 1950s,[1] should not be in doubt. The oblique and circumstantial intention is also important, for Blondel placed the strength of his evidence therein. They are joined in an early admission in a letter to Victor Delbos (May 6, 1889): "We try ceaselessly to invent a better and more beautiful ideal, a wider truth. As humanity grows, Christ arises. And the perpetual task of philosophy and apologetics (and for me, is it not the case that, at bottom, they are one and the same?) is to discover that he himself is greater and incomparable."[2] What follows is equally eloquent. The *Carnets intimes* abound with confidence concerning the possibility of producing an apologetic work in philosophy, that is to say, to reveal to his contemporaries the wealth of the knowledge of Christ. Blondel does not make any secret of his desire to communicate his profound and explicit faith: Christianity must take hold of philosophy and vice versa.

However, if philosophy is apologetics, apologetics must make itself philosophy. The apology for Christianity must be able to be presented as philosophy. Blondel had been led, partly by the necessity of a thesis at the Sorbonne, to emphasize this technical aspect of his enterprise.[3] From this follows his insistence on phenomenology and the dialectic of action, the postponement of the option to the borders of the philosophical analytic, and the teleological suspension of the ontological affirmation. In describing the necessity of the supernatural, he contends that he does not impinge upon

---

1 Referring particularly to the work of Henri Bouillard, *Blondel et le christianisme* (Paris: Éditions du Seuil, 1961), preceded by the article in *Recherches de science religieuse* 36 (1949) on "L'Intention fondamentale de Maurice Blondel et la théologie," and to the controversies that ensued with Henry Duméry. Note also Glé's thesis on H. Bouillard.

2 Maurice Blondel, *Lettres philosophiques* (Paris: Aubier, 1961), 18–19.

3 *Lettres philosophiques*, 37.

the effectiveness of the gift itself: "I have not gone beyond the domain of phi-losophy," he confirms to his judge Gabriel Séailles, "my intention has been to be committed to a rational examination of that which seems to me to be rational, even in the very notion of the supernatural."[4] There are innumerable declarations of this sort, for example, a quite beautiful one addressed to Georges Perrot, director of L'École normale: "If I speak of the supernatural, this is still a cry of nature, a call of the moral conscience and a demand of reason that I am making heard."[5] To Xavier Léon: "This study of 'theurgy' is still scientific, because it remains a pure phenomenon."[6] To Albert Bazaillas he speaks of a "pure phenomenology."[7] Henry Duméry described this "epoché" of the supernatural as an affirmation of the neutral characteristic of philosophy, unencumbered and uncommitted, set apart from the option. But to other correspondents, friends (Delbos, Wehrlé, Laberthonnière) or ecclesiastics, Blondel used another style of language and worried less about precautions. What is elsewhere presented as a hypothesis or a conjecture is here affirmed as a condition *sine qua non* and as an attainment. There is no rupture, no discontinuity, between the thoughtful requirements of action (*L'Action*) and what he calls metaphysics to the second power, or living truth, or panchristism. His book on Ollé-Laprune makes this clear. Blondel explains in a later letter (1910) to Wehrlé that the laborious nature of *L'Action* comes from an *ad hominem* argumentation, from the concern to "not upset the limited public of professors and intellectuals,"[8] who are more or less adherents of a "separated philosophy." He also, while he was drafting the text, reinforced the autonomy of philosophy, and, advised by Émile Boutroux, revised the final chapter in this way, the first version of which Fr. Henri Bouillard edited.[9] In the project submitted to the dean of the Sorbonne for the inscription of his thesis (March 22, 1887), he had already softened his intentions, but this shone through in his "barbarous" subtitle: "a study on the nature of the operation *ad extra* and concerning the value of literal prac-tice" (replaced by: "Essay on a critique of life and a science of practice"[10]).

---

4 *Lettres philosophiques*, 31.

5 *Lettres philosophiques*, 36.

6 *Lettres philosophiques*, 39.

7 *Lettres philosophiques*, 39.

8 *Lettres philosophiques*, 293.

9 In the tribute to Blondel (1961) from the *Archives de philosophie*.

10 *Lettres philosophiques*, 6–53.

Blondel took seven years, a biblical number, and went through at least seven versions to complete his book. It therefore has different layers. But, simplifying this great and mysterious book, one can see three aspects, three concerns, that are interpolated: 1. the most hidden but the most profound, the hard work of the demonstration of action, that is Christian philosophy, philosophical Christology, panchristism, and metaphysics to the second power; 2. the Pascalian problem of the meaning of life, the "natural desire for the supernatural," the conflict between the willing will and the willed will, which is an occasion for the argumentation; 3. the "scientific" elaboration of the phenomenology and the dialectic of action, the presentation of a "science of the subject"[11] and of practice. Persuaded that in act the impasses of the existential problem are found to be resolved, Blondel never ceased to provide the necessary demonstration by following the phases of a human act, to which the dialectical organization made him responsible. For the other intentional aspect, the implicit reasoning is apogogic: if Christianity is the response to human aspirations, elicited or not, as manifested by action, then it is necessary that one must opt for it, and it is pre-inscribed in the steps that lead there. It will be treated only as a phenomenon, for the needs of the apologetic cause, as if it were considered from the outside. But the juxtaposition of a philosophy of action and an apologetics only puts the subjective and objective conditions of the science of practice into relation with one another. *L'Action* is subtended and impregnated by a latent Christianity, which one would not seek if it were not already found. The belief and the practice of action lead to the justification of Christianity in its beliefs and in its practice, the Christian life. The hinge occurs at the demonstration of the "One Thing Necessary."

But the beliefs, the acts, the precepts, the rites, the dogmas . . . offer schematizations that are not only ingredients and milestones of action, but catalysts of its intentionality, of its deployment. So it is with the Eucharist. It emerges from the second option, the second section of the alternative, with the allusion to "the mysterious host."[12] It is the way to access the supernatural. But there is a prehistory to the philosophiscal problem of the Eucharist according to Blondel: the *Vinculum* of Leibniz, which he exhumes and explains.

---

11 *Lettres philosophiques*, 100.

12 *Action: Essay on a Critique of Life and a Science of Practice*, trans. Oliva Blanchette (Notre Dame, IN: University of Notre Dame Press, 1984), 374/345. [*L'Action* will be cited according to Blanchette's translation, listing first the French then the English page numbers. —Trans.]

THE SUBSTANTIAL BOND

In the revision of his Latin thesis, Blondel describes how he arrived "at exploring this notorious, and reputedly obscure, corner of Leibnizian philosophy." He was alerted to it by a lecture by the dean Henri Joly (from Dijon) during the winter of 1879. He already glimpsed in the *Vinculum* "the justification of 'incarnate truths,'"[13] "the real union of minds forming a body, like a 'new substance,'" without it therefore being limited to an occasional study of transubstantiation. The future enlargement of the Latin thesis is announced under the guise of a barbaric Latin:

> Quod autem apud Deum osculum dici potest, apud creaturas fit vinculum, quasi isto nexu vinceretur duplex rerum ordo et exprimeretur divinae naturae triplex in simplicitate operatio. Fons enim utriusque ordinis Deus, fons scilicet harmoniae non jam physicae nec dynamicae tantum, sed moralis et metaphysicae; adeo est illis, quae tanquam realia noscenda sunt, respondeant intelligibiles et verae subtantiae. Ideali monadum realium convenientiae consentit reale idealis harmoniae vinculum.

> What could be called a kiss in God becomes in creatures the bond, as if by this bond the double order of things was surpassed and the triple operation of the divine nature was expressed in a simple action. For God is the source of the two orders, that is to say the source of the harmony, not only physical and dynamic, but moral and metaphysical, so that to this knowledge, insofar as it is real, there corresponds true and intelligible substances. The real bond of the ideal harmony accords with ideal properties of real monads.[14]

THE CORNERSTONE

But Blondel realized that Leibniz did not take advantage of his intuition, that the *Vinculum* remains a hypothesis put forward for the needs of the system, and that it is even shamefully dismissed. In the revised addition of the thesis he admonishes the philosopher, he even berates him, for the shortsightedness that left the *Vinculum* "like an empty frame in the end," "a stillborn, an indifferent word, a sort of hook," an "adventitious glue," "opaque," "fake and extrinsic," an "aborted attempt," a "symmetry of fake windows." He does not hesitate to repeat a surgical metaphor: to "thor-

---

13 See the Latin thesis, *De Vinculo substantiali et de substantia composita apud Leibnitium* (Paris: Alcan, 1893), 52 (also 34 and 69).

14 *De Vinculo*, 64, cf. 63.

oughly bleed the secret wounds." Leibniz is rebuffed equally for his verbal transactions, his multiple and unsuspected deficiencies, "more like straw than grain," for his method is that of an "engineer-metaphysician."[15] This grievance consists in not having arrived at the *vinculum dilectionis et unio voluntatum.*

Such a parricide is only explained by the freedom of a philosophy that openly proclaims itself to be Catholic, without any more fear of the reprisals of secularism and buttressed by the gains in clarity made over time. He said of the *Vinculum* at the end of the Latin thesis: "invisible substance of visible things, real foundation of phenomena, formal truth of ideal things, synthetic unity of the analytic multiplicity, object for the application of the intellect, and common goal for the will that demands assistance. . . . It is at the roots that truth and reality both differ and agree."[16] Once Leibniz's failure has been noted, one can again raise the hypothesis and imply or even name the superior Bond, which is "composing rather than composed, uniting rather than a union." It is a uniting, therefore, that *fills the hole from above,*[17] that unites from above. Thus he acknowledges the following in the last line of the new edition of the thesis:

> Perhaps (at least) the hypothesis of the *Vinculum,* so archaic, so crude, and so obsolete as it might be, marks, like a rough-cut stumbling block, the place of the beautiful keystone, *Lapis Angularis.*[18]

The fine allegory of the bastion, which he addresses to Fr. Auguste Valensin, provides commentary on this comparison and its application: the keystone being loosened, the entire edifice is threatened with collapse and ruin.

This is the idea that attracted Blondel, extrapolating Leibniz, the idea of the substantial and universal Bond, whose true name is *Vinculum caritatis.* It belongs to the "metaphysics of the saints,"[19] for "philosophy is not able, of itself, to fasten these things . . . [but] must show that things are not fastened of themselves."[20] Christ is the ultimate Bond, "*vinculum omnium*

15 Maurice Blondel, *Une énigme historique: Le "Vinculum Substantiale" d'après Leibniz et l'ébauche d'un réalisme supérieur* (Paris: Beauchesne, 1930). [Quotations are drawn from, in sequence, 73, 130, 135, 131, 135, 92, 91, 93, 93, and 124. —Trans.]

16 Blondel, *De Vinculo substantiali,* 71.

17 Blondel, *Une énigme historique,* 136. Cf. 89 and 122.

18 *Une énigme,* 136.

19 *Une énigme,* 101.

20 *Une énigme,* 136.

vinculorum substantialium." "It is given from above—or rather, *primum movens et totum infrangibile.*"[21] It is an "original creation of God."[22] This occasional formula had, as we already know, sharply struck Blondel: *ex pluribus substantiis oritur una nova.* He glosses thus: *oritur nova substantia, perfectior et vinciens.*[23] "*Oritur*: truly a new being, a transcendent being that, in the order of time, can be posterior to its own conditions for existence, but which, according to the order of ontology, is anterior to its practical conditions and the chronological determinants . . . at the top of a hierarchy that it actuates and controls."[24] Still critiquing Leibniz in the passage, he superbly articulates the christological (and eucharistic) reality underlying the *Vinculum*:

> What Leibniz lacked the most is perhaps seeing the nature of the only materials capable of forming a connecting arch, *foederis arca.* The *Vinculum*, in fact, is not only a physical nature, a metaphysical essence, an immanent finality: it is also, without prejudice to all of that, the supreme magnet that attracts and links from above, step by step, the total hierarchy of distinct and consolidated beings, it is that without which, or rather without Whom "all that has been made would again become as nothingness."[25]

This last phrase is one of those that Blondel liked to emphasize.

The philosopher, in his flight of inspiration, does not forget that the hypothesis of *Vincula* was forged at the end of a eucharistic theory, regarding transubstantiation conceived of as a mutation of the *Vincula* of bread and wine. He himself, on his own,[26] resumes its application to the eucharistic mystery. The *Vinculum* is not only a binding agent; it is a "coagulant."[27] The double role of the Leibnizian *Vinculum*, to consolidate organic nature and to explain the Eucharist, inspires Blondel to proclaim the following:

> It is therefore the entirety of nature and all of metaphysics that is put in question by the theory of the *Vinculum*. On the other hand, it is the entire

21 *Une énigme,* 103, 100.

22 *Une énigme,* 89.

23 *Une énigme,* 100.

24 *Une énigme,* 88.

25 *Une énigme,* 105.

26 *Une énigme,* 105.

27 *Une énigme,* 136.

faith of the Church in supernatural charity that comes to be condensed in the belief in Transubstantiation: it is therefore, in an exact sense and according to the admission of Leibniz, all of Catholicism that is interested in the affirmation of the existence of the *Vinculum*.[28]

The hypothesis is applied with priority, or rather "par excellence to this *panis vivus et vitalis, Vinculum vinculorum, panis supersubstantialis* (Mt 6:11), principle and term without which there is nothing solid, nothing supported."[29]

How can that be? We must recall Blondel's maximal Christology and the continuity of the states of Christ. Like "charitism" and panchristism, the eucharistic mystery prolongs and perpetuates the Incarnation, it injects it into the marrow of existent beings. The patristic thought of *assimilation*,[30] which we saw in Rosmini, was relayed to the young Blondel in the spiritual texts of Bishop Charles-Louis Gay and Fr. Frederick William Faber, and helps to reinforce these connections. It is expressed in the densest passages of the new version of the thesis:

> Thus the body of Christ in the sacrament of the altar is substituted for the bread and wine, but he does not remain in the air, he does not eliminate the materiality that prolongs and enables the infinite perpetuation and the extension of the immensity of the Incarnation itself: *Verbum caro factum*, as if by skipping ahead, charity immediately linked the *initium creaturae* to the *terminus unionis consummatae*: a unique and privileged case that precedes, prepares, and anticipates the *Vinculum dilectionis in finem*, and thus serves not only as a particular and accidental example, but as the *Vinculum omnium vinculorum substantialium*. Analogically, on the humblest plane of nature, in all organic reality, there is a transcendent unity to the variable and indispensable, but subaltern, conditions.

And two pages later:

> I seek here to take up again, on my own, the Eucharist not only as *one* application, *una e multis*, of the *Vinculum*, but as the perfect example, the decisive vehicle, the total and perfect realization of the Leibnizian hypothesis pushed to the end of the perspectives that it opens up for us. What then do we see, considering things from this superior point of view?

28 *Une énigme,* 83–84.

29 *Une énigme,* 123. Cf. 122.

30 *Une énigme,* 135.

Transubstantiation, substituting the natural being of bread and wine for the *Vinculum ipsius Christi*, appears to us then like a prelude, under the veils of mystery, of the final assimilation, of the supreme incorporation of all that exists to the Incarnate Word: *Verbum caro factum ut caro et omnia assimilentur Deo per Incarnatum*. From this first grasp of the vital possession, the *Vinculum proprium Christi* prepares, even in the subconscious domain, the spiritual configuration which, without confusion or consubstantiation, ends in the transforming union, the normal term of the spiritual life and of the sacramental communion. For if the lower nature is to be transposed into a new earth and a new heaven where the Word, the α and ω, *primogenitus omnis creaturae*, will be the only light, the only food, and the universal "binding," *in quo omnia constant*, then for spiritual beings the *Vinculum* is not a transnaturalizing grip, but an embrace that binds them in respecting their nature; it is in some way, analogically, that *osculum* of the Spirit that consummates the Unity of the Trinity itself.[31]

The Eucharist is thus seen as an assimilation, a transformation of matter: conversion to the body of Christ, physical assimilation of the divine flesh and transformation into God, *eritis sicut Deus*. This was also Rosmini's perspective, though intertwined with his theological explanations with which Blondel does not trouble himself. Instead of an examination of the *how*, the mystery verifies its solid foundation by its richness of meaning, by the light that it pours upon the universe, man, and the relation to God. It is the unilluminated illuminator. It proves itself by the intelligibility that it promotes; it is the source of intelligence. The letters, less constrained than the philosophically reworked texts, declare, at times without precautions, how the eucharistic faith enters into the constitution of *L'Action*. Thus, in an early letter to Victor Delbos:

> The ideal of unity is found in the host that sums up in itself all of nature, the fat of the earth, the dew, the rays of the sun, until, by a sort of perfect nutrition, it becomes humanity and even divinity in order to form in us the new being, a reality, so to speak, more than divine, a truly universal synthesis.[32]

Let us continue to leaf through his letters. To Bazaillas: "Man, destined to be *sacerdos naturae*, elevates in himself the brute powers that contribute

31 *Une énigme*, 105–6.

32 Blondel, *Lettres philosophiques*, 19.

to his life, raising them to the dignity of reason . . . he has become thus the universal bond; he prepares for the universal transubstantiation by the mediation even of this body that must become a 'spiritual body.'"[33] The Incarnation prepares the Eucharist, which prepares the Resurrection. All the mysteries are connected. The idea of *assimilation*, with the determination of passivity, proceeds from the Eucharist: "ultimate fact, essential form of our knowledge and of the contingent life;"[34] "to be assimilated and to assimilate, mediating the entire universe to God the Emmanuel."[35] The eucharistic reference is perhaps slightly eclipsed by the Incarnation and panchristism, or the Doctrine of the Emmanuel. But it is a constant of Blondelian Christology never to separate the states of Christ, since they implicate one another. Let us turn now to see how the Eucharist is integrated into the demonstration of *L'Action*, and how a eucharistic philosophy is outlined therein.

L'ACTION

Access to the Eucharist is handled by the apology of the letter and of literal practice, the major lesson of *L'Action*. It is through the sacramental rite, where the desire and the will of religious action are fulfilled, that the dialectic reaches its goal in the Eucharist. But this conclusion, at the end of the demands of action, is preceded by preparations, so that in this approach to the revealed and incarnated supernatural, we can distinguish what presupposes eucharistic schematism and what designates the sacrament itself.

1. The first indication of a eucharistic allusion is the expression concerning "the mysterious host"[36] to which one must submit ("we must acknowledge—The host!"—Paul Claudel). We are here on the threshold of the option, which is still deferred, before the alternative: to be god without God and against God, or to be god by God and with God (356/328); the two branches being death or life, hell or the supernatural (the perfect action). Proximity to the Eucharist will then conform to the *preparations* and the exigencies of good action, that is to say, moral action: it is God who wills in us, who imposes the sacrifice of one's own will, thus instituting a

---

33 *Lettres philosophiques*, 58.

34 *Lettres philosophiques*, 75.

35 *Lettres philosophiques*, 75.

36 Blondel, *L'Action*, 374/345. [Here, Blanchette's translation has "mysterious guest," which has been altered to better reflect Tilliette's interpretation. "Guest" and "host" are both *hôte*. —Trans.]

principle of death and suffering. The eucharistic magnetization can still be detected from within human anxiety, as when Blondel writes that this concern feeds on action itself, "that must give us, with the satiating nourishment, this renascent vigor of health and this insatiable hunger which is the mark of a healthy and integral will" (386/355). But it is on the terrain of the "supernatural supposition," and thus of religious action in the form of cult, symbols, and signs (see the fifth part of *L'Action*: Completion of action, the end of human destiny) that the eucharistic schematism is specified.

2. From an "inner initiative," from immanence, "springs" the "notion" of Revelation. But to what does this refer? Eucharistic metaphors, like harbingers, explain this question: "But how could this quite subjective disposition recognize on the outside whether there actually is a nourishment prepared to calm this appetite for the divine? And after we have felt the unavoidable torment of the infinite, after we have summoned God to raise the veils of the world and to show himself, how can we discern this presence, if it is real?" (397/365).

Again, the principle of the solution is in action itself. Where can God be found? In the exterior reality itself, thanks to the mediation of an intercessor who is pontiff and savior (399/367). But submission is prior to the necessary help. It gives rise to "practical docility" (401/369), which inaugurates religious action, theandric action, as a hypothesis (403/371). Here begins, as is well known by Blondelians, the apology of the letter, the praise of rite, fidelity, and literal practice. There is no other way than practice, bruising and subjugating, because it reinforces the synthesis of man and God, consumed by action, "the only receptacle big enough to contain the coveted gift" (411/378). "Every act tends to be a communion" and only action is capable of obtaining "an assimilation of the whole organism to this principle of a higher life"; literal practice is "like a ferment," which produces "a slow work of transubstantiation and conversion . . . in our carnal mass, in our desires and in our appetites" (412/379). Of course, while he plays with the same words without naming the Eucharist, the entire discourse is obviously a eucharistic trope. After the necessity of the Incarnation, it is another incarnation that is now involved: an assimilation and a transformation, desire incarnated in acts and prescribed gestures, in *works*. Communion with God is coupled with a communion of men among themselves (413/379–80). Here looms the exigency of the sacrament, the vocabulary not being mistaken: the positive precepts must "contain its real presence and be its immanent truth" (416/382).

So far, we have followed, so to speak, a transcendental eucharistic guide to the demands of (religious) action. Henceforth, the schematism is translated into an object.

3. Indeed, "the religious act cannot be a symbol: either it is or it is not a reality" (417/383). But of which literal precept can one say that it is (a gift of) the divine reality par excellence, if not eucharistic communion? The magnificent pages 417–21/383–87 obviously apply to the Eucharist, though always under the guise of the analogy of action. This is the only possible interpretation. This end, which is the "clothing" or even the "body" of the transcendent, is the host, and "If God does not place Himself therein for man to find Him there and nourish himself thereby, man will not place him there" (417/383). A brief commentary:

a.   "The man of desire" wants to commune, and communion demands that the infinite accommodate itself to his littleness: "We must have the infinite as finite. . . . It is up to the infinite alone . . . to condescend to our littleness" (418/384). *Something* contains *everything*. Encrypted for the unbelieving reader, the text is immediately opened by the eucharistic key.

b.   The allusion becomes transparent: the divine "gives itself to all, like the manna which satisfied all tastes, it is under the most accessible and the most humble form." Further, this condescension is considered as a "sublime degradation," exinanition; and a very beautiful image evokes the mysterious radiance of the host as a distant star, a transposition of the sanctuary lamp.[37] The Eucharist is the "invisible hearth" of religious practice (418–19/384–85).[38]

c.   Assimilation, the key word, turns the order of thought and action upside down. It is the operation itself that becomes "nourishment and

---

37 The image is in *Énigme historique*, 109. This was able to induce the evocation of the star on the ocean (419/384), or to change to the memory, dear to Maurice Blondel, of the firefly, the little shining bug of his first communion (April 26, 1874). See the notes of February 11 and March 22, 1888, in the *Carnets Intimes (1883–1894)* (Paris: Éditions du Cerf, 1961). For the precocity of Blondel's eucharistic reflection, see Chrysologue Mahamé, *Spiritualité et philosophie chez Maurice Blondel de 1883 à 1893*, 100–20, a thesis from the Institut Catholique from 1967. See also Albert Raffelt, *Spiritualität und Philosophie: Zur Vermittlung geistig-religiöser Erfahrung in Maurice Blondels "L'Action" (1893)* (Herder, 1978), 30–34. Pages 417–21/383–87 of *L'Action* are also the richest in their allusions to spiritual writers, for example, Bishop Gay (the host, manna, annihilation, the inert thing, etc.) and Fr. Faber (smallness and immensity, the Eucharist as the light of the world, the Eucharist in the depths of creation, the key to creation, the magnet of souls, assimilation. . .).

38 [Slight alterations to Blanchette's translation. —Trans.]

light" for the spirit, vivifying thought and will. "Under the sensible wrapping that serves to give action a purchase, we touch, we possess the reality which the senses do not reach" (420/385), the act, namely communion, occurs in the absolute. "We absorb it into ourselves, and it is the one that absorbs us into it" (420/386).

d.   Then Blondel takes up the traditional analogy of the Eucharist and marriage, or the mystery of generation (an analogy that Fr. Pousset cultivates intrepidly). It is a graft, a natural magic—which refers metaphorically to "the insertion of a thought of faith and of a sacramental operation into our viscera." But the graft is only a primer; the latent comparison is impregnation: literal practice "insinuates" in the organism the "divine seed," and this "sacramental matter,"—"in which the living infinite seems annihilated and as though dead" (Fessard will remember this sentence)—resurrects a "life which is at once divine and human," God born in us, and we born in him, *theotókoi*, like the Virgin of Ephesus (Denz. 252). Man becomes, according to the words of St. Thomas, "the God of his God." The Augustinian analysis is equally evident.

e.   Communion produces an exchange and a reversibility. God is annihilated in order to be engendered anew by us (421/386–87). A great wonder, by which, in order to be, we must and can "bring it about that God be for us and by us." The act par excellence is a "true communion and like a mutual generation of the two wills living in us." In this perspective, death, the last act, is "the last, the complete, the eternal communion," because eternity is necessary to "receive and absorb God." This idea is particularly reminiscent of Rosmini, and Teilhard will take it up later.

The Eucharist is therefore the archetype of "[taking] the letter literally" (422/387). It reveals to us that "when we will fully, it is Him, it is His will that we will" (422/388). The eucharistic synthesis associates two seemingly incompatible natures; it marries the wills and manifests love. *Ut unum sint* (423/388).

4. The last part, "The Bond of Knowledge and Action in Being," is dominated by the *Vinculum*, and by the *Vinculum vinculorum*, Christ. The inspiring and illuminating mystery is the Incarnation, in the Scotistic and Franciscan perspective, and the christological schema emerges (for reasons that would be too long to analyze here[39]) starting from the objectivity of

---

39 See my chapter on Blondel in *Le Christ des philosophes: Du Maître de sagesse au divin Témoin* (Namur: Culture et Vérité, 1993).

the sensible: sensation is the real par excellence, and what Christ saw with his eyes of flesh is forever solidified in being. But all the states of Christ are interdependent, so that the eucharistic Christ is suggested by the expression about the "real presence" (437/400) of the entire system of objects, as well as by the expression "to feed" on the truth (438/401). The reminder of the exinanition also implies the eucharistic abasement and its relation to sacrifice: "If He [God] offers Himself to man under a form of annihilation, man cannot offer himself to Him except by annihilating himself as well, in order to restore to God his divine privilege" (442/404). Eucharistic symbolism is never far off when it comes to characterizing the close bond between man and God:

> For it is through this matter that the truth of the overwhelming infinite is intimately communicated to each individual; and it is through it that each one is protected against being overwhelmed by the infinite truth. To reach man, God must go through all of nature and offer Himself to him under the most brute of material species. To reach God, man must go through all of nature and find Him under the veil where He hides Himself only to be accessible. (449/410)

God in the sensible is not simply the sign of extreme condescension, it is the condition of the existence of the sensible: the sensible is assimilated, it produces that which he undergoes. The extraordinary evocation of God as both active and passive at the end of §IV, however much it applies directly to the Mediator and to the Incarnate Word, reached concomitantly through the memory of the Passion, applies par excellence to the reality of this religious action, the Eucharist. But, again, it is especially through the precept of communion, the literal observance of this letter, in which God gives himself most intimately, that *L'Action* situates the location of a eucharistic philosophy.

AFTERWARD

After the modernist controversy, during which he published the remarkable texts *The Letter on Apologetics* and *History and Dogma*, Blondel becomes timorous and silent. He only publishes sporadically, slowly preparing his great trilogy, *La Pensée*, *L'Être et les êtres*, and *L'Action*, which is at the same time a tetralogy if we add *La Philosophie et l'Esprit chrétien*,[40] which

---

40 Cf. *Exigences philosophiques du christianisme* (Paris: Presses Universitaires de France, 1950), 260.

demonstrates an inflection more in line with traditional philosophy. His language, now harnessed, no longer bursts forth as it did initially, nor is there that genius of discovery that drives the first *L'Action*. However, Blondelians are divided in their preferences, and the trilogy is and remains an imposing construction. But it shows little novelty and even a certain regression compared to the extraordinary beginning of 1893. The originality of the ideas of panchristism and of Christology inherent in philosophy has faded. Blondel proceeds by correspondences, by alternating questions and answers: philosophy proposes enigmas that the mysteries of Revelation solve. It is a fruitful idea that brings apologetic philosophy back to the quest for meaning, and that leaves behind the other, bolder idea of Revelation incorporated into and operative within metaphysics. This style appears especially in *La Philosophie et l'Esprit chrétien* and in the two studies to which Blondel (who died on June 4, 1949) dedicated his final thoughts, "Le sens chrétien" and "De l'assimilation," published posthumously together in a volume with the title *Exigences philosophiques du christianisme*.[41]

"De l'assimilation" is an ample development on the idea of supernaturalization, for which the eucharistic reference serves only as an index.[42] "Le sens chrétien" discerned the supernaturalization of transubstantiation (a single person multiplied by the Eucharist) or absorption, and even consubstantiation, "an inexact expression, which is either too strong or too weak."[43] Nature, capable of theogenesis, is a generating principle and an immanent cause of the life that it supports; it is a resisting and transubstantiatable wildling.[44] Supernatural life is "a vitalizing and transforming assimilation." There is no question of the Eucharist here, properly speaking.

On the other hand, the second volume of *La Philosophie et l'Esprit chrétien* presents an essay on the Eucharist at the end of the examination of the seven sacraments ("the Christian symbiosis and its mystery"). The "beautiful word Eucharist," along with what it names, refers to the vitalizing and supernaturalizing function of Christ incarnate, the mystical body, *totum in singulis*. It is "the initial and final principle" of the New Covenant. In addition, "all the solutions to ontological, ethical, social, eschatological, and mystical prob-

---

41 Translated into English by Oliva Blanchette as *Philosophical Exigencies of Christian Religion* (Notre Dame, IN: University of Notre Dame Press, 2021).

42 See the allusion to the allegory of the true vine from the farewell discourse in Blondel, *Exigences philosophiques du christianisme*, 222.

43 *Exigences*, 177.

44 *Exigences*, 271.

lems are concentrated in the consecrated Host."[45] This was a program of such magnitude that Blondel was no longer capable of completing it.

What is the new gift, the increase that the Eucharist brings? Stated briefly, "The real presence of the Incarnate Word," the tabernacle, immanence, food, the "residence" in "this living ciborium that every Christian has to become." Christ transubstantiates us into himself at the price of an inverse transubstantiation, marked by debasement, patience, and immolation. It is an "endosmosis," an inverted assimilation of terrestrial foods. One will never speak enough about the Eucharist.[46] It includes the supratemporal "drama" of the holy sacrifice, the assimilating union, a "symbiosis" or "unitive synthesis," the "deposit of eternal life." . . . The development of the dictation becomes more oratory than philosophical. It is completed by the twelfth "note" in the text.[47]

How is the Eucharist both viaticum and the bread of angels (a question he shares with Rosmini)? One must return to the institution narrative, to the Last Supper. The Eucharist before the immolation is related both to redemption and to incorporation into the mystical body of redeemed humanity:[48] center of worship, pledge of eternal life, but also already real presence, sanctifying permanence. The flesh nourished by Christ will be transfigured. That is why the Mass is the act par excellence of the Christian cult, its center, its epitome, the summary of all the truths and realities that make the coherence of the "divine plan for humanity." "Philanthropy" is concretized in this "invisceration" of a ferment, which does not lead to consubstantiation, but to "eucharistic transubstantiation." Possession and implicit presence are intended to be made explicit: on one side is viaticum, pledge, deposit; on the other side is the bread of angels, food of the elect, banquet of divinity. There is no opposition between these two aspects, for "the impossibility of depleting the inexhaustible" preserves a perpetual freshness, even unto beatitude.[49] The secret of the King must remain inviolable even after the foretastes, the first fruits, and the promises have been fulfilled.

---

45 *La Philosophie et l'Esprit chrétien*, vol. 2: *Conditions de la symbiose seule normale et salutaire* (Paris: Presses Universitaires de France, 1946), 165.

46 *La Philosophie*, 166–69.

47 *La Philosophie*, 323–28.

48 *La Philosophie*, 324.

49 *La Philosophie*, 325–26.

The Eucharist is the "Sacrament of the sacraments" and the "perfect realization of the Incarnation of the Divine Word."[50] Blondel, rediscovering the inspiration of his youth, confirmed all the meaning of his effort when he spoke of "the Christian truth and practice in which lies the secret that reveals our destiny to us."[51]

---

50 *La Philosophie,* 327–28.
51 *La Philosophie,* 327.

Chapter 9

Poetic Digression and the Pragmatism of Édouard Le Roy

No matter how isolated he may have been among philosophers at the end of a century in the full bloom of secularism, Blondel is, on the other hand, one of the witnesses of an intense eucharistic piety that ran throughout the nineteenth century. Even if, here and there, the evocation of the Eucharist is covered with revolutionary and sacrilegious trappings,[1] it also magnetized a pure and purifying lyrical vein among poets who were touched, in the depths of their misery, by the light of the Eucharist. When Baudelaire speaks of "the mystic food that would be their strength," or when Rimbaud "greedily waited for God," we can see that it was the Blessed Sacrament that ultimately moved their tormented souls. But the eucharistic poet whom the divine food revived is the author of *Sagesse*, Paul Verlaine, who was regenerated for a time by his Catholic faith and something very close to mysticism:

> Is this possible? To one day be able to find it
> In your bosom, on your heart which was ours,
> The place where the head of the apostle rested?
> . . . Then frankly and simply come to my table,
> And I will bless you with a delectable meal
> To which the angel himself will have only assisted,
> And you will drink the Wine of the immutable vine
> Whose strength, whose sweetness, whose kindness
> will sprout your blood to immortality.

The next sonnet of this mystical prosopopoeia continues:

> Then go! Keep a modest faith in this mystery
> of love by which I am your flesh and your reason,
> and most of all come back very often into my house,

---

1 See Frank Paul Bowman, *Le Christ romantique* (Geneva: Droz, 1973).

> To participate in the Wine that quenches,
> In the Bread without which life is treason,
> There to pray to my Father and to beg my mother. . . .

The poem "It is the feast of wheat, it is the feast of bread," which con-cludes the collection (and which was formerly learned by so many French schoolchildren), mixes the song of the "fruit of the earth and the work of men" with the hymn of the Blessed Sacrament.

> For on the flower of loaves and on the flower of wines,
> Fruit of human power in all places distributed
> God reaps and harvests, and disposes for his purposes
> the Flesh and the Blood for the chalice and the host!

The symbolism was, indeed, admirably predisposed to celebrate the mysterious reality and the profound symbol of the Eucharistic Christ. This would also flourish in the sumptuous verses of Paul Claudel (*La Messe là bas*), while more minor figures like Louis Mercier, Francis Jammes, Louis Le Cardonnel, and Marie Noël would pay homage to the sacrament, at times echoing Racinian accents. It is nevertheless surprising that Stéphane Mal-larmé, an unbeliever, dedicated an elliptical paragraph of the *Divagations* to the Eucharist, the theological correctness of which Jean-Luc Marion liked to emphasize, perhaps excessively. Here is this remarkable text:

> Our communion, or part of one in all and all in one, thus, withdrawn from the barbarous food that designates the sacrament—in the consecration of the host, however, the prototype of ceremonials, is affirmed, despite its differences from a tradition of art, the Mass. The enthusiast that one is, with regard to something, either would no longer know how to attend as a passer-by to tragedy, even if it included an allegorical return to the Self; and, at the very least, requires a fact—or at least credulity in a fact—in the name of results. "Real presence": or—the god had better be there—diffuse, whole, mimed from afar by the effaced author, known by us trembling, because of all the glory, if latent then undue, which he assumes then gives back, struck by the words' authenticity and luminescence, triumphant with Homeland, or Honor, or Peace.[2]

---

2 Stéphane Mallarmé, *Divagations*, trans. Barbara Johnson (Cambridge, MA: Harvard University Press, 2007), 246–47. [Translation slightly altered. —Trans.]

The text is taken from "Catholicism" in the "Services" section of *Divagations*. It is less elusive than it appears at the first reading. One simply needs to chant it. It is the Eucharist seen from the nave. Mallarmé, in search of alternative liturgies, which he seeks especially at the theater and the opera, also frequents the cathedrals dear to his friends, such as Huysmans or Villiers, and he gives a supremacy to the Mass over the ceremonies of the temples of art, calling it the "prototype of ceremonials." Further, he endorses a eucharistic realism against an allegorical interpretation. Mallarmé the theologian could instruct more than one contemporary exegete! I offer here some delicate caesuras: "either / would know no longer—words / and light—Honor / or Peace." The "barbarous food" is the bread, the matter of the host. "Enthusiast" is to be understood in the strong sense. "Passer-by" is ambiguous: it can be the enthusiast as a passer-by, or rather it can be the tragedy (the holy sacrifice), which cannot be transitory and ephemeral like a simple commemoration, but a tragedy that leaves, precisely, a "real presence." Credulity equals belief, as both equally result in transubstantiation. "Or" announces an opposition, not a disjunction. The effaced author is the one serving, *alter Christus*. "Mimed from afar" is the vision from the center of the nave. The latent glory that should be radiant is the glory of the hidden God. Finally, the light of peace is superior, victorious over the light of honor or the country.

The poet's vaticinations run the risk of being more orthodox than the reflections of the philosopher, as in the case of the great submissive Catholic, Édouard Le Roy. Because he also refers to action, and because his impugned book is titled *Dogme et critique*, Le Roy was sometimes attached to Blondel's boat, or better, attached to Blondel's boat as it was moored to the controversy with those faithful to Bergson. But the homonymy of action and their common adversaries should not mask the considerable gap that exists between the author of *Histoire et dogme* and Édouard Le Roy. Moreover, Fr. Wehrlé, a close friend of Blondel, was not mistaken when he strongly contested Le Roy's positions in his "Qu'est-ce qu'un dogme?" Of course Le Roy attempts to link Blondel to his cause in his reply: "I too use the term *Action* in the rich and full sense as in Blondel; and indeed it seems to me that I have repeated this with enough insistence."[3] He also approves of the method of immanence. But his explanation of nature and the supernatural is inspired more by Bergson than by Blondel, and as well as by the critique of intellectualism, as found in Bergson's *Données immédiates*.

---

3 Édouard Le Roy, *Dogme et critique*, 5th ed. (Paris: Librairie Bloud et Cie, 1907), 58.

Le Roy published the article "Qu'est-ce qu'un dogme?" in *La Quinzaine* on April 16, 1905, which caused a commotion in the small Catholic world. The fallout can be seen in the dozens of articles and reviews. Two years later, he took stock of the controversy by publishing a number of replies (to Wehrlé, Fr. de Grandmaison, Fr. Portalié, and Msgr. Turinaz), which, together with the contentious article, form the volume *Dogme et critique*, which was put on the Index.

Le Roy displayed a rather minimal conception of dogma. Dogma is at the same time a safeguard, a veto (against errors and heresies), and a guide for action, a practical guide rather than a theoretical truth. Dogma escapes proof and intellectual verification because it presents itself as a standard of action. It is vital, not speculative. This moral pragmatism, which does not deny the irreformable and infallible objectivity of doctrinal affirmations, seemed to him to lead directly to the act of faith. Theories, intellectual formulations, are superimposed; they are indispensable insofar as they respect the primacy and the meaning of the practical order. Le Roy quotes Laberthonnière in this regard.[4] Intellectualism gives way to action. A dogma is not a theorem, it is a rule for belief and action.

Among the examples chosen by the philosopher was the dogma of real presence. What is present is that which is perceptible by itself or by its effects. Now, the eucharistic presence is not like this at all; it is mysterious, ineffable, without analogy. The dogma does not positively state its content, but rather it excludes the idea, for example, that it is only a symbol or a figure of Jesus.[5] The dogma means "that one should have an identical attitude before the consecrated host as one would have before Jesus if he was visible."[6]

These insights are very thin. The replies to Wehrlé, and then to Portalié, will allow Le Roy to clarify his thought. Wehrlé, omitting the "for example" from the above-cited text, found the reference to the Council of Trent insufficient. But Le Roy agrees: the council aims, though negatively, not only at the sacramentarians (Zwingli and Oecolampadius), but also at the dynamic presence of Calvin and the impanation and consubstantiation of Osiander and Luther.[7] In the response to Portalié, the "example" of real presence has a smaller treatment compared to the disproportionate, and interesting, devel-

4 Le Roy, 25.

5 Le Roy, 18–20.

6 Le Roy, 26.

7 Le Roy, 84–85.

opment dedicated to the Resurrection. Le Roy maintains the negative function of doctrinal definitions and the freedom of speculation. He notes
Portalié's misunderstanding of the perceptible and the effectively perceived.
In any case, the presence is accessible to us only in terms of action. The
author refuses the intrinsic determinations of presence, and if the body of
the text demonstrates some caution while exploiting the vulgar, nontechnical
character of the term "substance" (even though the current vocabulary bor-
rows from ancient philosophy), the footnotes brush against some dangerous
areas: "The mystery of the sacramental presence is apprehended by us *under
the species* of *our* duties of attitude and conduct in relation to it."[8] Eucharistic
theology is summarized and reduced to four parts, a "purely regulatory and
legal" part, a part that is a negation of erroneous theories and attitudes, a
positive part "that is entirely pragmatic," and an explanatory part that is not
of the faith.[9] The object of faith, Le Roy emphasizes when concluding his
treatment on the Eucharist, is the intention of the definition. The *vehicle*, the
ideology, matters less. "Is not the body more than its clothing?"[10]

After distancing himself at the beginning from Blondel and Laberthonnière, he later seeks their support.[11] But, to repeat, Le Roy's practical
nominalism and theoretical relativism lend themselves to Blondel's thought
very poorly. In spite of his denials, he hardly distances himself from a philosophy of *als ob*, tempered, it is true, by the sincerity of his ecclesial faith.
This is why he chafes at the accusations; incrementally the tone becomes
more vigorous and he loses his temper. It required the extreme courtesy
and benevolence of Fr. de Grandmaison[12] and the simplicity of Fr. Sertil-
langes to come to meet the somewhat misguided layman and to offer him
a helping hand, one that he solicited more than he actually seized.

A proposition from the anti-modernist decree *Lamentabili* (July 3,
1907) unequivocally condemned his untenable thesis. "Dogmata fidei reti-
nenda sunt tantummodo juxta sensum practicum, id est tamquam norma
praeceptiva agendi, non vero tamquam norma credendi."[13]

---

8 Le Roy, 260, n. 1.

9 Le Roy, n. 3.

10 Le Roy, 262.

11 Le Roy, 108 and 307.

12 Le Roy, 84–110.

13 Denz. 3426, n. 26 of the decree.

Chapter 10

Teilhard de Chardin:
The Universal Eucharist

I t is surely intentional that the editor of the *Oeuvres complètes* of Teilhard de Chardin set apart the beautiful, admittedly very early, eucharistic texts: "The Mass on the World" and "Three Stories in the Style of Benson."[1] This would thus suggest the key role that the Eucharist plays in Teilhard's cosmic Christology. To prevent any misunderstanding, the preface to the *Hymne de l'univers* by Fr. N. M. Wildiers emphasizes that the admirable eucharistic trope of Teilhard—the radiance of Christ even in matter—should not be understood as detrimental to transubstantiation. But like Blondel, though with more boldness and lyricism, the Jesuit meditates on the cosmic meaning of the mystery: "Beyond the Transubstantiated Host, the priestly action extends to the cosmos itself. . . . The whole of Matter undergoes, slowly and irresistibly, the great Consecration."[2] Already in 1917, in "The Priest" (the first version of the "Mass on the World"), Teilhard wrote:

> When Christ, prolonging the movement of his Incarnation, descends into the bread in order to replace it, his action is not limited to the material fragment that his Presence comes, for a moment, to volatilize. But transubstantiation is surrounded by a real, albeit attenuated, divinization of the whole Universe. From the element of the cosmos in which he has been inserted, the Word acts to subjugate and assimilate all the rest.[3]

And in 1924 in "My Universe," speaking of "real and physical extensions of the Eucharistic Presence," he adds: "As we properly call 'our body' the local center of our spiritual diffusion . . . the initial Body, the primary Body,

---

[1] Pierre Teilhard de Chardin, *Hymne de l'univers* (Paris: Éditions du Seuil, 1961).

[2] *Hymne de l'univers*, 12.

[3] Pierre Teilhard de Chardin, *Écrits du temps de la guerre (1916–1919)* (Paris: Grasset, 1965), 287.

is limited to the species of bread and wine. But . . . the Host is like a fiery hearth from which it radiates and spreads its flame."[4]

Before the magnificent desert landscape of Ordos, in Asia, on August 6, 1923, Fr. Teilhard celebrated his "Mass on the World."[5] The altar is the whole earth, the offertory "the work and the sorrow of the world." The paten bears the harvest of effort, the chalice the lifeblood of "crushed fruit." Thus begins a magnificent paraphrase of the eucharistic mystery, enlarged to the dimensions of the universe. "This is my body, this is my blood" is pronounced on all life and on all death. The universe is an "immense Host." The World is consecrated, the universal Presence of God under the "Universal Species:" *ut nobis Corpus and Sanguis . . .* everything is the body and blood of the Word. Consecration leads to communion. To take bread is to be delivered, to be released and to be consumed, to take the chalice is to gather bitterness and taste death in advance (note that Teilhard does not speak of an intoxicating cup and a lavish wine). A vibrant prayer of oblation addressed to the Sacred Heart completes the contemplation.

The "Mass on the World" is followed, in this edition, by "Christ in the World of Matter: Three Stories in the Style of Benson." The "Style of Benson" refers to the English prelate Robert Hugh Benson (who died prematurely in 1914), whose mystical tale *The Light Invisible* Teilhard admired while a student at Canterbury. The fiction imagined by Teilhard is made up of three progressive visions: the Painting (a banal painting of the Sacred Heart begins to vibrate and undulate; it serves as an analogy for the extraordinary radiance of the figure of Christ); the Monstrance, where the glow of the host is communicated to the Universe, then the intense light *contracts* again on the host ("I heard then that they were singing the Ave Verum"); and the Pyx, a meditation on communion: *the Host gave way, its center vanished while attracting me*, and it was separated from the priest "by all the thickness and the surface of the years" that he had left in order "to live and to divinize."[6]

Teilhard conveyed there, in the middle of the war (October 14, 1916), some very personal details,[7] particularly the double nature of his love. The host refers to the universe and the universe to the host. The eucharistic con-

---

4 See *Hymne de l'univers*, 15. The first version (1918), "Mon univers," which is less eucharistic, is in *Écrits*, 263–79.

5 *Hymne de l'univers*, 17–37. See *Écrits*, 281–302 (1918).

6 *Hymne de l'univers*, 55.

7 The "friend" to whom he attributes the visions and who died at Verdun is evidently himself (see *Hymne de l'univers*, 41, note).

secration offers the beginnings of the transfigured Cosmos; it is the sign, the pledge, of a divinization of matter. This is again the fruitful perspective of Baader, of Blondel: not to explain the Eucharist, but to explain *by* the Eucharist. The sanctification of matter and human work that applies itself to it is the leitmotif of Teilhard's eucharistic thought. The *Hymn to Matter* includes a eucharistic invocation: "Sap of our souls, Hand of God, *Flesh of Christ*, Matter, I bless you."[8] And Teilhard's masterpiece, *The Divine Milieu*, follows the guiding eucharistic thread.

This work, like *The Human Phenomenon*, is not without a Blondelian rhythm: it insists on action ("communion through action"), the One Thing Necessary, the "Living Bond of the Pleroma," the infinite value of the smallest gesture, of the infinitesimal. The idea of food, of assimilation, though transposed to cosmic forces, is recurrent.[9] If a fragment of matter is deified, then all of matter is deified and diaphanous to the mind. Let us follow the guiding thread:

a. The Eucharist is enlarged to the dimensions of the Cosmos. "The Eucharistic Christ controls all the movement of the Universe."[10] "From the hands that knead the dough to those who consecrate it, the great universal Host should only be prepared and handled with *adoration*."[11] The Eucharist sums up the offering of the World, which is the Divine, Diaphanous, Milieu.[12]

b. The Mystical Body is the omnipresence of the Divine Milieu. The cosmic path relays or joins "the great path cleared in the Church by the pervasive worship of the Holy Eucharist."[13] The great sacramental operation in a way overflows the words of the priest. Teilhard speaks of the "extensions" of the Eucharist and, so as not to be misunderstood, he emphasizes: "There is only one Mass, only one Communion, only one Event": the Incarnation, realized in each individual by the Eucharist. This is what he calls the Great Communion and about which he comments that the "broad human communion" is only an approximate figure. It is concerning this deified world that, in a splendid paraphrase, he pronounces the consecratory word: "Hoc est Corpus meum."[14]

---

8 *Hymne de l'univers*, 72 (in *La Puissance spirituelle de la matière*). See *Écrits*, 445.

9 *Le Milieu divin, Ouvres*, vol. 4 (Paris: Éditions du Seuil, 1957), 50–53, 147, 149, 154.

10 *Le Milieu*, 153.

11 *Le Milieu*, 58.

12 *Le Milieu*, 163.

13 *Le Milieu*, 150.

14 *Le Milieu*, 153, 147, 151, 180–83.

c. The universal Eucharist is still *hidden*, being an object of faith. If the World is in our hands like a host, it is on condition of believing and of making the Real Presence of the Incarnate Word. Without faith, the world is opaque, a nondivine milieu. Faith sees more profoundly: "Make me adore it [the universe] by seeing you hidden in it. The great liberating word . . . repeat it to me, Lord: *Hoc est Corpus meum.*" The Eucharist is made up of these burdens and sacrifices that faith takes on. "Everything that terrifies us in our lives . . . [is] in fact only the Species or Appearances, the matter of the same Sacrament."[15]

d. Under the Species of the World and the "accidents" of Matter, God is present in our lives and the world is a sacrament. The actual Eucharist refers to this great *Sacramentum Mundi* where all energies are transmuted: "Our humanity assimilating the material World, and the host assimilating our humanity, the eucharistic Transformation overflows and completes the Transubstantiation of the bread of the altar. Gradually it irresistibly invades the Universe. It is the fire that runs on the heather. It is the gong that vibrates the bronze. In a second and generalized sense, but in a true Sense, the sacramental Species are formed by the totality of the world, and the duration of Creation is the time required for its consecration."[16] The sacramental Species mean that through Matter and the Universe God embraces me, God reaches me. With the metaphor of the "universal kiss," Teilhard joins Blondel and even Schleiermacher.

e. *The Divine Milieu* is not only a breviary of Christian cosmology; it is a work of spirituality. The grand perspective flows back into my life, my thought, in order to transfigure them. It determines the offering of *my life*: "One must always and everywhere commune. The Eucharist must invade my life. My life—the sacrament of life, of my life—is . . . a Communion by the World with you," in the adoration, the absorption, the annihilation, the "purification" by Matter. Over *our* lives, we must repeat the words of Consecration, so that "the world is transfigured for our use"—*ut nobis Corpus et Sanguis fiat Domini nostri Jesu Christi.*[17]

f. This is not easy. Darkness surrounds us, and the share of passivities needed to animate the divine Presence is heavy: "confronted by the powers of diminishment and death," it is necessary "to believe, more than anything

15 *Le Milieu*, 171–73.

16 *Le Milieu*, 154.

17 *Le Milieu*, 157, 135, 180.

else, in your active Presence." But the envelopment of the passivities does not prevent the previous Presence from acting: "To commune with you in them [the blessed passivities], of a communion at the font [at the Sources of life], I have only to recognize you in them, and to ask you to be there more and more."[18] Death is the ultimate passivity, and at the same time the supreme moment of communion. This leads to a beautiful evocation which ends as follows:

> So give me something more precious still than the grace for which all your faithful pray to you. It is not enough that I die while communing. Teach me how to *commune while dying*.[19]

It would be interesting to look for sketches of *The Mass on the World* and of the *Divine Milieu* in the early texts of *Genèse d'une pensée*[20] and the admirable *Écrits du temps de la guerre*—for example, the meditation on death chanted by the cry of bacchants: *Io triumphe*.[21] Also note "L'Âme du Monde,"[22] "Le Prêtre," "Forma Christi," with the praise of the Eucharist ("La Chair du Christ"),[23] and the commentary of the *Hoc est Corpus Meum*.[24] One could also find traces of these themes in later essays. We will rather seek these ideas through the work of recovery by one of Teilhard's followers, who is certainly not a simple epigone.

The inspiration of Fr. Teilhard crisscrosses, as a matter of fact, the book by Fr. Gustave Martelet, SJ, *The Risen Christ and the Eucharistic World*.[25] It is a valiant effort to rethink the Eucharist in christo-cosmic and anthropological categories. It is not actually the Eucharistic Christ who radiates and functions as an explanatory key to "man in the world," as it is for Blondel. And while Teilhard meditates on the "planetary dimensions" of the Eucharist and opens the world to eucharistic "extensions," Martelet would instead

---

18 *Le Milieu*, 74, 78–79.

19 *Le Milieu*, 96. The death card of Karl Rahner's mother contained this invocation.

20 *Lettres* (1914–1919) (Paris: Grasset, 1961).

21 *Écrits*, 147 (*Le Milieu mystique*), 151, 163.

22 *Écrits*, 215–32.

23 *Écrits*, 331–53.

24 *Écrits*, 375.

25 Gustave Martelet, SJ, *The Risen Christ and the Eucharistic World*, trans. René Haque (New York: The Seabury Press, 1976). Original French: *Résurrection, Eucharistie, Genèse de l'Homme* (Paris: Desclée, 1972). These ideas are resumed and reshaped in his 2005 bestseller, *Teilhard de Chardin, prophète du Christ toujours plus grand* (Brussels: Lessius, 2005).

like to start from the universal extensions that are identical to the body of the Resurrection to understand how, thanks to the body of the risen Christ, "the Eucharist is itself pre-eminently the sacrament of Presence."[26] The Eucharist is, therefore, part of a meditation on the Resurrection (of Christ) and on the body (with its generic and social dimensions), which leads significantly to a paraphrase of *The Mass on the World*.

The anthropology of the body, which helps to prepare us to understand the Risen Body, benefits from contemporary phenomenological contributions and the work of Maine de Biran. Above all, Martelet retains the critique of dualism and a commitment to being anchored in the world. The Resurrection is, in fact, the negation of dualism and the establishment of a new relationship with the world. In a sense, according to Teilhard's perspicacious intuition, the World is the body of the Risen One. A sentence from Teilhard is used by Martelet as a benchmark: "My matter is not a part of the universe that I would possess *totaliter*, it is the totality of the universe possessed by me *partialiter*."[27] It is man as a microcosm. What happened for Christ at the Resurrection and what will happen for the dead, of which he is the first fruits, is an interpenetration of the body and the world such that the opacity of the "objective body" has ceased and the "subjective" or "phenomenal body" no longer experiences any obstacle, any limitation to its presence in the world. The glorious body, the body of eternity, is already prefigured in the body of death. In the exemplary and unsurpassable case of Christ (in whom we have already risen), "the relation of the glorified Christ to our world is *constitutive* of the identity of the Lord and . . . his true nature, *presupposed* by the Eucharist, will be *revealed* only in the Parousia."[28]

Fr. Martelet pays great attention to the already dated and risky position of Édouard Le Roy in *Dogme et critique*, no doubt because it experienced a notable revival among certain Protestant and Catholic exegetes. In his explanation of the Resurrection, Le Roy, as Léon-Dufour will also do later, set about to eliminate the corpse and thus consequently envisaged the miracle of Easter on the model of our own resurrection. The separated soul is not reincarnated immediately, of course, but it is reborn, it re-forms a body, which is the body of eternity. "O great soul, it is time that you form a body!"

---

26 Martelet, *The Risen Christ*, 174.

27 Teilhard de Chardin, *Science et Christ: Oeuvres de Pierre Teilhard de Chardin* (Paris: Éditions du Seuil, 1965), 33–35. See 38–39, 79.

28 Martelet, *The Risen Christ*, 236 n. 91.

(Valéry). Martelet, who would willingly substitute "man" for "soul" (without examining the problem of immortality), rightly rejects the strict parallelism of the two resurrections. He does so in a very convincing way when it is about signifying the glory of the Firstborn, in brilliant language inspired by the Fathers and by Teilhard,[29] and in a less convincing way when he tries to represent the phenomenon of the Resurrection:

> Had the presumed witness been present in the tomb at the "moment" of the Resurrection, he would have seen nothing but an erasing flash, if I may use the phrase, which suppressed the death-relationship that still defined Christ's remains, by converting it into a glory-relationship."[30]

It is only an image, of course, but this kind of nuclear lightning is not much better than the famous "accelerated decomposition of the corpse" invented a short while ago by X. Léon-Dufour.

Why the detour through the Resurrection in order to develop a theory of the Eucharist? Because the body of Christ in the host is the Body of the Risen One and here there is an essential key, forgotten since the Church Fathers: the analogy between the Resurrection and the Eucharist.[31] This is Fr. Martelet's excellent intuition, and he successfully defends it on an exclusively theological level. The analogy extends, by virtue of christological premises, to man himself in his (future) eschatological state:

> In the Eucharist *whatever happens to a double element of this world must also happen to the entire world, and to man himself, when they are looked at in the light of the Resurrection.*[32]

Note that Martelet italicizes almost the entire sentence. The history of eucharistic theology, Martelet says, is that of a "widening gap" between the Resurrection and the Eucharist. It is due to this fracture, which generated heresies and misunderstandings, that it was necessary to speak of Body and not of substance.[33] He thus strives to repair this fracture by connecting,

---

29 See Martelet, *Résurrection, Eucharistie, Genèse de l'Homme*, 81, despite the hyper-physical-ism, and 185.

30 Martelet, *The Risen Christ*, 90.

31 Forgotten even by the encyclical *Mysterium fidei*. See Martelet, *The Risen Christ*, 119.

32 Martelet, *The Risen Christ*, 172. See also 120.

33 Martelet, *The Risen Christ*, 120.

thanks to a better understanding of corporeality, "*The paradox of Christ's eucharistic body . . . to the paradox of his resurrection.*"[34] The Eucharist, he writes in the course that served as preparation for the book, is submissive to the "metabolic push" of the Resurrection.

In fact, the transformation, the migration of bodily matter, is symbolized in the Eucharist as the mystery of death and resurrection in the Paschal moment sealed in impenetrable night.[35] For the substance of bread and wine, steeped in food, soaked in sweat, is the "fruit of sorrow and labor of men," and it is intended to be incorporated, assimilated. The analogy of the dying grain is always invaluable. It is perhaps in this way that the author could overcome the objection that the institution of the sacrament is at the Last Supper, which he seems to take rather lightly.[36] The first Eucharist, which Christ gave to Himself, contains the Body which is going to be immolated and resurrected, but it contains it "before suffering," and therefore it lacks the metabolism which would apply to the condition of a spiritual body. Hence the inevitable tendency to accentuate symbolism, which proved fatal to Léon-Dufour.[37] But Martelet, with his insistence on the reality of presence, protects himself against these deleterious consequences. However, the mutual inclusion of these mysteries allows him not only to anticipate, but to trace the Resurrection back into the Passion:

> The presence of Christ's transforming passion is, in fact, effected symbolically in the Eucharist . . . [and] realized for us. . . . For the risen Christ is still at work and even in agony, as Pascal said, "until the end of the world." The sovereignty he acquires over the universe through his resurrection does not cut him off from our sufferings: rather does it bring him into, "interiorize" him, in them, and it is bread that has known the mill and grape that has known the wine-press that become at his table his flesh and our flesh, the blood which allows us to consecrate our own.[38]

It is not at all certain that this is the same meaning that Pascal had in mind. But the intuition is profound. It also shifts the sacrament toward passivity, which is the most poignant, the most meaningful sign, as Blondel glimpsed

---

34 Martelet, *The Risen Christ*, 136.

35 See Martelet, *Résurrection, Eucharistie, Genèse de l'Homme*, 155.

36 See Martelet, *The Risen Christ*, 129.

37 The new version of his work is titled *Le Pain de la Vie* (Paris: Éditions du Seuil, 2005).

38 Martelet, *The Risen Christ*, 172. See also 178.

as well. In fact, the spontaneous trajectory of Martelet, if not Teilhard as well, is to make the Paschal Christ the agent, the author, of transubstantiation (integrating transsignification and transfinalization), tirelessly communicating his life and his light. The descriptions that he attaches to Christ are symptomatic: he is "the cosmic pruner of death's ill-governed powers," he is the Pantocrator, the *supreme 'mutant'* and the only "complete transgressor of the iron law which sets an inexorable term to all life's successes and imposes upon every living being the . . . annihilating yoke of the laws of nature," he is the "supreme bread," the "supreme living being for man and the world."[39] It is also symptomatic how he sidelines the notion of Christ *under* the species" in order to emphasize the dominion that he exercises *over* them. This dynamic conception of a resurrectional and eucharistic dynamism is reminiscent of the lively eucharistic force of Leibniz and the eucharistic accretions of the glorious Body according to Rosmini. But Martelet both responds and does not respond to what he calls "the prejudicial question par excellence," which was formulated by Cardinal Joseph Ratzinger: "What happens when nothing physical or chemical happens?"[40]

This concerns the question of whether to abandon or maintain a eucharistic physics, which some (Cipolla) hoped to see renewed in the wake of Teilhard. But the emphatic Christology of Martelet does not lend itself to providing this problem with updated features:

> Just as the risen Christ is much less contained in the world than the world is contained in him, so we may say that Christ is much less *in* the bread and wine than the bread and wine are *in him*, "converted" and changed in the newness of his life.[41]

Edward Schillebeeckx's notion of a "sacramental Parousia,"[42] which inspires Martelet, is only adequate if it retains its Heideggerian sense of presence.

39 Martelet, *The Risen Christ*, 82, 84, 175, and 179.

40 See Martelet, *The Risen Christ*, 229, n. 77. Ratzinger became Pope Benedict XVI in 2005.

41 Martelet, *The Risen Christ*, 178.

42 Martelet, *The Risen Christ*, 229, n. 75.

Chapter 11

Simone Weil: Eucharistic Hunger

Simone Weil represents the antithesis to the *theologia gloriae* or the eucharistic triumphalism of Teilhard. She is fascinated by the extreme exinanition of Christ into the host. Simone was marked with the stamp of affliction from the beginning. She was terribly cerebral and tortured by headaches, deprived of joy by an indelible fate imprinted on her sensibility, doomed to erasure and self-destruction. She dreamed of annihilation like others who had survived. She defined herself as a crossroads of ideas that had chosen her more than she had sought them. Her stubbornness, her Cathar gnosis and syncretism, can disconcert and even irritate, but the intensity of her love for Christ and the originality of her genius appeal even more.

She shows the passion of converts, the fire of witnesses. However, for reasons that she explains at length,[1] she did not request baptism and she excluded herself from communion, which she so ardently desired. She remained with her *hunger*. It was in keeping with her vocation to find God more in absence and deprivation than in possession (note the similarities with St. Thérèse of Lisieux). Exinanition is her way to God; through starvation she accesses the Eucharist, through spiritual hunger. She herself, voluntarily, suffered from hunger, and she died of deprivation, of anorexia, her eyes on the green countryside outside of London.

The Eucharist is connected to her conversion. It was, in fact, the offices of Holy Week, particularly through the liturgy of Solesmes, and a stay in Assisi that revealed to her the crucified Christ, the prototype of the wretched. More precisely still, it was then that she recited a eucharistic poem by George Herbert, "Love," when "Christ himself came down and took possession of me."[2] Such homesickness marks the end of the poem:

---

1 In the letters addressed to Fr. Perrin, in Simone Weil, *Waiting for God* (New York: Perennial Classics, 2001).

2 *Waiting for God*, 27; Simone Weil, *Pensées sans ordre concernant l'amour de Dieu* (Paris: Gallimard, 1952), 84.

"You must sit down," says Love, "and taste my meat."
So I did sit and eat.

As Simone never approached the altar, the Eucharist was offered to her only in the form of contemplation and fasting.

To understand her attitude, one must have recourse to her notes, which are entirely intuitive, penetrating, and scattered throughout the published books. The recurrent ideas make it possible to thematize an introverted thinker of extraordinary intensity and subjective logic.

Simone Weil searches for God in *decreation*, annihilation. One must fade away so that God can be. She would like to be no longer, to be no longer an I, a Self. The "taste for nothingness" is ambiguous, and she draws it from mysticism and Spinozism. This prayer is her heart's desire: "May God grant me to become nothing."[3] She adds: "In so far as I become nothing, God loves himself through me." She loved the death of Phaedra as portrayed by Racine:

> And death, robbing my eyes of their light,
> Restores to the day they sullied all its purity.[4]

She believes that she too does "disturb the silence of heaven and earth."[5] From this we can see her obsession with erasure, withdrawal, disappearing: "To see a landscape as it is when I am not there."[6] What others expect from possession, she obtains from deprivation, from a pure and ineffectual desire. She is filled with nothing. Her taste for affliction (which she considers the most beautiful word[7]), extreme affliction, comes from the fact that affliction crushes mercilessly, annihilates. The abandoned Christ, the leitmotif of her Christology, is the perfect image of affliction. She prefers failure, deficiency. "But perhaps God likes to use castaway objects, waste, rejects. After all, should the bread of the host be moldy, it would become the Body of Christ just the same after the priest had consecrated it."[8] Among the Christian mysteries, she is drawn to the Cross, to humiliation, and to the Eucharist, which brings humiliation to its peak. By a strange disposition of the soul and an

---

3 Simone Weil, *Gravity and Grace* (New York: Ark Paperbacks, 1987), 30.

4 *Gravity and Grace*, 36; Simone Weil, *Cahiers*, vol. 2 (Paris: Plon, 1953), 186.

5 Weil, *Gravity and Grace*, 37.

6 *Gravity and Grace*, 37; *Cahiers*, vol. 2, 198.

7 Cf. *Cahiers*, vol. 1 (Paris: Plon, 1951), 13.

8 *Waiting for God*, 30.

identification with the wretched, she is incapable of living other than in a state of perpetual suffering and therefore of patience, *hupomonè*. The beauty of the world, the image of necessity, acts as a foil to affliction, which also comes by necessity.[9]

These premises of Simone's intellectual temperament set the tone for her reflections on the Eucharist. Having never received communion, she knew the Eucharist only as hunger and desire, "a hunger that is already satisfied and that cries out eternally."[10] For she was literally nourished by being excluded from this living Bread, about which she copied the relevant verses from the fourth Gospel.[11] She tasted deprivation, she contented herself with eating it with her eyes: "Here below seeing and eating are two things. You have to choose one or the other."[12] "What is essential is to be hungry and to know that you are hungry," or even to "cry out that you are hungry and that you want bread:" "The important thing is that [the soul] announces its hunger by crying."[13] Simone has this remarkable sentence: "The eternal part of the soul feeds on hunger."[14] This is her original relationship to the Eucharist: abstinence, hunger.

Naturally, she turns to the starving Christ. Despite his hunger, he rejected the first temptation: turning the stones into bread.[15] Besides the sacrament of Christ as food, there is the Eucharist of the starving Christ. Giving food to the starving Christ in the person of the hungry beggar is an equivalent of communion. The bread with which one gives alms to the beggar becomes the flesh of Christ, "when it is given to the sorrowful in a movement of pure compassion."[16] "Just one piece of bread given to someone who is hungry is enough to save the soul," if it is "given with the attitude of a beggar."[17] Christ will say: I was hungry and you gave me to eat. . . . But also: I was hungry,

---

9 *Pensées sans ordre*, 83. Affliction and beauty are "the only two keys by which one enters into the pure country, a country where one can breathe, the country of the real."

10 *La Connaissance surnaturelle* (Paris: Gallimard, 1950), 252.

11 See *La Connaissance surnaturelle*, 51.

12 *La Connaissance surnaturelle*, 251.

13 *Pensées sans ordre*, 44–45; *Waiting for God*, 138.

14 *La Connaissance surnaturelle*, 252.

15 *Cahiers* vol. 2, 225, 230, 233, 277 (but also see *La Connaissance surnaturelle*, 267: "the stone that feeds, the Holy Grail, comparable to the Eucharist. Christ is also at the same time stone and bread"); *Pensées sans ordre*, 50; *Waiting for God*, 98 and 103.

16 *Pensées sans ordre*, 28.

17 *La Connaissance surnaturelle*, 43.

and you did not give me food. . . . Christ is hungry in his poor. "The Word that became incarnate is hungry that this beggar would be fed."[18]

He is both the food and the hunger. He is the living and supersubstantial Bread.[19] The Eucharist means eating God: "You are hungry and you ate me."[20] In communion "every day [God] makes himself matter in order to give himself to man and to be consumed by him."[21] In the poor as well, Christ is hungry and he is eaten. He is the hunger, he is the bread. And if "eating a piece of bread when you are hungry is communion with the universe and its creator,"[22] the carnal presence of Christ was like a communion made by humanity itself.[23] Sadly, it made a sacrilegious communion, and Christ was murdered.

The hunger of man "eats man," which is to say that it feeds on affection, feeling, love. But "when one stops eating man, one wants only to eat God."[24] Man eats God.[25] Conversely God eats him and man must be eaten: by death.[26] "If the grain of wheat does not die . . ." is Simone's refrain, accompanied by the myths: Persephone's grain of wheat, Kore's pomegranate seed, Dionysius's grape, and Attis's blood.[27] Death is the test of being eaten by God. "The beauty of the world is the mouth of a labyrinth . . . it is absolutely certain that he [man] will finally arrive at the center of the labyrinth. And there God is waiting to eat him. Later he will go out again, but he will be changed; he will have become different, after being eaten and digested by God."[28] Everything that crushes hands us over to the digestion of God: by fatigue and misfortune, as by death, which is itself a great fatigue, man is made matter and consumed by God.[29] Something of this inverted eucharistic mystery occurs in contemplation, "when a human being turns his eyes and his attention toward the Lamb of God present in the consecrated bread, a part of the evil

---

18 *Cahiers*, vol. 2, 233.

19 *Waiting for God*, 146.

20 *La Connaissance surnaturelle*, 250.

21 *Gravity and Grace*, 29.

22 *La Connaissance surnaturelle*, 85.

23 *La Connaissance surnaturelle*, 323.

24 *La Connaissance surnaturelle*, 251.

25 *La Connaissance surnaturelle*, 250.

26 *Cahiers*, vol. 1, 157.

27 *Cahiers*, vol. 2, 64; *La Connaissance surnaturelle*, 244; *Pensées sans ordre*, 61.

28 *Waiting for God*, 103.

29 *Cahiers*, vol. 1, 126, 157, 176; *Cahiers*, vol. 2, 43.

which he bears within him is directed toward perfect purity, and there suffers destruction. It is a transmutation rather than a destruction."[30]

God gives of himself in food, and man, through his death and work (which is a kind of death[31]), is food for God. The priest, as Fr. Chevrier said, is an eaten man. There is a reciprocity and an exchange. Like Christ in the Eucharist, man becomes matter, and the products of his incarnation in matter become the flesh and blood of Christ. This very beautiful idea is developed in a small text, touching on the idea of a Christian utopia, entitled "Christianity and Life in the Countryside,"[32] which was the result of reflections from her stay as an agricultural worker with Gustave Thibon, in Ardèche. Christ intentionally chose bread and wine in which "to incarnate himself."[33] The farmer transforms his energy, that is to say his blood and sweat, into bread and wine. His privilege is no less sublime than that of the priest, since his flesh and blood are transmuted in the Eucharist into the flesh and blood of Christ. This is the "circuit" of agriculture, "the cycle is complete." The grain is the "flesh of man become flesh of Christ, eaten by the miserable."[34] Simone suggests that we should establish tours of villages and vineyards to see the role of the preparation of the species of the Blessed Sacrament.[35]

Work is a form of sacrifice. From a different angle, Weil rediscovers the Teilhardian thought of a general transubstantiation.[36] Matter, food, turns into thought. Energies captured by matter, solar energy, physical energy, go back to vital and spiritual energies. Eating, she writes rather curiously, is like "absorbing springs."[37] Simple sensible perception is also a transubstantiation. Weil elaborates an energetics of consumption, which perhaps has its completion in the final work of death. The "supersubstantial bread" of the petition from the *Pater Noster*, connected elsewhere to the order of the world, is a "transcendent energy" and, when it is transubstantiated, "a moment comes when we cannot help doing [good]."[38]

---

30 *Waiting for God*, 124. *Attente de Dieu* (Paris: La Colombe, 1950), 191.

31 *Cahiers*, vol. 1, 126.

32 In *Pensées sans ordre*, 21–33.

33 *Pensées sans ordre*, 25, 29.

34 *Pensées sans ordre*, 25, 31; *La Connaissance surnaturelle*, 228–29, 315.

35 *Pensées sans ordre*, 27.

36 *Gravity and Grace*, 42; *Cahiers*, vol. 2, 35, 177.

37 *Cahiers*, vol. 2, 35.

38 *Gravity and Grace*, 42; *La Connaissance surnaturelle*, 335; *Attente de Dieu*, 216–17.

When she ventures to articulate a theory of the Eucharist, her good intuition penetrates the Catholic mystery. She does not get lost in her conception of the Eucharist, but is interested in the extreme kenoticism that emaciates the presence. *Waiting for God*, which only seems to be a purely scandalous text, exposes the Eucharist as a "convention."[39] Jean Guitton has provided some commentary on this word.[40] "Convention" would perhaps be shocking if it were not a convention established by Christ, who is God. Divinely instituted, it is infinite, absolute, creative, and therefore real, realizing. It also supposes, in order to be extended, a second convention, the institution of the priesthood.[41] Guitton wonders if this infinite convention is unreasonable. It is not, he replies, because matter is the most worthy receptacle, "the lowliest degree of creation is the most capable of the infinite." "The extremes touch."[42] The Eucharist thus realizes the kind of presence that is *absolute* and *pure*, something perfectly pure that arouses a perfectly pure religious act, contemplation. It is the true philosopher's stone.[43] Baader and Blondel are in agreement with this.

The eucharistic convention brings about a perfect and total presence, because it takes place in the purest secrecy.[44] Just as it is incomprehensible that pure geometry has technical applications, so the eucharistic "hypothesis" generates a marvelous reality. It is an "invisible, and somewhat conventional, miracle."[45] "A real convention is a supernatural harmony."[46] Those for whom the use of the word remains shocking should reflect on the terms of the convention and on the one who pronounces it. To say that the Eucharist is conventional "at a higher degree," that it is "placed at the central point," and that it represents "perhaps the perfection of purity here below,"[47] is to model it on the divine model and author: "all nonconventional purity"[48] is imperfect

---

39 *Waiting for God*, 122–23.

40 Jean Guitton, "Quelques observations sur la pensée de Simone Weil concernant l'Eucharistie," *Cahiers Simone Weil* (March 1982), 15–21.

41 Guitton, 17.

42 Guitton, 17–18.

43 Guitton, 19.

44 Guitton, 20.

45 Guitton, 8. See *Attente de Dieu*, 188.

46 *Waiting for God*, 122.

47 *Waiting for God*, 187, 189, 188.

48 *Waiting for God*, 188.

because it is not ideal, not mathematical. Eucharistic purity is contagious through contemplation. It is made of emptiness and the transparency of emptiness, the image of the annihilated Christ. It is loved in starvation, it offers itself in exinanition, it arouses "impersonal love,"[49] purified from the hunger of creatures, which is for Simone Weil the *nec plus ultra* of love.

> At the center of the Catholic faith is a little formless matter, a little bread. The love directed to this piece of matter is necessarily impersonal . . . it is this fragment of matter that is at the center of the Catholic faith. This is the most scandalous thing about it and that is where its most wonderful virtue resides.[50]

The Eucharist completes the kenotic incarnation: it is necessary that *God be emptied of his divinity* in order to love him; he is emptied of his divinity by becoming man, and emptied of his humanity by becoming a corpse (bread and wine), matter.[51] "The host is really the Lamb of God which takes away sin."[52] Conversely, Simone, who usually strongly distinguishes Catholic from Protestant faith,[53] expresses the adventurous idea that "consecration does not make it so that God can be found" in matter, but only that it "makes a fragment of matter," at this instant of time, transparent, the object of a "real contact with God." It is true that she says consecration and not communion. She adds, as by a paradoxical encounter with Teilhard: "The use of the Eucharist consists in understanding that every bit of matter is eucharist."[54]

Simone Weil's eucharistic outlook is summarized by "if the grain of wheat does not die." Food is associated with sacrifice and death. "The blade of sacred grass that gives us bread" dies in order to come to life again and in order to be eaten. Christ dies in order to serve as food, *factus cibus.* Hunger is a kind of death that, beneath the species of unappeased and always quenched desire, sustains the soul eternally. Affliction and the attention pursued in endurance are the sacraments of contemplation. As fever nourishes, so deprivation of the Eucharist kindles purification. Daniel and

49 *Waiting for God*, 198.

50 *Waiting for God*, 198.

51 *Cahiers*, vol. 2, 183.

52 *Waiting for God*, 123.

53 *Gravity and Grace*, 117.

54 *Cahiers*, vol. 2, 231–32.

his companions after their fast "looked healthier and better fed than any of the young men who ate from the royal table" (Dan 1:15). The "hunger strike" can be a eucharistic behavior (!) and, as the remedy sometimes consists in a cure by means of famine, the soul *feeds* its hunger by turning in an effort of attention toward the supernatural bread. Being eternally hungry and thirsty could be the definition of hell. In Simone Weil's heterodox mentality, this is the condition of heaven. Blessed are those who hunger and thirst, for they will never be satisfied.

Chapter 12

Eucharistic Research and Theories of the Twentieth Century

PAUL CLAUDEL

The Catholic poet Paul Claudel, a great poet of the Blessed Sacrament, drafted a small, dense treatise on the Eucharist while in Prague in 1910, which was published in *Positions et propositions II*[1] with the title of "The Physics of the Eucharist." These fifteen pages are more than a summary of St. Thomas and more than a paraphrase of the Catechism of the Council of Trent. Instead, Claudel demonstrates that precise language and a strict orthodoxy are not incompatible with the spiritual radiance of faith and the stirrings of devotion. "The Physics of the Eucharist" is a fragment of a theologically poetic art, more of which is found elsewhere in his prose writings. It recalls the style of Bossuet.

His physics conforms at all points to the letter of dogma and also that of philosophy, although "contrary to philosophical reasoning." This is not unlike Blondel, in that the nature of the intelligible schema takes on the mystery, though beyond the deception of common sense:

> This mystery, which puzzles our spirit, is accepted at once by our heart, with neither reserve nor hesitation, as if it were a simple, easy thing, like a gift that is as supremely proper as it is gratuitous. Our stomach does not accept the bread better than our heart does, which precedes our foolish reason and throws itself ahead, and goes to the Eucharist, not only without a single doubt, but with a voracity and a violent desire, as toward food that is coveted by all our being. Nature elevated by grace, deaf to our arguments, speaks as itself before its creator with a violence that bewilders us. This is the opposite of philosophical reasoning that occurs, as it were, outside of us, which the inner heart takes so long to accept. Here it is being that goes directly to being.[2]

---

1 Paul Claudel, *Positions et propositions II* (Paris: Gallimard, 1934).

2 Claudel, 59–60.

The idea of the heart's precedence and presence was like that of Fr. Faber (which was also impressed on Blondel), as also was the priority of the will (previously perceived by Leibniz, which is at the origin of the "new substance," the eucharistic bond). Guided by the intuition of faith, Claudel states: "that which we find under the substance itself is the will, it is the special intention of God who created it. 'My words,' the Word says, 'are spirit and life!' God speaks, and the entire universe responds."[3] Moreover, this performative divine intention not only reaches down to the fibers of a thing, but brings it into communion with its source, for that is where it both reaches and stops. The following lines constitute a perfect commentary on the "God of his God" of Thomas Aquinas and Maurice Blondel:

> What more intimate union? He desires to associate us with what is deepest in him, deeper than thought and deeper than the heart itself. He makes us co-exist with him, he associates us with his center, to his intimate life as Christ the Redeemer, as he forms this body and permits it to be Jesus Christ. His most holy body is in the substance, which is in us like an effect in its cause. Not a beating of his heart in which our heart is not able to experience the source. The Eucharistic Christ is precisely the same one who conversed with the apostles: but they saw him from the outside in and we nurture him, as it were, from the inside out.[4]

It is not until he arrives at the expression of the bond that he finds the right explanation:

> When we commune, we receive a substance that is at the same time united to the accidents of bread, by the power of the sacrament, and united to the dimensions and to all the accidents of the sacred body, by natural concomitance. The Eucharist, between these two worlds, forms an indissoluble bond and something that is shared by him.[5]

This bond also unites, unifies the communicants to Christ in his current state of glory: "by this temporal sacrament, we are communed, united to Christ in his eternal state of being [earlier, Claudel evoked "the perfect fruit that is the body of glory, the spiritual body, firstborn among the dead, bright,

3 Claudel, 56.
4 Claudel, 63–64.
5 Claudel, 58.

agile, subtle, impassible"[6]]. It is not he who moves, it is the veil of this world that is opened, it is we who are, in a sense, removed from time and space in him."[7] The wonderful contrast that follows recalls Pascal:

> Christ, during the days of his human life, only delivered to us his hands or his face, his husk, and did not give us his substance. The Eucharistic Christ withdraws his hands and wants to deliver to us only his heart and his substance, which includes all the rest.[8]

For the Eucharist as for the other modalities of Christ, the maximal interpretation is always the best. The Claudelian realism does not hesitate to mention "an eatable God" (edible), "a drinkable God"[9] (*caro cibus, sanguis potus*). He emphasizes, with the whole tradition, that the spiritual food that we absorb assimilates us to it:

> You will devour it entirely, according to what is written in the book of Exodus (concerning the Paschal lamb). You will make it entirely pass within. No longer for your sight, but for your nourishment . . . Jesus . . . entrusts to us his own key, he causes us to act with him with regard to everything in our inner life that builds up Christ.[10]

Ultimately, it is the effect that attests to the cause, and the Eucharist is proven by its use, which Claudel exclaims elsewhere: the proof of bread is that it nourishes, the proof of water is that it quenches thirst.

The theological and spiritual considerations of the poet are not frustrated in the least bit by eucharistic philosophy. The Eucharist is a deep and penetrating mystery that philosophy must take into account and benefit from; it is "at the center of our intellectual life," and the failure of Cartesian philosophy regarding the Eucharist brings about the collapse of an entire section of modern philosophy: "as opposed to everything that all modern philosophy since Descartes affirms . . . extension does not have its own existence besides the concrete quiddity that serves as its root, its support, and origin . . . it is neither a substance, as Spinoza, Gassendi, and even Malebranche affirm . . .

6 Claudel, 59.

7 Claudel, 62–63.

8 Claudel, 63.

9 Claudel, 58.

10 Claudel, 64–65.

nor is it a preexistent form of the spirit, as in Kant's delusion."[11] Further, dogma establishes that the substance is fundamentally inaccessible to the senses. As for accidents without a substance, this philosophical *hapax*, Claudel compares it to the glimmer of a dead star, or the thaumaturgical virtue of the bones or clothing of a saint.[12] How the sacrament produces that which it signifies is explained by the (re-)creative, performative intention: "Natural things signify to us some of the attributes and benefits of God. But the sacrament produces for the soul that which was signified by it for the body. It becomes eminently true that the water cleanses and that the oil penetrates and confirms, yes, and that the bread and wine are food and beverage at last."[13] The conversion of the *tota substantia panis* into *substantia corporis Christi* can be further elaborated, due to the heterogeneity of the substances, which was already such a concern for Descartes and Leibniz, such that one is entitled to judge it as luminous: "the substance of Christ replaces that of the bread, but in wedding his mode of manifestation to our senses."[14] The formula avoids the turmoil of Rosmini.

GABRIEL MARCEL

Gabriel Marcel indicates where and how to look for the traces of the Eucharist in his thought. It is at the end of the fundamental text, "Position and concrete approaches of the ontological mystery,"[15] which is his discourse on method and a charter, so to speak, of his concrete philosophy. He writes: "some will say: in reality, everything that you say implies a reference— unconfessed and, besides, unformulated—to the givens of Christianity, and it is only positively illuminated in its light. It is in this way that we understand that which you understand by presence when we evoke the Eucharist, and by creative fidelity when we think of the Church."[16] These notions are the major elements of a concrete philosophy, and at their origin they are a Christian product. But, given that in the analysis of presence the eucharistic watermark is closely intertwined with his notion of survival, it will not be useless to recall the content of Marcel's Christian philosophy. The objection

---

11 Claudel, 52–53.

12 Claudel, 53–54.

13 Claudel, 57.

14 Claudel, 61.

15 *Du refus à l'invocation* (Paris: Gallimard, 1940).

16 *Du refus à l'invocation*, 298.

that we cited above allows him to explain himself, briefly, and when the question reappears, he refers again to this explanation.[17] His Christian philosophy, more by suggestion and inspiration than by a formal intention, is, in a sense, pre-Christian, inasmuch as it is prior to conversion and was already secretly polarized and magnetized by the unknown faith. It is developed subconsciously in an inspiration by an unrecognized Christianity, or in a naturally Christian soul. It is moreover pre-Christian in the sense that the theme undergoes, in its circular quest, in the elaboration of its own categories, the influence of a sensed or welcomed faith, the irradiation of a sensed or perceived hearth—but always with discretion and a *clair-obscur* that the intuited, nondiscursive, and nonsystematic character of Marcelian philosophy makes somehow inevitable and beneficial:

> The existence of the Christian fact, just as that of positive science, only plays a role here as a fertile principle. It fosters in us the blooming of certain thoughts that, in fact, we perhaps would not have accessed without it. This fertilization is able to be accomplished in what I will call peri-Christian areas, and I personally find proof of them in the fact that it occurred to me almost twenty years before I even had the most distant idea of converting to Catholicism.[18]

When it is a question of determining and justifying the Christian content or impregnation of his philosophy (spontaneous and not calibrated, as it is for Blondel), Marcel constantly appeals to a situation of fact: the *fact* of the authority of existential and revealed Christian data, the *fact* that the philosopher, despite his claim to autonomy, bathes in a Christian milieu and that he cannot abstract himself from the tradition of Christianity, the *fact* that the philosopher, even apart from adherence to a positive religion, is a *committed* being and therefore receptive to Christian revelation. The *fact*, again, of Gabriel Marcel himself. It is unthinkable that he should be exiled from his own self, that he would set aside his conversion and his life and replace it with an impersonal thinker.

That said, we must keep the strict distinction between the natural and supernatural. Between the mysteries inherent to human experience, such as love, evil, and death, and revealed mysteries, such as the Incarnation and Redemption, there is an insurmountable distance. If, however, the same

---

17 Cf. *Du refus à l'invocation*, 110, 225, and *Présence et immortalité* (Paris: Flammarion, 1959), 193.

18 *Du refus à l'invocation*, 299–300.

word is used for both orders of things, it is not a coincidence, for there are "intakes," "points of insertion," of the supernatural into the natural, and even in the natural there is "the anxious anticipation of another order."[19] The "recognition of the ontological mystery" in fact emanates from "a sort of fruitful irradiation of revelation itself"; it allows us to glimpse "the possibility of such a revelation." A philosophy of this type "goes along an irresistible movement to meet a light which it anticipates and by which it undergoes a secret stimulation in its depths, like an accommodating burn."[20]

Given these premises, the stimulating capacity of Revelation, such as the eucharistic mystery, puts pressure on his chosen notion of *presence*. This must be understood precisely. The Eucharist is not the object as such (as it is in Blondel's proleptic approach to the ultimate requisites of action), it is implicit and underlying, and not the only target. Its light illuminates a mystery of human experience, which is connected to ethical and religious categories in the widest sense: the mystery of presence. This is joined to fidelity and is not otherwise defined,[21] but fidelity to a presence implies from the start that it is not a matter of a sensible, external, or immediate presence. The still-unnamed Eucharist will act as a talisman and as a compass, but without ever being envisaged for itself, or brought into consonance with the question of the afterlife (for it is the food of immortality). The notion of real presence, however, signals collusion, collaboration. The eucharistic presence gives rise to a deepening of the notion, which provides analogies for the absent presence of the loved one. More precisely, because presence goes beyond the case of *a* being and the circumstance of death, and because it refers to the ontological mystery, it does not exhaust itself in the *test* that affects it. It is fidelity to being and therefore to mystery.

Presence is a mystery, and fidelity is the "actively perpetuated presence,"[22] prolonging "a certain hold of being on us." Then Marcel begins to apply this to the relationship of the living and the dead. If one examines faithful presence, it is not the attachment to a simulacrum, to an effigy of a disappearance (Marcel's plays, especially *Le Mort de demain* and *La Chapelle ardente*, criticize this idolatrous conception, admirably described in the stories of Henry James in *The Altar of the Dead* and *Maud-Evelyn*); it is

---

19 *Du refus à l'invocation*, 301.
20 *Du refus à l'invocation*, 301.
21 *Du refus à l'invocation*, 288.
22 *Du refus à l'invocation*, 228.

rather something that goes beyond the object on all sides. Death is its test or counter-test. Instead of allowing the memory to degrade into an effigy, fidelity perpetuates it as presence. Obviously one can say, and Marcel heard this objection many times, that this is a completely subjective feeling. Almost his entire journal, *Presence and Immortality*, which is also striated with eucharistic motifs (communion, eternity, memory, sacrifice), counters this objection. It is indeed the reality of a protecting and graceful presence that inverts the Orphic quest of memory and regret. Presence is not hoped for in vain. "A presence is a reality, a certain influx," which one cannot elicit. This old word "influx" escapes or spontaneously comes out of Marcel, which, as in Leibniz, has a eucharistic origin. Those with fidelity make themselves permeable, responsive: a "mysterious exchange" takes place "between the free act and the gift." The eucharistic imprint is flawless; it is licit to visualize the community of the upper room. However, the philosopher justifies the term "influx" ("too spatial, too physical") without resorting to a religious schematism. But the metaphor of the eyes of faith is recovered in the form of a second reflection "that refers to an underlying intuition that is blinded but effective and from which it experiences the secret magnetism."[23] The "world of pure charity, of total spiritual availability," which he then evokes, is the eucharistic atmosphere of the reciprocity of gift, about which Blondel also insisted. And it is the necessity of the thing itself, for Marcel was quite incapable of planning his meditative development, which leads presence and availability to consecration (meaning the Eucharist and the priesthood): "the most available soul is . . . the most consecrated, the most internally dedicated."[24] The parallel reflection on holiness, Christ being the Saint *par excellence*, is connected with this original approach to consecration and the priesthood, which is accessible to secondary reflection.

We are in the "meta-problematic" and the domain of higher analogies. Certainly, the eucharistic host is something more than and different from an *analogon*. But the operation that signifies presence (effecting what it signifies), that is to say, active and offered fidelity, belongs to the same ontological sphere that the eucharistic institution assumes and elevates. The metaphysics of the Eucharist and its applications cannot be confined to the theory of transubstantiation and its consequences, for it finds in human

---

23 *Du refus à l'invocation*, 292.
24 *Du refus à l'invocation*, 297.

existence and intersubjective relationships these arguments of fittingness and of conformity that have always enriched and saturated the understanding of the mystery. These significant pages of Gabriel Marcel are worth more than a whole treatise of laborious theology.

GASTON FESSARD

With Fr. Gaston Fessard (1897–1978), Marcel's close friend, we do not leave the realm of allusions and analogies, but here the Eucharist is openly thematic and its ramifications are exposed. Again (and, as is perhaps obvious for a close reader of Hegel, Blondel, and Marcel), it is the sacrament which enlightens and the act of faith which is a generator of thought.

In *La Dialectique des Exercices spirituels*,[25] the Eucharist appears at the hinge of the Third and the Fourth Week, and this placement, in a system that values the quaternary division, already marks the central role of the sacrament:

> If it is true that the *Exercises* lays out the structure of the free act . . . , one of the first, and not one of the least, results of Ignatian reflection is to emphasize the Eucharistic Mystery, to the point of designating it as the central point to which everything converges and from which everything derives.[26]

How is that the case? By the decisive determination of the *Hoc est Corpus meum*, which, pronounced on Holy Thursday on the eve of the Death and Resurrection, inaugurates a new presence of "thanksgiving," transforming the *body of sin* into the *body of grace*, "the beginning of the *conversion* of the world of Nature into a world of the Spirit."[27] The authority of the *Hoc* is the landmark for several aspects of Fessard's reflections: "This *hoc* marks, so to speak, the extreme point of the divine Freedom going out from itself, the two intermediate stages of which were, on the way out, Creation and the Incarnation, and on the way back, Redemption and the sending of the Spirit (*nova creatio*). From this point of view, the eucharistic *hoc* becomes the hinge around which the turn, the conversion, takes place, in which the whole life of Christ makes the World submissive."[28] By the place

---

25 *La Dialectique des Exercices spirituels de Saint Ignace de Loyola* (Paris: Aubier, 1956).

26 *La Dialectique*, 110.

27 *La Dialectique*, 110.

28 *La Dialectique*, 111.

that he gives to the Eucharist, St. Ignatius underscores "the union of God and the *hoc*, the Universal and the singular," which conditions our freedom (which Fessard understands in a way similar to Kierkegaard's "becoming Christian").

Even without being intimately familiar with the rigorous and undaunted thought of Fr. Fessard, one can know the importance that he gives to the conception of the symbol: reason operates in symbols that dialectic has the task of articulating and scrutinizing from all sides. In accordance with the hermeneutical method of the *Exercises*, which is a theory of the spiritual conversion of the free and temporal *subject*, the agent is subjective freedom, and this freedom is reflected in archetypal events, without prejudice to their original meaning. Therefore, in this case (contemplation *de Coena Domini*) it is freedom that pronounces, about itself, the "This is my body, which is given up for you." But by pronouncing its death sentence as an individual, it takes on the body of grace and the "germ of Resurrection" in a Community.[29] "The substance of the old man is converted into that of the New Man, *Transubstantiation*." Time is involved too, to the extent that it represents and actualizes the transition from Being to Non-Being, from the present to the past under pressure from the future. This passage is a *Passion*. Transubstantiation and Passion behave (as in Hegel) like the interiority and exteriority of conversion, where Fessard plays on the ambiguity of the term "conversion."

The application of the freely-willed Eucharist to vocation and the exercitant's election obviously refers to the archetypical freedom of Jesus. He offered himself because he desired to. This is so in such a way that the Eucharist is the "true cause of the Passion": "if the former precedes the latter, it is . . . because the Passion is only the material execution . . . of a spiritual movement which leads to the *Hoc est Corpus meum*. Without the freedom of Christ going out from itself, which is translated into this word, no Passion is possible."[30]

The Eucharist is therefore the intermediary link, the middle term between the Before of the individual and the After of the Universal Community, the "body of grace" mediating from the "body of the flesh" to the "spiritual body." It is the sacrament of passage, of the Passover: "the Passover is the memorial of the *passage*; the Last Supper, the memorial of the essential

---

29 *La Dialectique*, 113.

30 *La Dialectique*, 114.

passage which is the Passion."[31] Everything is consummated and consumed in the Agony and the Passion, in death, which holds the seed of the Resurrection. The Eucharist contracts times. Without it the deed of Christ loses its true significance. In a laconic though striking manner, which echoes Teilhard, Fessard writes: "On the Cross, he is the first human fragment consumed by the Universal Eucharist."[32]

These connections, which are frequently overlooked, identify a theological reasoning. They show the immanent spiritual sense of action, of gestures, which are much more important than the fixism of things. This is how such phrases are to be understood, phrases which pursue the striking parallel between the sacrificed and consumed Christ and the novice consumed by the decision: "As for its sensible being, this body [of grace] is still only a resolution, a word which aims to represent a social state. Similarly, the Eucharist, at the Last Supper, is only the *Hoc est . . .* applied to what we call bread. But likewise, in its deep and true being, the Eucharist is the movement of transformation in God that believers will undergo upon contact with him, by virtue of their faith, in the course of time, just as the being of this young man will gradually undergo" "a movement of transformation in God."[33]

This schematism of the eucharistic conversion applied to the election of religious life continues unabated, to include the descent of the corpse into the tomb ("if the grain of wheat does not die"[34]) and the beginnings of the Resurrection: from that of a "martyr," a "Eucharistic death," to that of "a social life of the resurrected body."[35] But the mystery of the host displays quite remarkable patterns in the extraordinary interval of the night of Good Friday. This meditation on the Pietà insists on the momentary priestly function of the Virgin Mother, although Fr. Fessard knew the Magisterium's hesitancy with regard to the theme of the Virgin Priest (a hesitancy that he shared). But Mary was invested with this unique role: as the representative of Humanity, holding in her arms, as in the Pietà, the "body of grace" (not yet risen), the "pure *hoc*" of the incorruptible corpse, placed on her, entrusted to her, handed over to her "discerning conscience" as the "pure means" of her act of faith:

31 *La Dialectique,* 115.
32 *La Dialectique,* 115, n.
33 *La Dialectique,* 114. Cf. 121–22.
34 Cf. *La Dialectique,* 121.
35 *La Dialectique,* 132.

At this hour when Mary is definitively full of grace, Mother of all grace and Queen of the priestly race, it is the Host about which she can say in all truth: *Hoc est Corpus meum*, offering to God the Father the Eucharistic sacrifice of his Son and of Humanity.[36]

In the womb of Mary there is also the beginning of a "perpetual presence," until the end of the ages.

The Fourth Week, in this "phenomenological dialectic"[37] of the Christian mysteries, highlights the *hoc* of the After, which is the spiritual body, the nonlocalizable body of the Risen One. He exhibits "the pure being of freedom."[38] One might think that, as a result, the body of grace disappears. This is not so, for Christ invites the disciples, at Emmaus, in Galilee, in Jerusalem, to "find the *hoc* where he shows it to them, when he says: *Hoc est Corpus meum*."[39] The *Hoc* is always the pivot of all these concentric circles. Thus, the purpose of the mysteries, from the Incarnation to the Resurrection, is to weave a bond of "indissoluble life" (to use the expression dear to Schelling), to which Fessard, at the instigation of St. Thomas, also interlaces the virgin birth.[40]

It is not easy, on a limited topic, to account for the coherence of a form of thought that constantly marks out "the path from theology to philosophy." It does not cultivate the obscure, but it also does not always explain its presuppositions. Its track is more accessible to those who have benefited from having conversations with Fr. Fessard, such as Fr. Yves de Montcheuil and Édouard Pousset.

GEORGES MOREL

But before exhibiting other recent attempts of eucharistic discernment, I would like to provide a place for the virulent criticisms of Georges Morel,[41] a longtime trusted advisor for the training of young French Jesuits. He helped somewhat to weaken eucharistic belief in the ranks of the clergy. It is entirely without pleasure that I am replying here to his attack, as our long

---

36 *La Dialectique,* 122.

37 *La Dialectique,* 121.

38 *La Dialectique,* 128.

39 *La Dialectique,* 128.

40 *La Dialectique,* 131, n.

41 In his *Jésus dans la théorie chrétienne* (Paris: Aubier, 1977).

years of common life have left me with a certain human sympathy. His book is not a good one; it feels a little rushed. He conducts the discussion with epigones (except for Ratzinger, of course), which does not facilitate the altitude of thought. However, flashes of his former vigor sometimes appear.

Even the earlier *Sens de l'existence selon saint Jean de la Croix* tended to minimize the symbolism and the reality of the Eucharist.[42] The more recent work could dispense with dealing with the Eucharist altogether, as once the divinity of Christ has been denied, the real presence goes down at the same time. But Morel is interested in the embarrassments of dogma and theology. He takes no account of the valuable distinctions of Innocent III (Denz. 782–783): *sacramentum et non res, sacramentum et res, res et non sacramentum,* bread and wine, body and blood, union and charity. According to Morel, the Catholic faith is entangled in a fundamental aporia, which results from its invincible tendency toward identity, rather than difference and alterity. Theological language oscillates between an ontological register (reifying) and a semiotic register (the sign), without being able or wanting to choose. Morel reserves his criticisms for several contemporary theologians whom he selected, notably Martelet, then Leenhardt (a Protestant), Ratzinger, Baciocchi, Durrwell, and secondarily Teilhard via Martelet. He tends to merge the terms from these various authors at the risk of confusing them. Morel latches onto a rhetorical phrase that is, indeed, unsatisfactory.[43] But by attacking the "mythological climate," "the fetishism," the process of identification and enslavement, the "fantasies of master and slave," a consumer society that would govern eucharistic behavior (!), he only manifests a stubborn refusal to enter into the difficulty and the reason of the mystery. Above all, he demonstrates a panicked and quite singular fear, a kind of phobia of "altering alterity,"[44] which freezes all things in their difference (that is to say, its nature: the bread remains bread[45]) and which leads to this tremendous declaration: "one does not honor bread by imagining that it could become the body of a god and thus cease to be bread."[46] Likewise, the virgin conception and birth, and Jesus' sinlessness and his absolute purity and transparency, are absolutely unbearable deviations from the ordinary human

---

42 See volume 2 (Paris: Aubier, 1960), 337–38, the Eucharist as less than the symbol of nature.
43 *Jésus dans la théorie chrétienne,* 149.
44 Cf. *Jésus dans la théorie chrétienne,* 151.
45 *Jésus dans la théorie chrétienne,* 152.
46 *Jésus dans la théorie chrétienne,* 152.

condition. As if the creature's "indelible wish" were not a pure being, a being without sin!

The eucharistic "illusion" is nevertheless a *sign* of the passage ("Jesus passing by") of an exceptional individual, and the sign remains, at least until his memory is in turn lost in the mists of the past. Like the Passover meal, the eucharistic meal, *an active memorial*, maintains and perpetuates a "real, effective contact" with his disciples. This is part of the question of the relevance of the Gospels of the "Rabbi Jesus."[47] The Gospel, certainly, is not enough, but it can help those who are attached to it "to hold fading questions very high."[48] It is slim. It is fragile. However, for lack of anything better, the Gospel can be "an exceptional sign."[49] Morel then measured himself against a "notable Christian,"[50] Pascal, about whom he gave a lecture in semiology.[51] He accuses Pascal of looking for miraculous signs and, not without some inconsistency on the part of our critic, of handling "oppositions" and "contraries," "this incapacity to be oneself,"[52] and finally, and again not without some inconsistency on the part of our thinker, of not loving the hidden God.[53] Saint John of the Cross is treated better, although he remained "partly captive" to the "prison of dogmas."[54]

The Eucharist is ultimately trivialized with the old refrain that it is a community meal and a commemorative banquet around the materials of bread and wine. In this way, according to Morel, the transient, banal being of Jesus is respected. It is therefore a question of "breaking with the Christian system of signs,"[55] but not with certain questions arising from this system. Christianity is a contradictory, eroded, half-dead system, whose problems persist. But we must not expect the decayed boat to sink itself. In fact, there is no shortage of axes, and the demolition crew is hard at work.

47 *Jésus dans la théorie chrétienne*, 191.

48 *Jésus dans la théorie chrétienne*, 195.

49 *Jésus dans la théorie chrétienne*, 205.

50 *Jésus dans la théorie chrétienne*, 205.

51 *Jésus dans la théorie chrétienne*, 210.

52 *Jésus dans la théorie chrétienne*, 210.

53 *Jésus dans la théorie chrétienne*, 212.

54 *Jésus dans la théorie chrétienne*, 216.

55 *Jésus dans la théorie chrétienne*, 216.

JEAN LADRIÈRE

With Jean Ladrière we are back to a Christian philosophy that is applied to the intelligibility of the Eucharist. But in this case it is not, as in Blondel, Marcel, and Fessard, an intelligible light that emanates from the eucharistic mystery to illuminate other subjects, with the Eucharist finding its justification in this illuminating capacity. It is rather the beam of philosophical reflection that is focused on or directed toward the Eucharistic Christ in order to better discern and penetrate its mysterious reality.

Ladrière is a philosopher of language. His paper at the Toulouse symposium, which was preparatory for the Eucharistic Congress in Lourdes (1981), entitled "Approche philosophique d'une réflexion sur l'Eucharistie,"[56] obviously gives importance, though not exclusively, to language and expression. After general considerations on faith and reason, philosophy and theology, which preserve the autonomy of philosophy (defined as "the effort of human reason to seize the more general conditions of experience"[57]), Ladrière defends the legitimacy of reason in the service of faith. That is to say, reason provides or proposes concepts to faith. It is up to theology to examine its appropriateness, its suitability. The medieval philosophical vocabulary was used for the Tridentine theory of the Blessed Sacrament. Ladrière does not at all say that this medieval vocabulary has had its day, but he indicates new concepts by which modern thought could make its way to the Eucharist: event, performativity, corporeality, historicity, order of ends, action.

a. The structural order is opposed to the order of the event, which is itself distinguished from the historical order. What happens is the event. And the pure, unconceptualizable event is evil. Salvation or deliverance will therefore belong to the order of events, to the gratuitous intervention and the unforeseeable initiative of God. The Eucharist, as a memorial of the Passion, is an event in the strong sense. And Ladrière means *each* Eucharist, and he is right to emphasize each, because if the Eucharist is magnified into something larger, the Eucharist is then often trivialized in its details, because of the multiplicity and quantity of the hosts. Multi-presence must not erase uniqueness. The monotony of the eucharistic currency is suppressed by the novelty and originality of each Eucharist, which is always sufficient for enriching the Church.

---

56 Published in the collection *Responsabilité, Partage, Eucharistie* (Paris: Éditions S.O.S., 1982).
57 *Responsabilité*, 138.

b. The heart of the event is constituted by the founding words of the Consecration (today modestly veiled in "the words of institution"). The word of the priest, the representative of Christ, is effective in what it signifies. Now, the notion of performativity (Austin) helps to some extent to understand the creative power of the word, the power of the creative word. Different from the statements which simply report ("the moon is red," "I have a headache"), performative statements convey an intention, incite an action: "read this book," "block the road," "I'm going over there," "stop the operation." Austin added to this distinction the pregnant notion of the "illocutionary force"—in short, the virtue of the verb—that characterizes and diversifies everything uttered within its contextual environment. Specifically, it is the illocutionary force of a promise, a commitment, a testament, an oath, or even an appointment, a declaration, a promotion, when the authority of the one who is speaking is invested with *ad hoc* power. This is where the instantaneous force of the creative word comes to light. *Dixit, et creata sunt.* Similarly, words like "I like," "I refuse," "I swear" can engage a whole purpose or destiny and can give shape to a series of events. History is spotted with these words that imprint on it the seal of the will, and that determine or force its course. Religious language (opaque to Wittgenstein) puts into play even more specific categories, if I dare say so, whose illocutionary force is part of an existential whole (for example the symbols of faith). And, within religious language, sacramental words form a case that goes beyond the act of speech strictly speaking, Ladrière remarks, and therefore it is not reducible to a magical rite.[58] Thus, the eucharistic word is the reproduction, the "re-actualization" of an originary and instituting word. It is not a quotation; it effects what it signifies, it inscribes an intention of an agent, the Church. Ladrière does not make use of the term *tautegory*, but the term would not be inappropriate. It is a performativity, and therefore it is *sui generis* and sacramental, derived from "the Eucharistic intention of Christ himself."[59]

c. The Eucharistic Christ is present in his body, which is the confounding point. Corporeality or incarnation helps us to understand "the connection between the body and presence." In short, corporeality is the subject-objectivity of the body, or the union of the soul and the body as a third substance, or the being and the having of the body, or the duality of

---

58 *Responsabilité*, 144.

59 *Responsabilité*, 146.

the objective body and the lived body. The analysis of corporeality is an advantage of modern philosophy. The body is the expression and instrument of the "self," that is to say, of presence. Concerning the risen body, philosophy is obviously neither very explicit nor very informed. But the eucharistic presence does take place, is real, in the form of food. Thus we have not left the sensible world behind. Food in general "makes our solidarity with the cosmos fully effective."[60] Here, one has the impression that Ladrière is following in the footsteps of Martelet, but it is only a quick shortcut. The body of Christ, in accordance with the remarkable analogy, connects us to the transfigured cosmos, makes the resurrected life emerge in us conspicuously, really incorporates us into the growth of the Mystical Body. By means of this, a dimension of sacred history is introduced that is correlative to the future of temporal existence.

d. The Eucharist "scans" the history of salvation.[61] This history is to be considered in the structural mode (of existential historicity), and the Eucharist "is at the heart of Christian historicity,"[62] it commemorates the "founding events" in the present tense of a re-actualization. "A sort of multiplied present makes all Eucharists coincide with the Last Supper," just as they make present the risen Body and thereby open up "to future realities." Temporal dimensions overlap in the Eucharist, leaving between those dimensions, however, the interval of faithful expectation, the condition of the itinerant. Eucharists mark the stages of a journey. The present of the Eucharist is both "a present of contemporaneity" and a present of an interval, of a path. How then is it possible to depict the end? The Kantian notion of an order of ends may be useful here.

e. Indeed, what is in question is "the establishment of an order of interhuman relations" (of an institutional system) that guarantees the recognition of freedoms, of free beings treated as ends and not as means. The concept of an order of ends allows us to think about this teleology. Kant resorts to analogies or parables of nature, the city, and the mystical body. A second nature, an ideal city or a city of ends, an ethical and spiritual community. It is the ultimate story of reason and action. By restoring the theological meaning of the *corpus mysticum*, the order of ends is given back its eschatological meaning, its meaning about the *eschaton*. But the Eucharist

60 *Responsabilité*, 150.
61 *Responsabilité*, 152.
62 *Responsabilité*, 153.

exhibits this eschatological dimension of salvation history, the growth of the body of Christ. It is a "realizing anticipation,"[63] the "place where what is to come is superimposed" in the present, the "two moments of salvific action." But it remains to think about the path, and the concept of action is helpful there.

f. Finality is abstract; concrete action effectively mediates, or conveys, free will and corporeality, the phenomenal reality. Action is this free initiative, this novelty, but one that reassumes the powers of the body. Its central moment is the decision[64] that unites all the forces in a "single thought." But action that sets the decision in motion is spread out over time, according to the requirement of action, which is finality.

"Action is interaction," reciprocity. But ultimately how is the horizon of reciprocity founded, how is action founded? Self-positioning is correlative to an "originary gift";[65] it is a call "to equal the magnitude of the gift." The gift of self responds to the originary donation. But evil is an internal, ontological obstacle, so that the (good) will can only accept *actual* signs by which salvation is thereby announced.

The Eucharist, which gives birth to a new man,[66] "assumes the action of man into the action of Christ"; it establishes an order of charity. "Nourished by the Eucharist," it "takes charge of its Christic efficacy" and becomes an "effective participation in the building up of the body of Christ." To put it concretely, it is by rejoining men in their fleshly being, in their corporeality, and also in their destitution, a destitution that Christ shared, overcame, and transformed into glory.

Jean Ladrière returned a certain number of concepts to their proper theological framework, thus restoring their supernatural destination (*kairos*, Word, incarnation, *Heilsgeschichte* or economy, mystical body and eschaton, action and service of Christ), and applied them to the Eucharist. The meditation on the Eucharist controlled the choice of terms, so to speak, on the other side of their philosophical significance. It is an excellent method for presenting the eucharistic mystery within an articulation of the truths of salvation. Here, the Eucharist, with the insistence on the word that accomplishes it in its articulation, is seen in the movement of the becoming and

---

63 *Responsabilité*, 158.

64 *Responsabilité*, 159.

65 *Responsabilité*, 160.

66 *Responsabilité*, 161.

the history of the Kingdom of God. It is conceived as a privileged moment or time of grace, an instrument of action and a call to action, as an action itself that is realized in the order of charity. There are so many "concrete approaches" that legitimize a very human and a very spiritual view of the Eucharist. But the givens of the mystery properly speaking are presupposed and are not made the subject of an exposition. That was the stance of the previous authors we selected (except Morel, of course).

YVES DE MONTCHEUIL

Ladrière's reflections are indeed "approaches," means of access that, presupposing the sacramental reality (transubstantiation and real presence), are brought to a synthetic view of the mystery. They witness to the desire to seek other paths for a theological elaboration, while not excluding what came before. It was an attempt of the same order, though in an extremely reserved and timid form, that appeared in Fr. Yves de Montcheuil's widely read article, "La raison de la permanence du Christ sous les espèces euchar-istiques d'après saint Bonaventure et saint Thomas."[67] Truth be told, at that time there also existed more or less clandestine texts in which Fr. de Mont-cheuil was more daring. But the "technical" article we are discussing is inter-esting insofar as it favors, in a way, St. Bonaventure. This relates to the problem of the fate of species, linked to the question of stercoranism. The solution of St. Thomas is well known: only the corruption of the species brings about the disappearance of the body and blood of Christ; nothing that externally affects the species can cause this disappearance: "to admit the cessation of the presence of the body of Christ for a reason other than the corruption of the species endangers the 'truth' of the sacrament."[68] However, it is not the same for St. Bonaventure. Without entering into a detailed discussion, the following is the conclusion that Yves de Montcheuil provides. The sacrament is for humanity. If this relationship disappears, Christ ceases to be present, regardless of the state of the species. The sacra-ment, that is to say the symbolic value, is essential to the Eucharist. Where the value of the sign ceases, as normally happens by the alteration of the species, Christ disappears. But it is because the symbolism is suppressed

---

67 Yves de Montcheuil, "La Raison de la Permanence du Christ sous les espèces eucharistiques d'après saint Bonaventure et saint Thomas," *Recherches de Science Religieuse* 29 (1939): 352–64.

68 de Montcheuil, 363.

that the destruction of the species leads to the disappearance of the real presence: all that ruins the sign undoes the real presence. It is therefore an analysis of the idea of the sacrament that controls the cessation of the presence, rather than the respect due to the body of Christ (when, for example, it is devoured by the mouse).[69]

Thus, under the guise of Bonaventure, Montcheuil sketched his preference for the sacramental aspect of the Eucharist and he inaugurated or relayed this period of eucharistic symbolism, which we are still living in (arising after some ten centuries of Catholic realism), a eucharistic symbolism that is not necessarily to the detriment of the reality of the real presence, as we see in Martelet.

ÉDOUARD POUSSET

The article of the late Fr. Édouard Pousset, SJ, published at the same time as Paul VI's encyclical *Mysterium Fidei,* is an original contribution, even if it relies on the unpublished notes of Fr. Joseph Moingt and, tacitly, on the intuitions of Fr. Fessard. The article is entitled "L'Eucharistie: Présence réelle et transsubstantiation"[70] and is principally concerned with the sacrament. It begins, however, with an overview dealing with the close interrelation of sacrament and sacrifice, and this through the necessity of death for the purpose of food and nuptial union, as well as the close interdependence of the Last Supper and the Cross. This last point had been emphasized by Fessard, who also recommended bringing together the Eucharist and Marriage, but Pousset's insistence strikes me as a bit forced.

In accordance with new trends in eucharistic theology, though they are also found earlier (recall the impulses of Fr. Faber), the eucharistic transformation, *mysterium fidei,* is a simple, ineffable act, like creation and the Incarnation, and it is not a miracle,[71] as nothing has shifted in the natural order. The author therefore endeavors to describe transubstantiation by its end, the nourishment of the body of Christ, and thus the result of the process more than the process itself. The result is the real presence, and it is this that we must first understand or clarify. The understanding of presence, in particular the relationship of an entirely spiritual presence (spiritual

---

69 "La raison," 360.

70 Édouard Pousset, "L'Eucharistie: Présence réelle et transsubstantiation," *Recherches de science religieuse* 54 (1966): 177–212.

71 Pousset, 204, 209.

nourishment) to a material and local presence, prepares the way for an understanding of the eucharistic conversion, in particular of the relationship between the feeble substance of bread and wine and the strong substance of the Body and Blood. The guiding thread of Pousset's sometimes adventurous considerations is Christ "being-food." A meditation on the *factus cibus viatorum* brings us back to everything else that is implied. It is framed by the Incarnation and the death of Christ, the Church as spouse, and the history of salvation. It therefore joins itself to a theological perspective, but its reference to "existential phenomenology" and to scholasticism gives it a philosophical relevance.

The prevailing dimension of personal, relational, and spiritual presence cannot be separated from a raw and local presence; the two are in dialectical relationship, just as the unity of the various moments of Christ forms a "total presence."[72] The subject's simple unity as "being there" must be understood simultaneously with all of his or her relationships.

Christ is present as (spiritual) food (and here there is a brief and unnamed reminder of Fr. Fessard's categories on corporeality): "He is present in the Eucharist as food";[73] he is there as substance. Pousset privileges a dynamic notion of substance: it is the unifying and totalizing principle of accidents and phenomena, though it is illusory to search for substance through them. Inert and slack thinking makes substance into a "substrate." Energetic thinking brings back its concrete aspect. In fact, there is a certain play between "substance" and "accidents," and the autonomy of the substance is defined by its capacity to "die" to its accidents, to be abstracted from them "without ceasing to be itself."[74] A weak substance, like a pebble, has almost no play in relation to its accidents. This is why a weakly substantial element (bread, wine) does not resist "the action of God who makes his own body therein."[75] Even as a natural substance, bread is easily eaten and transformed, *a fortiori* it is capable of undergoing a supernatural transformation.

Substance is not at all something physico-chemical, it is not a physico-chemical entity,[76] and this is why transubstantiation is not a physical process, nor is it based on the concept of nourishment. Substance is an active

---

72 Pousset, 187.

73 Pousset, 190.

74 Pousset, 196.

75 Pousset, 198.

76 Pousset, 200.

principle that unites the idea and the entity. Likewise, the substance of the body of Christ is the totalizing unity of both the whole and its accidents, as it is for every person. But the divinity in him introduces a process of radical death with a view to redemption. This capacity for a salvific self-destruction manifests itself in "an intermediate form of existence . . . the sacramental existence according to which he becomes food and is given to men."[77] The Eucharist is at the end of a "supernatural work" when it "comes to coincide with the work of men."[78]

The host is inseparable from a "natural, human, and divine history"[79] (and here again Fessard has left his mark). But transubstantiation can be analyzed in itself. Here one of Pousset's key ideas is verified, namely, that a feeble substantial element (bread), which itself results from the negation of a substance (wheat), lends itself to conversion into a spiritual nourishment, the body of Christ. But the accidents do not remain "in the air," as St. Thomas had thought, thus he had to resort to a miracle in order to explain their persistence. For they have an "intrinsic relation" to the nourishment of the Body, to the Body as spiritual nourishment. It suffices to keep them alive.

Does the rule of Christ being made present as food give an exclusive privilege to Mass and communion? This would be an erroneous thought. Eucharistic communion is relational, interpersonal. It must therefore be encompassed by a whole network of relationships that entail the reservation of the sacrament and all the worship that accompanies it.

Pousset's article opens up unexplored paths in certain respects, notably due to a differentiated concept of substance and to the consistent theme of the Eucharist as spiritual nourishment. Once the reality of presence and the change of substance are presupposed, the speculation unfolds boldly. The joint between the two substantial, or rather desubstantializing, processes is the food-substance. How one substance takes hold of the other is not made entirely clear in a study that showcases the transforming *action*, with its attendant risk of suggesting magic, a magical body. The high spiritual content of these pages nevertheless preserves the author from any semblance of idolatry. The exchange of the two substances under the sign of "suprasubstantial food" replicates the convergence of the Last Supper and

---

77 Pousset, 203.

78 Pousset, 204.

79 Pousset, 205.

the Cross. The Eucharist is the middle term of the two negations, eating and immolation. Pousset has thus also remembered the lessons from Hegel.

JEAN-LUC MARION

In order to partner with the Eucharistic Congress of Lourdes (1981), the journal *Communio* published the collection *L'Eucharistie pain nouveau pour un monde rompu*, in which a study by Jean-Luc Marion, "Le présent et le don,"[80] shines. Marion places himself on theological terrain, because, along with Heidegger, he does not accept the concept of Christian philosophy. But he restores philosophy by means of a critique of "the Eucharist submitted to metaphysics,"[81] *optimo sive pessimo*.

The presentation begins with a lively denunciation of the critics of the theology of transubstantiation. "Without a doubt there remains a definite presence of Christ, but it moves from the thing to the community,"[82] from the inertia of the thing to the life of consciousness. But this substitution makes the presence "strictly coincide" with the collective consciousness and perdures with it. It is "the immediate consciousness of the collective ego" that determines at present "the presence of God to the community." This presence is therefore affected by a "double dependency": that of the human consciousness—its presence and its attention. "The intermittencies of attention provoke the interim of presence."[83] One has thus traded a supposed idolatry for a subtle spiritual idolatry, precisely the one that Hegel attributed to Lutheranism. On the contrary, the exterior gift of the sacramental body assures the *distance* that thwarts the idol.

On the other hand, this new idolatry is an unwitting prisoner of a metaphysics of presence that has nothing to envy in the "reification" that it pretends to critique. What remains then is to "think the eucharistic presence without ceding to idolatry," "whether that of the (supposed) transubstantiated thing, or, evidently, that of the consciousness of the self, or that of metaphysics with its 'ordinary conception of time.'"[84] What to do then? J.-L.

---

80 "Le présent et le don," in *Revue Catholique Internationale Communio* 2, no. 6 (November 1977), reprinted in *L'Eucharistie, pain nouveau pour un monde rompu* (Paris: Fayard, 1981), 100–30. Citations are from the latter. [This article is modified and published in *God without Being*, 2nd ed. (Chicago: University of Chicago Press, 2012), 161–82. —Trans.]

81 "Le présent et le don," 113.

82 "Le présent et le don," 107.

83 "Le présent et le don," 110.

84 "Le présent et le don," 114.

Marion strives to think theologically of "the presence of the eucharistic gift."[85] The gift is temporalized in memorial and in the "epektasis" that governs the presence of the gift, the daily manna of time.[86] The present is a present, a gift. "The eucharistic present arranges . . . the temporality that is properly Christian"[87] and even christic.[88] It is within this ecstatic temporality that the "real presence" is situated and received. It is *received*: it is a demand. The real presence is exterior to and transcends the present of consciousness. In order to somehow deduce it, one should have recourse to a "logic of charity" or of the Cross, and all the rest is figurative, as Pascal says.[89] "The eucharistic present is deduced from an engagement with charity,"[90] initiated by the Incarnation, and "by the real building up of the ecclesial body of Christ."[91] The material union to the eucharistic body indicates a spiritual communion stricter than any "spiritual" union (here also, Pascal and Blondel would be welcome). Finally, against the profane conception of the *here* and *now* that governs the presence, a "theological gaze considers the eucharistic present as mystical," which does not diminish reality, but rather the contrary. *Res et sacramentum*, the real and the mystical body signified by the sacrament of the species (the *res* is *virtus unitatis et caritatis*). "The eucharistic present is deduced from the only theological 'reality,' which is mystical."[92]

Marion concludes with the necessity of a logic that is radically theological, supported by prayer. For the difficulties of the "theology of transubstantiation" only lead one to reflect on the *aporia* or the test of the "end of metaphysics" that was implicated here in "the vulgar concept of time," "and therefore the metaphysical discourse on presence." But, we must ask ourselves, what benefit should one assign to a Eucharist in which being and substance is time?

85 "Le présent et le don," 115.

86 "Le présent et le don," 120.

87 "Le présent et le don," 121.

88 "Le présent et le don," 116.

89 "Le présent et le don," 124.

90 "Le présent et le don," 125.

91 "Le présent et le don," 126.

92 "Le présent et le don," 128.

Conclusion

The Eucharist is a mystery of faith, *the* mystery of faith. The effort of theological reflection, and *a fortiori* philosophical reflection, must endeavor to illuminate the mystery, but while respecting it, while safe-guarding its character, which is supernatural, absolutely supernatural. This is not always the case, and the tendency, if not the temptation, of thinkers is to interpret this mystery of faith *par excellence* in rational or symbolic terms, so that it becomes comprehensible and explicable. Protestantism and modernism have evacuated the essence of the mystery by reducing it to a symbolism of shared bread and a community meal: the rite, the gesture, and the liturgy all bear their meaning in the performance itself, as the significa-tion absorbs the signifier. This is not to say that the ceremonial is without importance, for the sacramental mystery takes place at the heart of a sym-bolic and sacrificial ceremony, and sacraments cannot be detached from the ceremonial. The unbloody sacrifice of the altar, reiterating that of the Cross, and the sacramental consecration are of one piece, a single frame that is designated by the term "Eucharist," even with the ambivalence of its meaning. But, today, the laudable purpose of bringing out into relief the "bond of unity and of charity" leads to, or could lead to, a recognition and a preaching of a Eucharist that is simply figurative. This tendency (which is only a tendency, for one cannot prejudge the intentions) can be seen in the Dutch Catechism and the exegetical work of Léon-Dufour, for example. It may be that this satisfies some catechists. Frequent communion, very rec-ommendable in itself, has led to the banalization of communion, and the danger would be to consider the Eucharist as a simple agape meal, a banquet among friends, even if stylized and solemnized. In this banquet the host would only be the sign of a communion of faith and love and a presence of He who said that where two or three were gathered in his name, He would be in their midst. In reality, the *mysterium fidei* is the center that radiates outward, and besides the visible gathering of the faithful, it originates from the institution and the gift, and consequently it infinitely transcends those assembled and the presiding priest. Without this center, the gathering is only a parish meeting.

Reducing the revealed mysteries in order to make them more accessible, easier to digest, is not limited to the Eucharist, although it is the most refractive element of the Catholic economy. For the Incarnation, the virginal conception, and the Resurrection are equally reduced to rubble. Rationalism, therefore, whether latent or conscious, begins to unravel the foundation of the faith. The articulation of truths is such that, if one yields a point, the rest is disintegrated little by little and washed away: Christianity is treated like a "Christian theory" that can be contested as any other theory. But the pernicious action of rationalism (which reaches all the way to catechesis), and its poor sibling, modernism, must not throw us into the arms of a blind, vulnerable fideism. And fideism should not be confused with the faith of those who are simple, which is suitable to them insofar as they are simple, but, as believers, the simple can rise up to an effective and affective understanding of the supernatural that envies nothing of the practiced theologian.

The fact remains that speculative dexterity (whether that of the theologian or of the philosopher who often comes afterward) is repeatedly in danger of betraying the nature of the mystery that it is attempting to define, to specify. However, Descartes's first goal was not to provide an explanation, but, being solicited by theologians, to justify his teaching and its ability to be applied to the Eucharist, that is to say, not to contradict it and to render it unthinkable. But the intervention of the median extension leaves intact the conversion of the substances, which it presupposed, and is thus shown to not contradict the permanence of the accidents. In fact, when Descartes advances toward the dangerous question about the mode of Christ's real presence in the Blessed Sacrament, he understands it as a transforming, metabolic union of the soul of Christ with the materiality of the bread and wine. The suspicion (and it is only a suspicion) of impanation renders the hypothesis doubtful, and, even before having been disseminated, invalid. Descartes withdraws in good order, retires his conjecture, and, good Christian that he is, takes refuge behind the Council of Trent's partial confession of impotence. This is also Malebranche's almost discouraged conclusion after a series of arguments that are all the more embarrassing because they respond to false problems. And Leibniz, likewise directed to the question about the permanence of the *species*, formulates the famous hypothesis of the substantial bond for the sake of Fr. Des Bosses. The substantial bond relates to his concern to not touch the monads and their representations, which is simply out of the question for him. But the expression "substantial bond" is equivalent to "substance" in the theory of transubstantiation; the substantial bond is substantializing, it realizes phenomena, it substantializes the monad or monads, it is the invasion, or at least the indication, of a "superior realism" in the universe reflecting and reflected by the Leibnizian monadology. But Leibniz's responses, as well as those of Descartes, are concentrated on this difficult question: what has changed if nothing has changed in appearance? In any case, the instantaneous mutation occurs in the eucharistic object itself, and philosophy has the task of giving an account of the invisibility of the process of substantial mutation.

Leibniz's and Descartes's theories, especially the latter's, are physical theories, as they crudely pose the question of a eucharistic physics. Can one ignore this by abstracting from the physical aspect of the eucharistic transformation? Is eucharistic physics at an impasse, and is it an obsolete area of research? Has it made its last desperate attempt, after three centuries of discussion, in the quarrel that was ignited during the 1950s between Fr. Filippo Selvaggi and Msgr. Carlo Colombo? Is this "quarrel of another age" definitively closed? Colombo outright declared (in the footsteps of Fr. Josef Ternus, who, according to Clark, leaves us as "orphans in the world of intelligence") that the composition of matter, atoms, molecules, and protons have absolutely nothing to do with eucharistic transubstantiation. Ultimately, he pronounces a eucharistic agnosticism. According to him, in the host as such, in the eucharistic object, nothing happens, and the finest analysis will not discover anything, and with good reason! The change is metaphysical, without impacting the physical plane. Colombo, who in fact won the debate, unintentionally lent a hand to all the symbolists and sacramentarians who transfer the mystery of transmutation to the *subject* of the Eucharist. Selvaggi had begun with a good intention, but this was spoiled by his eucharistic concordism. It seemed to him that he had found in the atomic structure of matter, as modern physicists analyze it, the split between substance and accidents. Consequently, one could predetermine materially that which changes and that which does not. Put on the defense, he was constrained to a position of despair, such that even if achieved by the most powerful instruments, the ultimate recesses of the consecrated matter would reveal nothing more and nothing less than the corpuscles that were there before. It was necessary for him to have the courage to say that our senses and our intelligence deceive us and that we should see the body of Christ where the elements of bread are found. *Visus, tactus, gustus in te fallitur. Sed auditu solo tuto creditur.* Thus Selvaggi conceded much to Colombo and to his subjective fideism, except as regards the absolutely undetectable reality of a physical mutation.

Is a material transubstantiation a false problem such that every scientific foray into the question is doomed to failure? It is reckless to say so, because the species at least are not metaphysical. But one would be mistaken to transpose a theory of physics onto a eucharistic theory. Moving away from the Charybdis of a miniature Christ shriveled up in the Blessed Sacrament by replication and penetrability, one falls into the Scylla of a substitution of heterogeneous atoms and an incredible quantitative upheaval! Science should not be taken completely out of play, provided that one considers physicality and matter from another angle, as a source of analogies, as a clarifying and re-clarifying area for the subject of the Eucharist. The abstract network of signs and calculations and formulas, which is how the modern scholar, instructed by quantum theory, ultimately considers reality, renders the Eucharist's coalescence of thing and sign, without distance, less strange to a scientific mind. Fr. Richard G. Cipolla notes that physical reality is not, in the end, a series of instruments; it is rather "holistic," interrelational, ineffable, mysterious. The well of matter has no bottom, it is inexhaustible. The sacramental world is not discontinuous with the physical world.

At the same time, an extrapolation would be dangerous, and this line of thought does not go beyond comparisons or beyond a physical analogy. More fruitful, because more magnificent, is the direction set out by Teilhard's eucharistic speculation, which is at the heart of the divinization of matter. The consecration of the universe precedes and envelops the consecration of the host. A fragment of matter is able to concentrate in itself the fire of sacrifice, because all matter radiates from the substance of God like a rising sun. But the mode of the physical presence of Christ in the universe, the Cosmic Christ, the universal Christ, acknowledged by the Pauline hymns, is difficult to characterize. The identity of the cosmic Body, even as it is glorified, is at least as puzzling as the identity of the human Body and the Eucharistic Body (see Martelet). Also, by no means does Teilhard mean to deny transubstantiation by replacing it with the adoration of matter, for he suggests above all a mystical vision, the world illuminated by the eucharistic revelation.

Indeed, Teilhardian realism is a sacramentalism, as the elements of the world, kneaded by human work, are transmuted into manifest and pregnant signs of presence. It is the great patristic doctrine that has never separated the eucharistic mystery from the life of grace and the organic whole of sanctification, from the world and men. This is the point of view of spiritual authors, rediscovered in our day by theologians and philosophers of the Eucharist: to deploy the intelligible riches of eucharistic belief, to extract the multiform understanding of the simple truth of the *Hoc est Corpus . . .* and this only by the power of that which is given to thought, for the Eucharist itself is its own proof. But the peril is that the beauty and the pregnancy of the symbol would obliterate the realism of the affirmation, and that the signifying host would only function as an analogue. What is admirable in the eucharistic sketches of Rosmini, Blondel, and Simone Weil is that the opulence of significations does not stifle the simplicity of the ontological affirmation (without ignoring the gnosis and syncretism of Simone Weil). Rosmini, with his intense idea of a life that is eucharistic, mysterious, and hidden, resituates the Eucharist in its native place, the subject: that of Christ or the faithful. The objectifying perspective, which was dominant for many centuries, has been downgraded for the subject's act or word, the subject for whom presence is its term, result, and horizon. The traditional image of food, then, of nourishment—*factus cibus viatorum*—takes precedence over the substantial mutation, which does not do equal justice to a subjective process.

Is a eucharistic physics always already outdated, then, and should one impose silence on the problems that it raises? It seems that one removes nothing of the plenitude of Christ's eucharistic presence in leaving aside the problems of quantity, of the position of the members, of perception, which freeze the difference between the appearance and reality and deprive the species of their full signification: "under [*sous*] the species" does not mean "underneath [*en dessous*]," even though we say "under [*sous*] the veil" or "below [*par-dessous*] the veil," for it is *as species* of bread and wine, in a specific mode. Many more or less idle considerations, even those that have provided beautiful developments for spiritual writers, should not be revived. They are bygone theological examples, venerable intellectual relics, but they respond to a dated mentality. The questions that surround stercoranism or the "problem of the mouse" thus belong to an excessive scholastic subtlety. For instance, Rosmini's conception of the consecrated bread and wine as so many local appendices of the glorious body of Christ. However, the same glorious Christ is integrally and really present *in* the sacrament, and Pius XII, before Paul VI, energetically pronounced warnings against the debilitating explanations that only note a "real and essential relation of volume and presence" between the species and "the Lord in heaven." *A fortiori* if one turns the consecrated species only into efficacious signs of a spiritual presence. The pope rises up against this tendency to "remove Christ from the Eucharist" and to leave in the tabernacle only the species with the kind of relationship just mentioned. This is a useful precaution in a time where, as a consequence and as a reaction against the reification of the Eucharist, there is a backlash of symbolism that is equipped with a *sui generis* but impalpable reality. Besides, it suffices to read St. Thomas's articles in the *Summa* (III, qq. 73–83), which are so weighty and balanced, in order to avoid believing too much or believing too little, as it were.

By means of the Eucharist, Christ becomes present under the species; by means of the Eucharist, he makes himself food, he is our food. *Factus cibus*. This is not at all to diminish the permanence of the real presence, the devotion to the tabernacle, processions, the reservation of the Eucharist, visiting the tabernacle, or perpetual adoration, but only to insist on the original act of communion, on the sacred bread as a vehicle of spiritual nourishment. The idea of the "divine prisoner in the tabernacle," of Christ who expects the silence of his adorers and friends "who keep him company," is very beautiful and comes from an irreproachable spirituality, but this act of passivity comes second. The gesture of communion (of Christ and of the faithful) evokes the initiative of the subject who gives himself in his gift, with an absolutism that is precisely the leading edge of the mystery. In this sense, the image of the legendary pelican—*Pie pellicane, Jesu Domine*—is even more eloquent than that of the lamb. The Eucharist as communion, as a union and relation of subjects, is the key to the sacrament. This is not to reduce the identity of the human body of Christ and the eucharistic body— "this is my body which will be given up for you"—but only to situate it in the words of the memory of the institution with the echo of the eucharistic discourse. The meaning of communion would, then, appear in the very will of Him who institutes it, and in the immediate relationship of the word with food. From this point of view, the intuition of Rosmini, who centers his eucharistic explanation on the communion of Christ, on the food that Christ transubstantiated by communing, appears to me to be far reaching and rich in promises.

The best eucharistic theory is not the one that isolates some aspects from others, and which decomposes the sacrament into a multiplicity of objective givens, but is rather the one that embraces the amplitude of the mystery and synthesizes as many aspects as possible. Blondel, who only treated the Eucharist indirectly, manages to leave nothing dissociated and to show the Eucharist as the goal of the theandric or hypostatic union inaugurated by the condescension of the Incarnation. Here again, the Eucharist is the bond par excellence, for it attaches all the truths of the Credo to one another.

A philosophy of the Eucharist presupposes at the same time the permanent conceptual help that philosophy (logical and metaphysical) gives to theology, and on the other hand the speculative benefit that faith brings to Christian philosophy. However, at times philosophy withdraws or declares itself incompetent. Edouard Le Roy's pragmatism leaves the proof of faith up to gestures and behaviors, leaving the formulation of dogmas at liberty. But this eucharistic agnosticism leads to a philosophy of *as if*, of *als ob*, which deprives the faith of intellectual certitude with all its harmonics. On the other hand, the mystery as a proof of the ontological affirmation, for example as in Gabriel Marcel, reveals its capacity to clarify the categories of existence.

Indeed, there is a "logic of the Eucharist" that comes to light, according to Jean Guitton,[1] in three types of philosophy: that of nature (realism), that of the spirit (idealism), and that of existence (existentialism). The existential type adds a commitment, a subjective implication, to the other two, rather than being numbered with them. Guitton dreams of a philosophy that could combine the advantages of the three perspectives and, naturally, he sees it in the suggestion of Leibniz. But Pascal is equally close to such a "logic of charity." The only question is whether philosophy as such will rise to the *ordo amoris*, as Max Scheler said.

The philosophy of the Eucharist is legitimate when the Eucharist is offered to the mind as a given that is to be understood, while the decision has already been made in faith. Hegel assumes to himself the right to give different interpretations of the sacrament of the Last Supper and to attribute to them a speculative value. Thus, eucharistic mysticism is relativized. It is the Protestant philosophy of the Eucharist that suffers from the diversity of belief. The philosophy of the Eucharist is only a eucharistic philosophy in Catholicism, for only in Catholicism does it call the intelligence to be elevated to the heights of so great a mystery: Leibniz had to borrow the Catholic belief in order to elaborate the theory of the substantial bond; Simone Weil, who was unbaptized, meditates intensely on the statements of the catechism. Eucharistic philosophy is very close to the metaphysics of charity, so dear to Blondel and Laberthonnière. It tries less to extract implicated truths from the Eucharist than to orient itself in relation to this landmark, according to this compass needle. It considers the mark of Christ on

1 Jean Guitton, "Logique de l'Eucharistie," *Revue Catholique Internationale Communio* 2, no. 5 (September 1977): 56–60.

philosophy, especially from the impression made by the Eucharist. *Panis vitae et intellectus.* This is why there are few examples of philosophical research into the sphere of influence of the Eucharistic Christ, and, where it actually does appear, it is said in few words. But if one takes the trouble to gather the grain, even to glean what has fallen to the ground, then indeed the crop can bring about beautiful first fruits for a great eucharistic work for our times. The heroic Fr. Yves de Montcheuil hoped for this and began himself to collect the materials.

Thus this long path, which perhaps has wearied the attention of the reader, concludes with a question, since the mystery must keep its obscurity. However, it will not have been pointless if one has followed the effort of the philosophers, which supported the theologians, to account for the vicissitudes of the remarks. Certainly, there is not, strictly speaking, a eucharistic philosophy that would supply the kind of physics that has disappeared since the work of Descartes and Leibniz. But the integration of the mystery into philosophy, especially as seen in Pascal, Rosmini, and Blondel, has been beneficial to philosophy (Blondel's metaphysics of charity) and advantageous for devotion, for example, in Fr. Faber, Bishop Gay, and Dom Marmion. This is a different story from that of the growth of the Blessed Sacrament in the life of the Church, the liturgy, and mysticism. Happily, there is no shortage of historians and spiritual writers to recount this story and to be nourished by it. Despite its austerity, eucharistic philosophy is no stranger to piety, and it daily feeds priestly meditation:

Sub diversis speciebus
Latent res eximiae.

May the adoration of the Blessed Sacrament, the Eucharistic Congress, and the *Katholikentag* time and again maintain the sanctuary lamp, the flame of the tabernacle.

The Year of the Eucharist
Paris, June 12, 2005

Bibliography

Agamben, Giorgio. *The Omnibus Homo Sacer*. Meridian Crossing Aesthetics. Stanford, California: Stanford University Press, 2017.

Armogathe, Jean-Robert. "Dom Desgabets et Port-Royal." *Chroniques de Port-Royal* 17–18 (1969): 68–87.

———. Review of *Pascal et Descartes*, by M. Le Guern. *Archives de Philosophie* 36, no. 3 (1973): 460–61.

———. *Theologia Cartesiana: L'explication physique de l'Eucharistie chez Descartes et Dom Desgabets*. Archives internationales d'histoire des idées 84. La Haye: Nijhoff, 1977.

Baader, Franz Xaver von. *Sämtliche Werke*. Edited by Franz Hoffman and Julius Hamb. 16 vols. Aalen: Scientia Verlag, 1963.

Balthasar, Hans Urs von. *Theologik I: Wahrheit der Welt*. Einsiedeln: Johannes Verlag, 1985.

Billot, Louis. *De Eucharistia*. Rome: Spellani, 1889.

Blondel, Maurice. *De vinculo substantiali et de substantia composita apud Leibnitium*. Paris: Alcan, 1893.

———. *Une énigme historique: Le "Vinculum Substantiale" d'après Leibniz et l'ébauche d'un realisme supérieur*. Paris: Beauchesne, 1930.

———. *La Philosophie et l'Esprit chrétien*. 2 vols. Paris: Presses Universitaires de France, 1944–6.

———. *Exigences philosophiques du christianisme*. Paris: Presses Universitaires de France, 1950.

———. *Carnets intimes (1883–1894)*. Paris: Éditions du Cerf, 1961.

———. *Lettres philosophiques*. Paris: Aubier, 1961.

———. *Dialogues avec les philosophes: Descartes, Spinoza, Malebranche, Pascal, Saint Augustin*. Bibliothèque Philosophique. Paris: Aubier, Éditions Montaigne, 1966.

———. *Le lien substantiel et la substance composée d'après Leibniz*. Louvain-Paris: Nauwelaerts, 1972.

———. *Action: Essay on a Critique of Life and a Science of Practice*. Translated by Oliva Blanchette. Notre Dame: University of Notre Dame Press, 1984.

Boehm, Alfred. *Le "Vinculum Substantiale" chez Leibniz: Ses origines historiques*. Études de Philosophie Médiévale 26. Paris: Vrin, 1962.

Bouillard, Henri. "L'intention fondamentale de Maurice Blondel et la théologie." *Recherches de Science Religieuse* 36 (1949).

———. *Blondel et le christianisme*. Paris: Éditions du Seuil, 1961.

Bouillier, Francisque. *Histoire de la philosophie cartésienne*. 3 vols. Paris: Durand, 1854.

Bowman, Frank Paul. *Le Christ romantique*. Histoire des idées et critique littéraire 134. Genève: Droz, 1973.

Catholic Church. *Compendium of Creeds, Definitions, and Declarations on Matters of Faith and Morals*. Edited by Peter Hünermann, Helmut Hoping, Robert L. Fastiggi, Anne Englund Nash, and Heinrich Denzinger. 43rd ed. San Francisco: Ignatius Press, 2012.

Chardin, Pierre Teilhard de. *Le milieu divin*. Oeuvres de Pierre Teilhard de Chardin. Paris: Éditions du Seuil, 1957.

———. *Genèse d'une pensée: Lettres 1914–1919*. Paris: Grasset, 1961.

———. *Hymne de l'univers: La Messe sur le monde, Trois histoires comme Benson, La Puissance spirituelle de la matière*. Edited by Fernande Tardivel. Oeuvres de Pierre Teilhard de Chardin. Paris: Éditions du Seuil, 1961.

———. *Écrits du temps de la guerre (1916–1919)*. Paris: Grasset, 1965.

———. *Science et Christ*. Oeuvres de Pierre Teilhard de Chardin. Paris: Éditions du Seuil, 1965.

Chauvet, Louis-Marie. *Symbol and Sacrament: A Sacramental Reinterpretation of Christian Existence*. Translated by Patrick Madigan and Madeline Beaumont. Collegeville, MN: Liturgical Press, 1995.

Chrétien, Jean-Louis. *The Ark of Speech*. Translated by Andrew Brown. New York: Routledge, 2003.

Claudel, Paul. *Positions et propositions*. 2 vols. Paris: Gallimard, 1928.

———. *La Messe Là-Bas de Paul Claudel*. Edited by Marie-Joséphine Whitaker. Annales littéraires de l'Université de Franche-Comté 850. Besançon: Presses Universitaires de Franche-Comté, 2009.

Couture, Léonce. "Commentaire d'un fragment de Pascal sur l'Eucharistie." *Bulletin théologique, scientifique et littéraire de l'Institut Catholique de Toulouse* X (1898).

de Maistre, Joseph. *St Petersburg Dialogues, or, Conversations on the Temporal Government of Providence*. Edited by Richard Lebrun. Montréal: McGill-Queens University Press, 1993.

Descartes, René. *Principles of Philosophy*. Translated by Valentine Rodger Miller and Reese P. Miller. Dordrecht, Netherlands: Reidel, 1983.

———. *Meditations, Objections, and Replies*. Edited and translated by Roger Ariew and Donald Cress. Hackett Classics Series. Indianapolis: Hackett, 2006.

———. "Selected Correspondence of Descartes." Translated by Jonathan Bennett, 2017. https://www.earlymoderntexts.com/assets/pdfs/descartes1619_4.pdf.

Döllinger, Johann Joseph Ignaz von. *Die Lehre von der Eucharistie in den drei ersten Jahr-hunderten*. Mainz, 1826.

Falque, Emmanuel. *The Wedding Feast of the Lamb: Eros, the Body, and the Eucharist*. New York: Fordham University Press, 2016.

Fessard, Gaston. *La dialectique des exercices spirituels de Saint Ignace de Loyola*. Théologie. Paris: Aubier, 1956.

Feuerbach, Ludwig. *The Essence of Christianity*. Translated by George Eliot. London: Kegan Paul, Trench, Trübner & Co., 1890.

Fichte, Johann Gottlieb. *The Way towards the Blessed Life; or, The Doctrine of Religion*. Trans-lated by W. Smith. London: Strand, 1849.

Flamand, Jacques. *L'idée de méditation chez Maurice Blondel*. Philosophes contemporains. Textes et Études 15. Louvain: Nauwelaerts, 1969.

Goldman, Lucien. *Le Dieu caché: Étude sur la vision tragique dans les Pensées de Pascal et dans le Théâtre de Racine*. Bibliothèque des idées. Paris: Gallimard, 1955.

Gouhier, Henri. *La pensée religieuse de Descartes*. Études de philosophie médiévale 6. Paris: Vrin, 1924.

———. *Essais sur Descartes*. Essais d'art et de philosophie. Paris: Vrin, 1937.

———. *Les premières Pensées de Descartes: Contribution à l'histoire de l'Anti-Renaissance*. De Pétrarque à Descartes 2. Paris: Vrin, 1958.

———. *Blaise Pascal: Commentaires*. Paris: Vrin, 1966.

———. *Cartésianisme et Augustinisme au XVIIe siècle*. Paris: Vrin, 1978.

Guitton, Jean. "Logique de l'Eucharistie." *Revue Catholique Internationale Communio* 2, no. 5 (September 1977): 56–60.

———. "Quelques observations sur la pensée de Simone Weil concernant l'Eucharistie." *Cahiers Simone Weil*, March 1982, 15–21.

Hamann, Johann Georg. *Sämtliche Werke*. Edited by Josef Nadler. 3 vols. Vienna: Herder, 1949.

Hegel, Georg Wilhelm Friedrich. *Lectures on the History of Philosophy*. 3 vols. London: Kegan Paul, Trench, Trübner & Co., 1896.

———. *On Christianity: Early Theological Writings*. New York: Harper, 1961.

———. *The Phenomenology of Spirit*. Translated by Terry P. Pinkard. Cambridge Hegel Translations. Cambridge: Cambridge University Press, 2018.

Henry, Michel. *Words of Christ*. Translated by Christina M. Gschwandtner. Interventions. Grand Rapids, MI: William B. Eerdmans Publishing Company, 2012.

Hölderlin, Friedrich. "Bread and Wine." Translated by Susan Ranson. sites.google.com/site/germanliterature/19th-century/hoelderlin/brot-und-wein-bread-and-wine.

Kant, Immanuel. *Religion within the Boundaries of Mere Reason*. Edited and translated by Allen Wood, George di Giovanni, and Robert Merrihew Adams. Cambridge: Cambridge University Press, 1998.

———. *Anthropology from a Pragmatic Point of View*. Edited by Robert B. Louden. Cambridge Texts in the History of Philosophy. Cambridge: Cambridge University Press, 2006.

Kaplan, Francis. *Les Pensées de Pascal*. Paris: Éditions du Cerf, 1982.

Labrousse, Élisabeth. *Pierre Bayle*. 2 vols. La Haye: Nijhoff, 1963.

Lacoste, Jean-Yves. *L'intuition sacramentelle et autres essais*. Philosophie. Paris: Ad Solem, 2015.

Ladrière, Jean. "Approche philosophique d'une réflexion sur l'Eucharistie." In *Responsabilité, Partage, Eucharistie*. Paris: Éditions S.O.S., 1982.

Latourelle, René, and Gerald O'Collins. "Is a Philosophical Christology Possible?" In *Problems and Perspectives of Fundamental Theology*, translated by Matthew J. O'Connell, 135–50. New York: Paulist Press, 1982.

Le Guern, Michel. *Pascal et Descartes*. Paris: Nizet, 1971.

Le Roy, Édouard. *Dogme et Critique*. 5th ed. Paris: Bloud et Cie, 1907.

Leclerc, Marc. "La Finalité chez Leibniz. Introduction à l'interprétation Blondélienne." Catholic University of Louvain, 1982.

Leibniz, Gottfried Wilhelm von. *Gothofredi Guillelmi Leibnitii: Opera Omnia*. Edited by Louis Dutens. 6 vols. Geneva, 1768.

———. *Lettres et opuscules inédits de Leibniz*. Edited by Foucher de Careil. Paris: Ladrange, 1854.

———. *Nouvelles lettres et opuscules inédits de Leibniz*. Edited by Foucher de Careil. Paris: Durand, 1857.

———. *Die philosophischen Schriften*. Edited by Karl Immanuel Gerhardt. 7 vols. Berlin: Weidmann, 1870.

———. *Leibniz*. Edited by Jean Baruzi. La pensée chrétienne: Textes et études. Paris: Bloud, 1909.

———. *Sämtliche Schriften und Briefe: Allgemeiner politischer und historischer Briefwechsel*. 10 vols. Berlin: Akademie Verlag, 1979.

———. *L'être et la relation: Avec trente-sept lettres de Leibniz au R.P. Des Bosses*. Edited and translated by Christiane Frémont. Paris: Vrin, 1981.

Leibniz, Gottfried Wilhelm von, and Antoine Arnauld. *The Leibniz-Arnauld Correspondence: With Selections from the Correspondence with Ernst, Landgrave of Hessen-Rheinfels*. Translated by Stephen Voss. The Yale Leibniz. New Haven: Yale University Press, 2016.

Lemaire, Paul. *Le Cartésianisme chez les Bénédictins: Dom Robert Desgabets.* Paris: Alcan, 1901.

Léon-Dufour, Xavier. *Le pain de la vie.* Parole de Dieu. Paris: Éditions du Seuil, 2005.

Mahamé, Chrysologue. "Spiritualité et philosophie chez Maurice Blondel de 1883 à 1893." Institut Catholique de Paris, 1967.

Malebranche, Nicolas de. *Oeuvres complètes de Malebranche.* Edited by André Robinet. 20 vols. Paris: Vrin, 1958.

Mallarmé, Stéphane. *Divagations.* Translated by Barbara Johnson. Cambridge, MA: Harvard University Press, 2007.

Marcel, Gabriel. *Du refus à l'invocation.* Paris: Gallimard, 1940.

———. *Essai de philosophie concrète.* Paris: Gallimard, 1940.

———. *Présence et immortalité.* Homo sapiens. Paris: Flammarion, 1959.

Marion, Jean-Luc. "Le présent et le don." *Revue Catholique Internationale Communio* 2, no. 6 (November 1977): 50–70.

———. *Sur la théologie blanche de Descartes: Analogie, création des vérités éternelles et fondement.* Philosophie d'aujourd'hui. Paris: Presses Universitaires de France, 1981.

———. *God Without Being.* Translated by Thomas A. Carlson. 2nd ed. Religion and Postmodernism. Chicago: University of Chicago Press, 2012.

Martelet, Gustave. *Résurrection, Eucharistie, genèse de l'homme.* Paris: Desclée, 1972. Translated as *The Risen Christ and the Eucharistic World.* New York: Seabury Press, 1976.

———. *Teilhard de Chardin, prophète d'un Christ toujours plus grand.* Au Singulier 10. Brussels: Lessius, 2005.

Mathieu, Vittorio. *Leibniz e Des Bosses, 1706–1716.* Turin: Giappichelli, 1960.

Mayes, Robert J. H. "The Lord's Supper in the Theology of Cyprian of Carthage." *Concordia Theological Quarterly* 74 (2010): 307–24.

Monaco, Matteo, ed. *Bibliografia di Xavier Tilliette.* Trieste: Edizioni Università di Trieste, 2002.

Montcheuil, Yves de. "La raison de la permanence du Christ sous les espèces eucharistiques d'après Saint Bonaventure et Saint Thomas." *Recherches de Science Religieuse* 29 (1939): 352–64.

Morel, Georges. *Sens de l'existence selon Saint Jean de la Croix.* 3 vols. Theologie. Paris: Aubier, 1960.

———. *Jésus dans la théorie chrétienne.* Présence et Pensée. Paris: Aubier-Montaigne, 1977.

Muzio, Giuseppe. "Il senso ortodosso e tomistico delle quaranta proposizioni rosminiane: Testi di Rosmini e di S. Tommaso." *Sodalitas Thomistica*, no. 6–7 (1963).

Nancy, Jean-Luc. *Corpus*. Translated by Richard Rand. Perspectives in Continental Philosophy. New York: Fordham University Press, 2008.

———. *The Disavowed Community*. Translated by Philip Armstrong. Commonalities. New York: Fordham University Press, 2016.

Pascal, Blaise. *Pensées et Opuscules*. Edited by Léon Brunschvicg. Paris: Hachette, 1909.

———. *Thoughts, Letters, Minor Works*. Translated by W. F. Trotter, M. L. Booth, and O. W. Wight. The Harvard Classics 48. New York: P.F. Collier & Son Co., 1910.

Pickstock, Catherine. *After Writing: On the Liturgical Consummation of Philosophy*. Oxford: Blackwell Publishers, 1997.

Pousset, Édouard. "L'Eucharistie: Présence réelle et transsubstantiation." *Recherches de Science Religieuse* 54 (1966): 177–212.

Raffelt, Albert. *Spiritualität und Philosophie: Zur Vermittlung Geistig-Religiöser Erfahrung in Maurice Blondels "L'Action" (1893)*. Freiburger Theologische Studien 110. Freiburg: Herder, 1978.

Rahner, Karl. "The Theology of the Symbol." In *Theological Investigations IV*, translated by Kevin Smyth, 221–52. London: Darton, Longman, and Todd, 1974.

Rex, Walter. *Essays on Pierre Bayle and Religious Controversy*. International Archives of the History of Ideas 8. La Haye: Nijhoff, 1965.

Rosmini, Antonio. *Opere edite ed inedite di Antonio Rosmini*. Edited by Enrico Castelli and Michele Federico Sciacca. 80 vols. Rome-Stresa, 1966.

———. *Introduction to Philosophy*. Translated by Robert A. Murphy. Durham, UK: Rosmini House, 2004.

Russo, Antonio, ed. *Xavier Tilliette inedito*. Collana di filosofia italiana 19. Milan: Franco Angeli, 2020.

Schillebeeckx, Edward. *The Eucharist*. London: Sheed & Ward, 1968.

———. *L'économie sacramentelle du salut: Réflexion théologique sur la doctrine sacramentaire de saint Thomas, à la lumière de la tradition et de la problématique sacramentelle contemporaine*. Translated by Yvon van der Have. Studia Friburgensia 95. Fribourg: Academic Press Fribourg, 2004.

Schleiermacher, Friedrich. *The Christian Faith*. Edited by Hugh Ross Mackintosh and James S. Stewart. Edinburgh: T & T Clark, 1928.

Schrecker, Paul. "G.-W. Leibniz: Lettres et Fragments Inédits." *Revue philosophique de la France et de l'étranger* 118, no. 7/8 (1934): 5–134.

Seils, Martin. *Theologische Aspekte zur gegenwärtigen Hamann-Deutung*. Göttingen: Vandenhoeck & Ruprecht, 1957.

Sokolowski, Robert. *Eucharistic Presence: A Study in the Theology of Disclosure.* Washington, DC: The Catholic University of America Press, 1994.

Stancampiano, Simone. "Xavier Tilliette: Fede e sapere in dialogo." *Il giornale di filosofia,* April 30, 2007. http://www.giornaledifilosofia.net/public/scheda.php?id=78.

Tilliette, Xavier. *Schelling: Une philosophie en devenir. 1, le système vivant: 1794–1821.* Bibliothèque d'histoire de la philosophie. Paris: Vrin, 1970.

———. *Schelling: Une philosophie en devenir. 2, la dernière philosophie: 1821–1854.* Bibliothèque d'histoire de la philosophie. Paris: Vrin, 1970.

———. "Problèmes de philosophie eucharistique." *Gregorianum* 64, no. 2 (1983): 273–305.

———. "Problèmes de philosophie eucharistique II." *Gregorianum* 65, no. 4 (1984): 605–34.

———. *La christologie idéaliste.* Jésus et Jésus-Christ 28. Paris: Desclée, 1986.

———. *L'absolu et la philosophie: Essais sur Schelling.* 1. éd. Épiméthée. Paris: Presses Universitaires de France, 1987.

———. *Le Christ de la philosophie: Prolégomènes à une christologie philosophique.* Cogitatio fidei 155. Paris: Éditions du Cerf, 1990.

———. "Henri de Lubac: The Legacy of a Theologian." *Communio: International Catholic Review* 19, no. 3 (Fall 1992): 332–41.

———. *La semaine sainte des philosophes.* Jésus et Jésus-Christ 53. Paris: Desclée, 1992.

———. *Le Christ des philosophes: Du Maître de sagesse au divin Témoin.* Ouvertures 10. Namur: Culture et vérité, 1993.

———. "Notes and Reflections on the Virtue of Hope." *Communio: International Catholic Review* 23, no. 3 (Fall 1996): 441–47.

———. "The Chastity of Jesus." *Communio: International Catholic Review* 24, no. 1 (Spring 1997): 51–56.

———. *Schelling: Biographie.* Les vies des philosophes. Paris: Calmann-Lévy, 1999.

———. *Les philosophes lisent la Bible.* Philosophie & théologie. Paris: Éditions du Cerf, 2001.

———. "Trinity and Creation." *Communio: International Catholic Review* 28, no. 2 (Summer 2001): 296–310.

———. *Jésus Romantique.* Jésus et Jésus-Christ 85. Paris: Desclée, 2002.

———. *La mythologie comprise: Schelling et l'interprétation du paganisme.* Bibliothèque d'histoire de la philosophie. Paris: Vrin, 2002.

———. *L'Église des philosophes: De Nicolas de Cuse à Gabriel Marcel.* Philosophie & théologie. Paris: Éditions du Cerf, 2006.

———. *Philosophies eucharistiques de Descartes à Blondel.* Philosophie & théologie. Paris: Éditions du Cerf, 2006.

———. *Eucaristia e filosofia.* Translated by Giuliano Sansonetti. Filosofia. Nuova serie / Morcelliana 52. Brescia: Morcelliana, 2008.

———. *Eucaristia e filosofia.* Translated by Ubenai Lacerda. Rio de Janiero: Editora Santuario, 2011.

Vacant, Alfred, and Eugène Mangenot, eds. *Dictionnaire de théologie catholique, contenant l'exposé des doctrines de la théologie catholique, leurs preuves et leur histoire.* 15 vols. Paris: Letouzey et Ané, 1899.

Voltaire. *Oeuvres complètes de Voltaire.* Vol. 9. Paris: Garnier, 1877.

———. *The Ignorant Philosopher.* Girard, KS: Haldeman-Julius Company, 1922.

Weil, Simone. *Attente de Dieu.* Paris: La Colombe, 1950

———. *La connaissance surnaturelle.* Paris: Gallimard, 1950.

———. *Cahiers.* Vol. 3. Paris: Plon, 1951.

———. *Pensées sans ordre concernant l'amour de Dieu.* Paris: Gallimard, 1962.

———. *Gravity and Grace.* New York: Ark Paperbacks, 1987.

———. *Waiting for God.* New York: Perennial, 2001.

Žižek, Slavoj, and John Milbank. *The Monstrosity of Christ: Paradox or Dialectic?* Edited by Creston Davis. Short Circuits. Cambridge, MA: MIT Press, 2011.

Zubiri, Xavier. "Reflexiones teológicas sobre la Eucaristía." *Estudios eclesiásticos* 56, no. 216–17 (1981): 41–60.

Index